Joshua Brooking Rowe

Contributions to a history of the Cistercian houses of Devon

Joshua Brooking Rowe

Contributions to a history of the Cistercian houses of Devon

ISBN/EAN: 9783337150709

Printed in Europe, USA, Canada, Australia, Japan

Cover: Foto ©ninafisch / pixelio.de

More available books at **www.hansebooks.com**

CONTRIBUTIONS TO A HISTORY

OF THE

CISTERCIAN HOUSES

OF

DEVON.

BY

J. BROOKING ROWE,
FELLOW OF THE SOCIETY OF ANTIQUARIES;
FELLOW OF THE LINNEAN SOCIETY;
MEMBER OF THE ROYAL ARCHÆOLOGICAL INSTITUTE OF GREAT BRITAIN AND IRELAND
HONORARY MEMBER OF THE ROYAL INSTITUTION OF CORNWALL;
AUTHOR OF "A FAUNA OF DEVON;"
"THE ECCLESIASTICAL HISTORY OF OLD PLYMOUTH;"
ETC. ETC.

PLYMOUTH:
W. BRENDON AND SON, 26, GEORGE STREET.
1878.

ERRATA.

Page 5, paragraph 6, last line, for "among' read *in*.
  „ 39, for Sir George Augustus "Heathfield" read Sir George Augustus *Eliott*.
  „ 85, paragraph 123, line 12, for "Bishop" read *Abbot*.
  „ 105,   „   143, „ 4, for "Erne" read *Erme*.
  „ 123,   „   179, „ 1, for "Churstowe" read *Churchstowe*.
  „ 141,   „   205, „ 6, for "M" read *B*.
  „ 142, line 5, for "hortis" read *hostis*.
  „ 142, „ 6, for "Trivarunt" read *Triverunt*.

NOTE.

THE following papers are reprinted from the *Transactions* of the Devonshire Association. Referring to an observation in paragraph 2, page 4, as I arranged my materials, I found it unnecessary to carry out my original intention of giving a concise history of each Abbey, as by so doing I should have been repeating to a great extent what is already in print. Buckland and Buckfast I have treated somewhat fully. What I have said of Newenham is only additional to the collections of Mr. Davidson, and the whole may be considered as supplementary to the works of Dugdale and Oliver, and may be of assistance to the author who at some future period undertakes to write a full history of these religious houses, the inmates of which did so much to make our county a good land — a land of wheat and of barley, of flocks and of herds.

16, LOCKYER STREET,
    PLYMOUTH.

CONTENTS.

	PAGE
INTRODUCTORY	3
THE CISTERCIAN ORDER	4
BUCKLAND	8
DOCUMENTS RELATING TO BUCKLAND	25
THE ABBOTS OF BUCKLAND	36
PEDIGREE OF THE REDVERS FAMILY	37
PLATES. [See par. 61, page 51.]	
BUCKLAND DOCUMENTS, ETC.	41
BUCKLAND MINISTERS' ACCOUNTS, 31 AND 32 HENRY VIII.	45
BUCKFAST	52
THE ABBOTS OF BUCKFAST	130
DOCUMENTS RELATING TO BUCKFAST	131
NEWENHAM	139
THE ABBOTS OF NEWENHAM	157
DOCUMENTS RELATING TO NEWENHAM	193
DUNKESWELL	159
THE ABBOTS OF DUNKESWELL	170
FORD	171
THE ABBOTS OF FORD	192

THE
CISTERCIAN HOUSES OF DEVON.

INTRODUCTORY.

I.
BUCKLAND.

THE

CISTERCIAN HOUSES OF DEVON.

1. WE have in this county (for although Thorncombe was in 1842 made a part of Dorsetshire, I include Ford Abbey as belonging to Devon) examples both of the earliest and latest foundations of the Cistercian order of monks.
Always excepting the most valuable work of the late Dr. Oliver, little attention has been hitherto paid to the monastic institutions and ruins of the county. Perhaps this neglect has arisen from the unfortunate state of decay into which nearly all the buildings have fallen. Devonshire seems to have suffered more than any other part of England, and cannot be said to possess any monastic ruin of importance, and there is none perhaps except Dartington and Ford, in which the existing remains give any idea of its former architectural glories. And yet Devonshire possessed upwards of thirty religious houses, some of the first importance, and ranking among the noblest in England. The bare mention of the great Benedictine monasteries of Exeter and Tavistock, the Cluniac house at Barnstaple, the five abbeys of the Cistercians distributed over the county, and last, but by no means least, the Augustinian Priory of Plympton, to say nothing of the numerous smaller establishments of the preaching orders and friars, will show how much of interest there is in the investigation of the subject.

2. Unfortunately, the task is not easy; and to work out properly the history of even one of these, requires an amount of time which few are able, and still fewer willing, to devote. But even by a person whose time is much occupied, and with whom the labour is one of love, a something can be accomplished; and I think that a concise history of each house,

embracing all the known facts of interest connected with it, such as I am about to endeavour to give, will be of some little use. I propose to give a short history of each of the Cistercian abbeys from its foundation to its fall, to refer briefly to the various abbots, to enumerate the possessions of the monks, and their holders after the dissolution, and to describe from personal examination such of the buildings as remain. And without giving in every particular my authorities, I may say that I have consulted every author who has touched upon the subject, from the ponderous folios of Oliver and Dugdale and Polwhele, and the less unwieldy quartos of Pole, Prince, and Lysons, down to the more concise but not-to-be despised pages of the traveller's hand-book and the local guide, and even to the magazine article and the newspaper paragraph.

3. But before proceeding to the special subject of each abbey, it will be convenient to consider briefly, by way of introduction, the history of the order, the objects its members had in view in its formation, and their rule of life, and also to refer to the buildings, and to show how they were especially constructed to meet the wants of the community.

4. As is well known to those who have looked into the history of the monastic orders, the Cistercian sprang in the eleventh century from the Benedictine order, and had its rise in an attempt to abridge the luxury and put an end to the worldly spirit which then pervaded monastic life.

5. In 1098 a few monks of the Abbey of Molesme, in the diocese of Langres, took counsel, and resolved to endeavour to stem the tide, and leaving their own monastery, wandered forth under the leadership of their abbot Robert, and settled down in a desert spot about fifteen miles south of Dijon, and on St. Benedict's day laid the foundation of that famous order which in its day and generation exercised such an important influence throughout Europe, which sent forth so many men distinguished for their piety and their learning, which gave to the church many a pope and bishop, which in less than a century possessed nearly two thousand monasteries, each and for many a year the centre of a life of self-denial, piety, frugality, and industry, each spreading around it an atmosphere of well-directed labour, each exercising an influence felt, at least in England, perhaps even to the present day.

6. Although Alberic and Stephen Harding (the latter an Englishman, and one of the West Country, a native of Sherborne), who succeeded Robert in the government of the newly-established order, did much in laying down the lines

which were to be the rules for future guidance, neither were very successful in inducing others to follow their example in living a life of such austerity as they proposed. But Harding was comforted by the vision vouchsafed to him of a great multitude washing their white robes in a fountain, which he took to be an assurance that his labours would one day be rewarded. It was not until the great St. Bernard, who in 1113 with thirty companions had knocked at the gate and obtained admission to Citeaux, had joined the monks, that the order, in spite of the criticisms, the scoffs, and the jealousies of its brethren, began to grow in popular favour. From that time the vision of Stephen Harding began to be fulfilled, and soon the poor buildings of Cistercium were too small to accommodate those who applied for leave to enrol themselves among the ranks of the new brotherhood.

7. Before the Reformation it is estimated that the order possessed about 3500 houses, 109 of which were in England. The first founded in this country was that of Waverley, in Surrey, in 1129; and one of the earliest was that of Buckfastleigh, in this county.

8. What were the objects which these men set before them? What was it that gave them such a reputation? What was it that made men exclaim that the whole church was full of their high reputation and opinion of their sanctity as it were with the odour of some divine balsam, and there is no country or province wherein this vine loaded with blessings has not spread its branches?* An endeavour to answer these questions would be out of place here, as it would necessitate an investigation, not only into the causes which moved the founders of the order to separate themselves from their former associates in the religious life, but also to consider the history of the time, and the social and political state of the people in the twelfth and thirteenth centuries. Briefly, however, it would seem that the secret was in the unquestionable sincerity and honesty of purpose which characterized the order in its early days, in the selfsacrifice shown, and the labours to which the monks gave themselves up; in their appealing by their simple mode of life to the feelings of the lower classes, and in their avoidance of the ease and luxury which even then was too frequently a scandal and a blot on the religious life.

9. In the eleventh, twelfth, and thirteenth centuries, the lot of the Cistercian monk was a hard one. The rules drawn up by Harding in his *Carta caritatis*, the Charter of Love, were

Cardinal de Vitry. Fox, p. 293.

strictly enforced, and it must have required no small confidence in his powers of endurance when the novice took the vows binding him for life to the austerities of the order. The monasteries were situated in such secluded spots as to render any intercourse with the outside world difficult. The food of the inmates was of the plainest kind, silence was rigidly enforced, communication was carried on within the walls mainly by signs, the fratry or day-room had no fireplace, and was exposed to the rigour of the weather, one end being left open to the air; and when the poor monk, after perchance his supper of fruit and herbs, sought his dormitory, the cold night air played about his hard couch, admitted by the slits in the long wall, unglazed and unshuttered, which served as windows. The stranger or wayfarer was welcomed and hospitably treated, but he was not allowed to enter the refectory or cloister. Luxury, ease, and the ordinary comforts of life were frowned upon, and for a long time banished. Labour and prayer, prayer and labour, alone occupied the thoughts of the Cistercian.

10. They were the farmers proper of the monastic orders. While other communities had their mills and granges mainly for their own use, and the use of those about them, the Cistercian made agriculture his business, and sent the products of his land forth for the use of the outer world. It is somewhat difficult to realize the scale on which farming was conducted on the estates of a great Cistercian abbey. I think our Devonshire houses were small in comparison with those in other parts of the country; but when we recollect that a Continental one had soon after its foundation 10,000 sheep, 1,000 goats, 2,000 pigs, 500 cows, 200 mares, and 100 horses, we can easily understand that extensive buildings were required, and a large staff necessary for the conduct of such a business. How then was the labour accomplished? Not by the monks; for they were few in number.

11. In every Cistercian house were two classes—the monks proper and the conversi, the masters and the servants. Both classes took the vows; but the lives of the conversi were spent mainly in labour upon the farms and other menial work, performing such religious duties only as might be reasonably expected from lay folk, who had to obtain their livelihood by the sweat of their brow. They were the poorest of the poor, and often the vilest; and many sought the convent when no other door was open to them, and death stared them in the face. Taken in hand then by the monks, compelled to earn their bread, they soon became useful, and the outcast of

society found in the Church a shelter denied him by the world. The number of monks proper was comparatively small; the conversi were numerous. At Clairvaux it seems that preparation was made for about 350; and at Fountains Mr. Sharpe calculated that 200 could be accommodated. Where were such numbers housed? Mr. Sharpe answers this question very satisfactorily, and to his recently-published books on the subject of Cistercian architecture I must refer all interested in the general subject. I will, however, briefly indicate the ordinary features of the arrangements of the buildings.

12. In the first place, the church was to be provided. This, according to the rules, was always to be in the form of a cross, and dedicated to the Blessed Virgin. The choir, or more properly chancel, was of small dimensions; no Lady chapel; but chapels are frequently found in the transepts. The tower was low. There were to be no representations of the human figure. Stained glass was forbidden; pictures and organs were not allowed; but as time crept on these rules were neglected, and the Cistercian church in its architecture became less severe. It would seem that the rule was, that the church should be on the north, and the other buildings on the south; but we shall find that there were exceptions to this. Supposing ourselves leaving the church on the south side through the transept, we should have on the east the chapter-house, and on the west the east walk of the cloister, and beyond the fratry or day-room of the monks, over which would be their scriptorium and dormitory, connected by a flight of steps with the church. Turning to the west, we should enter the south walk of the cloister, and have on our left hand successively the kitchen, refectory, and offices, and following the same walk, leaving the western arcade on our right, we should enter that part of the building, the special home of the servants of the monastery, to which Mr. Sharpe has happily given the name of the Domus Conversorum. In the greater monasteries this was sometimes 300 feet long. Those who know Fountains will doubtless recollect the noble vaulted building which is foolishly called the cloister, measuring about this length. This is the Domus Conversorum, and over it was the dormitory of the conversi.

13. You will see from Mr. Sharpe's model plan, given in the first part of his work, that access was thus easily gained to the church by all. It was divided, probably by means of wooden partitions, for the use of, firstly, the monks, who took the east end; secondly, the conversi, who used the

aisles and the last bays of the nave; thirdly, the outsiders, the inhabitants of the adjoining villages and others, to whom was allotted the centre of the nave.

14. Hills and highlands were always avoided in the selection of a site for an abbey. The Cistercian's habitation was far from the haunts of men; in a valley, and as far as possible in the narrowest part of it, and close to a river, the settlement was made; and in such a situation in many a fertile spot throughout England the farmer-monk made his home. In five of such localities in our fair county, members of the order, at varying intervals, took up their abode. The earliest house was founded in 1137, only nine years after the first—that of Waverley, in Surrey—was planted in England; and the remaining four were established at different times—one in the twelfth, and the other three in the thirteenth century. While we can boast one of the first, we can also claim one of the latest in England. The one I am now about to speak of is the last founded.

15. The Abbey of Buckland was founded by Amicia, the mother of Isabella, wife of William de Fortze, Earl of Albemarle, a lady connected with both those great families which had shown such love for the Cistercian, which had done so much to extend his order, and which had endowed it with so many rich possessions. Baldwin Earl of Devon had founded Quarr, in the Isle of Wight; and William le Gros, Earl of Albemarle, had founded the Abbeys of Meaux and Vallis Dei, both for the Cistercians, besides houses for other orders; and we may conjecture that it was the consideration of what had been done by her ancestors and the ancestors of her son-in-law, and the good results which were apparent from their benefactions, which induced Amicia, the widowed countess of Baldwin, seventh Earl of Devon, to provide another place of settlement for Cistercian brethren.

16. The monks having already houses in other parts of the county, and the south-west being unprovided, none being nearer than Buckfastleigh, Amicia resolved that her new colony should be planted amidst the family possessions on the banks of the Tavy. She therefore acquired, either by purchase or gift from her daughter Isabella, certain lands which were vested in her by deed, dated 1273, the King's confirmation of which is dated 1275; and in the eighth year of Edward I. (1280) she signed the foundation deed of Buckland Abbey, vesting in the monks and their successors the manors of Buckland, Bickleigh, and Walkhampton, with the advowsons thereof, and the hundred of Roborough, for

the use of the abbey dedicated in honour of God and the blessed Mary, mother of God, and the blessed Benedict. From 1273 to 1280 the pious Amicia was, we may conclude, busily preparing the site and buildings for the reception of the monks and their servants.

17. The foundress did not go to Ford, as might have been expected, for men to fill the new house, but she asked the Abbot of Quarr, the house founded, as I have mentioned, by the restless Baldwin, the second earl, to send her some monks, and accordingly Robert the first abbot* and others were sent from the Isle of Wight to Buckland. As frequently happened, there was trouble to begin with. It was one of the rules of the order that there should be no interference with the parish priest, and that the houses should be under the jurisdiction of the bishop. But when the monks came to Buckland they seem to have broken both these rules; they began to celebrate divine offices without any consent or license of the bishop. The bishop of the diocese, the famous Walter Bronescombe, was not a prelate to view with indifference any encroachment upon the privileges of his see, or to permit any interference with, or contempt of, the spiritual jurisdiction rightly belonging to him, and when he heard that the newly-arrived monks had begun to exercise spiritual functions in the neighbourhood of their house, he quickly placed them under an interdict. We do not know the date of this, but, as we have seen, there were buildings used by or for the use of the monks before the charter of Amicia. The interdict is referred to in a deed of Bronescombe's, dated 27th May, 1280, in which he recites, that having been petitioned by the Queen Eleanor (who had doubtless been urged to take up the cause of the monks by Amicia), he thereby removed the interdict, and permitted them to celebrate divine service until the feast of Pentecost next following. In June, satisfied with the conduct of the new-comers, the bishop extended the time to Michaelmas; but on the following St. Mary Magdalene's-day (the day of his death, 22ud July, 1280) Bronescombe released the monks from all further supervision, and gave them permission to perform all divine offices for ever thereafter.

18. As I said just now, the Foundation charter vesting the land in the abbey is dated 8th Edward I. It is interesting to notice how careful grantees of land in those days were to have their rights confirmed by all persons in whom there could be possibly any claim, or right of claim, therein. We con-

* Foundation Deed, Appendix C.

stantly find deed after deed professing to quit claim to land which we might have thought was effectually vested in the holder. Here, besides the deed of foundation from Amicia and the grant from her daughter, the wealthy and powerful Isabella de Fortibus, it was thought necessary also to obtain confirmation of the latter from the King, of whom the lands were to be held in *capite*. And later, in 1291, when it would appear that the Countess Amicia, "*nobilis mulier mater nostra carissima domina Amicia*," was dead, another confirmation was obtained from her daughter.* The deeds are very interesting, containing the names of places very familiar to us. The neighbourhood does not seem so utterly desolate and uncared-for as might have been supposed. We find mention of stone walls, boundaries, roads, paths, and houses. Soon after the foundation the title of the abbey to the hundred of Roborough was called in question, and the abbot was cited in the king's courts to show his authority in opposition to that of the crown; and although he produced the charters and confirmation by the king, as the hundred was not mentioned in the latter, judgment was given for the crown. But this difficulty must have been got rid of; for the abbey held the hundred down to the dissolution.

19. From the registers of the bishops of Exeter, so diligently searched by Dr. Oliver for the purposes of his *Monasticon*, from a few old deeds, and from leases granted by the various abbots, we gather some scanty knowledge of the history of the abbey. No Cartulary, or any other important record of the abbey, is to be found in any public office or library, or, as far as I can ascertain, in any private one.

20. In 1336 (11 Edward III.), not 1328, as stated by Dr. Oliver, the royal license was granted to the abbey and convent to crenellate the abbey. *Mansum abbatiæ suæ, Abbas et conventus de Buckelond*. Perhaps the fear of the foreigner had something to do with this fortification. It was not long after this (1339), that the French landed and burnt a great part of Plymouth; and William, the then abbot, might have thought that the herds and well-stored barns of the monks would prove a source of temptation to the roving Breton, and needed protection, and the abbey was battlemented.†

* Appendix E.
† "Very few houses of any importance were built in the thirteenth, fourteenth, and fifteenth centuries without being fortified; and the law required a licence from the crown before any house was allowed to be fortified."— *Parker*. The following is an extract from a licence to fortify (1482) given

21. The monks appear to have lived a quiet, unostentatious life—not greedy of wealth, or desirous of adding to their possessions, not quarrelling with their neighbours, as monks often did, and as landowners sometimes do even in our more enlightened times, but still occasionally involved in disputes with reference to their rights. Indeed, almost the first mention we have of the doings of the monks is to be found in the record of legal proceedings taken against them by a servant of the Abbot of Tavistock—his forester, one Thomas Gyreband—who complained, that having charge of the wood of Blakemoresham, and coming to a place in it called Ivyoak, he found Robert the Abbot of Buckland and others felling the wood and oaks there, and that on his attempting to prevent this, the abbot and the others with darts and hatchets assaulted and beat him, and with a bow and an arrow made of ash, headed with iron and steel, wounded him in the right arm, and afterward stole from him an outer garment. The Abbot and Convent of Buckland pleaded firstly their clergy, and denied the assault and robbery. Thomas got the worst of the affair; for he contradicted himself, and the abbot and his monks were acquitted, and Thomas committed to gaol for making a false accusation. And later in the pleadings we find the whole history of the affair. Blackmoresham wood was, I expect, on the opposite side of the Tavy, and belonged, as the forester said, to the Abbey of Tavistock, but the Cistercians had on the river a weir, and were obliged to keep it in order, and had a right to take from this place wood for its repair. Whilst obtaining wood, Thomas assaulted the defendants, and drew blood, and

by Mr. J. H. Parker: "Edward by the grace of God King of England & France and Lord of Ireland, to all to whom these presents shall come, greeting. Know ye that we considering the good & gracious services which our dearly beloved subject Edmund Bedingfeld Esqre, hath before these times rendered to us from day to day, and which he still continues inclined to render: of our special favours have granted and given *license* and by these presents do grant and give licenso, for us and our heirs, as far as in us lyeth, to the said Edmund, that he at his will and pleasure, build, make, and construct, with stone, lime & sand, *towers* and *walls* in and about his manour of Oxburgh in the County of Norfolk, and that manour with such towers and walls to inclose, and those towers and walls to *embattle*, *kernel* and *machecollate*: and that manour so inclosed, and those walls and towers aforesaid so embattled, kernell'd, and machicollated, built and constructed, to hold for himself and his heirs for ever, without perturbation, impeachment, molestation, impediment, or hindrance from us or our heirs or others whomsoever. And besides, of our abundant grace, we pardon, remit, and release to the aforesaid Edmund, all transgressions, offences, misprisions, and contempts, by him the said Edmund before these times, however done or perpetrated, on account of his enclosing such walls and towers, embattled, kernelled, machecollated, and built as aforesaid, in and upon his said manour," &c. &c.

in self-defence one of the Buckland men shot Thomas with an arrow in the arm, whereupon he fled, leaving his coat, bow, and hatchet, which William le Pye and another carried away, not as a robbery, but because they were left there. And the jury found that the defendants were rightly in the wood and not trespassers, and they were acquitted.*

22. In 1448 the monks considered themselves aggrieved for that the Lord of the Manor of Stonehouse, James Derneford, had, in defiance of the rights of the abbot and monks as lords of the hundred of Roborough, set up at Stonehouse a pillory and tumbrel, and had held a court of frank-pledge there. This was a usurpation, and gave rise to much trouble and unpleasantness. The monks would not allow James Derneford to use these marks of authority, and he would not admit that he was wrong, or remove them. At last, as recited in the award, the whole matter was referred, by the mediation of friends, to the decision of William Hylle, the Prior of Plympton, and James Chudlegh, Esq. The award was in favour of the abbey; and besides removing the pillory and tumbrel, James Derneford had to pay £20, as a fine for his encroachment.†

23. Thirty years later we find the monks defendants in a case, which was apparently brought against them, on behalf of the Crown, for the purpose of ascertaining the rights of the Duchy of Cornwall in the Forest of the Dartmoors.‡ The Abbot, Thomas Oliver, was cited to appear at Lydford, for that he did on the fourth day of October (18 Edward IV.), 1478, intrude and make claim upon land in Dartmoor within the bounds and marks of the forest, and was found culpable; and the jury also found that all the lands within the precincts, marks, and bounds of Dartmoor were of the ancient demesnes of the said prince, and were called the Fenfield and Common of Devonshire; and that all waives, strays, escheats, and presentments of assaults and bloodshed, plaints, writs of right according to the custom of the manor of Lydford and assizes of land, were appropriate to the court of Lydford. As doth appear, says Westcote, by ancient record remaining in the castle of Lydford.§

24. The agreement in the muniment-room at Powderham, which has been quoted by Oliver,‖ proves how much the later Cistercians had departed from the strictness of the early

* Oliver, p. 385. † See Appendix F.
‡ The forest of Dartmoor was permanently attached to the Duchy of Cornwall in 1337.
§ Westcote's *Devon*, p. 85. ‖ Oliver's *Monasticon*, p. 381.

rules of their order. It is dated 28th May, 1522, and is made between Abbot Whyte and Robert Derkeham, and shows how Robert, in return for assisting daily in the choir and teaching four boys of the convent, and also teaching the boys and any monks who might wish to learn music and the organ, was to be paid an annuity of £2 13s. 4d., to be provided with a decent table, to have a furnished room over the west gate of the monastery, and a gown of the value of 12s. every year; to have the reversion of a tenement at Milton, and until it fell in, feeding for two cows, and a garden, he paying half the rent. One would have thought that this was very fair pay as times went for Robert's work; but his room over the west gate was cold and dreary in the winter, so he had also five ounces of bread, a quart of beer, and a wax candle every night throughout the year, and thirty horse-loads of faggots. With these and his books and organ he ought to have made himself tolerably comfortable. He apparently appreciated them, and continued in their enjoyment for some time, for he was alive at the dissolution, and the grant was allowed by the Augmentation Office, 18th December, 1540.

25. The list of the abbots is incomplete; the following account contains all that I can glean with reference to them.

The names of the first and second abbots are somewhat uncertain; from Robert being mentioned in the Foundation charter, and as the abbot complained of in the proceedings by the forester Thomas Gyreband, it may be concluded that he was the first abbot, and, if so, it may be taken for granted that the second was William, who is mentioned in a grant, 17 Edward I., 1288, by Margaret de Ripariis, the widow of Baldwin, fifth of that name and eighth Earl of Devon, the only son of Amicia, the foundress, by which deed she released to William the Abbot of Bocland and his convent her claim of dower in the churches of Bocland and Walkhampton, in consideration of an annuity of £8 paid to her clerk William de Brenton, for which in default of due payment the sheriff was to levy by writ of *fieri facias* on the goods of the abbey.* Bishops Quivell and Bitton confirmed the grant of Buckland Church to the Abbey.

Galfridus was the next abbot. During the time of his rule there were many disputes as to the injury done to the property of the Abbey by the working of the silver mines in the neighbourhood. The complaints of the monks and the proceedings thereupon are to be found in the *Rolls of*

* *Archæol. Journal*, vol. v. p. 58.

Parliament.* Thomas Bitton, the Bishop of Exeter, in an instrument dated 1305, appropriated the church of Walkhampton to the use of the monks who were its patrons, and it recites the enormous devastation done to the woods and lands of the abbey by the working of the silver mines by the crown in and around them. The late Sir E. Smirke supposed these to be the silver mines of Beer, which were about this time worked with success, but as I do not find that the abbey ever had any property on the western side of the Tavy, it is rather difficult to see how their lands could be injured, and I think there may be some mistake in the identification.

Thomas was abbot as early as 1311, and in 1316 we find that he and the prior of Plympton entered into an arrangement (upon the intervention of the Bishop, Walter Stapeldon, with reference to suit and service of the latter at the hundred court of Roborough in respect of the lands of the priory in Old Blakeston, which was situate within the hundred, and it was agreed that the attendance should thenceforth be limited to three courts a year instead of, as I suppose, four, as theretofore.

The fifth abbot was a second William; he was party to an agreement with Ralph de Bellworthy, also with reference to suit and service at the hundred court of Roborough. He was succeeded by Thomas Wappelegh, John Bryton, and Walter, successively abbots in 1356, 1385, and 1392.

In 1418-19 we find, from a lease granted to William Pomeroy and his wife and daughter at Buttyckyswordy, in the manor of Walkhampton, for 65 years, that John was prior. In May, 1442, William Rolff, who had the protracted litigation with James Derneford, of Stonehouse, succeeded. Of the abbots following him we know little. John Spore succeeded Rolff, 28th September, 1449, and John Hylle, October 21st, 1454. Thomas Olyver became abbot 20th March, 1463, and it was against him that the proceedings at Lydford were taken for the monks' trespass upon Dartmoor forest, and during the long time that he was head of the monastery, we find him granting many leases of land for terms of years determinable on lives. He espoused the cause of the Earl of Richmond, afterwards Henry VII., and was proscribed by Richard, but lived to see the success of the former, and continued abbot of Buckland for several years after his accession. John Brundon, the next, was abbot for a short time only. Thomas Whyte succeeded, and was abbot before 1511 and after 1527. It was with him that Robert

* *Rot. Parliam;* see also Oliver's *Monasticon,* p. 385.

Derkeham, the organist, entered into the agreement I have referred to.

The sixteenth and last abbot was John Toker, or Tucker, a member of a Devonshire family and brother to Robert Tucker, alderman, and afterwards, in 1543, Mayor of Exeter, who, Prince says, in his memoir of his grandson William Tucker, Dean of Lichfield, " with great honour discharged the office."*
The family was settled at Moretonhampstead. The later pedigree will be found in the *Visitation* of 1620. He was blessed by the bishop as abbot of Buckland, 7th June, 1528, and just ten years afterwards he surrendered the house and its belongings to the king. During the twelve months, immediately before the surrender, he had granted leases (no doubt for a consideration) of the rectorial tithes of the parish church of Buckland, and of Walkhampton, Bickleigh, and Sheepstor, and also of Bampton, to his brother Robert and his nephews William and Hugh Tucker.

26. At the dissolution there were twelve monks in the house, to all of whom pensions were granted. No complaint was made as to their conduct; no breath of scandal or word of reproach rested on this or any of the Cistercian houses; or indeed, as far as I know, and judging from the pension lists, on any of the religious houses in the west country. Thus, after only about two centuries and a half, the land dedicated to God, and set apart for pious uses by Amicia, was snatched from its holders, who had so well discharged the trust committed to them, by a tyrannical king and his rapacious courtiers, aided by a compliant and time-serving parliament. With miserable pittances the monks were sent forth into a world to which they were unaccustomed, while the buildings which had been handed down to them, some of which they had erected, and the lands they and their predecessors had tilled and improved, were given to those who had no love for the monk, who had thus toiled for the stranger who now entered into his labours; while, worst of all, the church was gutted and ruthlessly converted into a dwelling-place for the usurper. Whatever opinions may be held as to the expediency of the existence of monasteries, it is impossible to look impartially into the history of their dissolution without coming to the conclusion that a grievous wrong was done to the people of England, and an injury inflicted upon the commonwealth, from which perhaps it has not yet recovered. This is not the place to enter upon a defence, and I do not now wish to attempt to extenuate, or to say anything upon the religious

* Prince's *Worthies*, ed. 1810, p. 735.

bearings of the subject, but the fact remains, that while before the dissolution these houses were sources of immense good, mingled perhaps with some things that were undesirable, on their extinction, their belongings were squandered, and no effort made to use them for the benefit of the people who had so largely profited by them in former days. It is very evident that in such an establishment as that of Buckland, where there was no grasping after an accumulation of wealth, no endeavour to extend the possessions of the house, that the labours of these monks must have been productive of great good to the locality, and its loss severely felt by the lower and middle classes of the neighbourhood.

27. The revenues of the abbey were at this time £241 17s. 9½d. per annum, and it was easy to pay out of them, or out of the proceeds arising from the sale of the plunder, the pensions granted to Tucker, the last abbot, and his monks. The abbot had £60 per annum; and the monks various sums, beginning with Thomas Maynard, who received £5 6s. 8d., down to John Jordan, who had only £3 6s. 8d. a year.

28. What then were the possessions of the abbey at the time of the dissolution? I have said that the monks were not avaricious. From the foundation charter, and the grants and confirmations, we know that it was originally endowed with the manors of Buckland, Bickleigh, Walkhampton, and Collumpton, and the hundred of Roborough, with the advowsons of Buckland, Bickleigh, and Walkhampton, and much later, in exchange for a part of the hundred of Roborough, given up to the Corporation of Plymouth in 1464, the church of Bampton. We find from the *Valor Ecclesiasticus* that at the end of the two hundred and sixty years of its existence the abbey possessed very little more than is mentioned in the original grants, the additions consisting only of a house in Exeter, doubtless for the use of the abbots on their visits to the bishop, worth £1 6s. 8d. per annum, and a tenement in Saltash worth 8s. per annum. How these were obtained we do not know.

29. Before going further, I may refer very briefly to the seals of the abbey. One, apparently the earliest, is from an impression attached to a deed dated 1310, in which we see in the centre, under a canopy, the Blessed Virgin and Child, and below is a shield with what appears to be a lion rampant, probably representing the arms of the Redvers, Earls of Devon. Between the shield and the canopy the word "Amicia" appears. There is around the margin the legend "SIGILLVM ECCLESIE LOCI S'CI BENEDICTI DE BOCLAN."

Another, of about the same date, is said to be a counter or private seal of the abbot; but I am inclined to think that it does not belong to Buckland, at least I can find no abbot who was named Stephen, which word appears in the legend. The seal is from an impression in the British Museum.

Another, mentioned by Dr. Oliver, very similar to the last mentioned, has a figure of St. Benedict holding the crozier or pastoral staff in his right hand, and a book in his left. In the centre, between the figure, is the name Ami-cia divided. The legend is "✠ S. ABBATIE BOCLAND SANCTI BENEDICTI."

A fourth has a right hand grasping a pastoral staff, from which is suspended an olive-branch. The staff passes through the letter A. The legend is "✠ S. COMMUNE ABBIS ET COVENT' S'CI BENEDICTI." This last seal is very similar to that used by St. Bernard himself soon after the establishment of Clairvaux in 1115,* and probably this device was used by many houses.

The arms borne by the abbey were, quarterly, argent and gules, a crozier, in bend or.

28. After the monks came George Pollard, of London, for whom the former were ousted from their valley home. The lands, church, conventual and domestic buildings, were then intact, and were granted to him the year after the surrender, 14th December, 1539, for a term of 21 years, at a rent of £23 3s. 5d., reserving to the king and his successors all great timbers, as well as all trees and wood in and upon the premises being or growing.

29. From the next document it would seem (although it is not so recited) that George Pollard must have disposed of his interest under the royal lease, for we find that May 26th, 1541, the king granted, in consideration of the good, true, and faithful service which his well-beloved servant, Richard Greynfeld (or, as we are accustomed to call him, Grenville), of Bideford, knight, heretofore done to us, as for the sum of £233 3s. 4d. paid by the said Richard Greynfeld, the reversion of the site of the monastery, houses, buildings, barns, tenements, meadows, pastures, feedings, and also all the church, belfry, and burial ground, and all houses, buildings, barns, dove-houses, orchards, gardens, pools, vivaries, land and soil, as well within as close and near to the site, sept, circuit, and precinct of the late monastery, as fully and wholly, and in as ample manner and form, as the last abbot and late convent held or enjoyed the same, paying £2 6s. 4½d. yearly. And thus a descendant of the Sir Richard Grenville, who in his

* See *Archæol. Journal*, vol. xiv. p. 15.

devotion in 1134 had founded and erected the Cistercian monastery of Neath, in Glamorganshire, became a participator in the spoil of another house of the same order.

30. I may mention here that it is said that the bells in the tower of the abbey were given to the church of Egg Buckland. I do not know how this could happen, as there was no connection between the abbey and this church. In the tower at Egg Buckland there are at present three bells, one an ancient one, with the inscription, "✠ 𝕹𝖔𝖈𝖊 𝖒𝖊𝖆 𝖇𝖎𝖇𝖆 𝖉𝖊𝖕𝖊𝖑𝖑𝖔 𝖈𝖚𝖓𝖙𝖆 𝖚𝖔𝖈𝖎𝖛𝖆;" but this might have come from any place. The two others are dated respectively 1682 and 1768, but may have been recast from older bells, as there were three bells at Egg Buckland in 1553 mentioned in the inventory of church goods of Edward VI.*

31. The Grenvilles did not long continue the owners of Buckland Abbey. In 1580 the abbey site, house and lands, were sold by Sir Richard and Lady Mary Grenville, after obtaining the royal license to alienate them, in December, 1580, to John Hele and Christopher Harris for £3,400; and nine months later these conveyed the property to Sir Francis Drake, whose descendants still retain them.†

32. The manor and lands of Collumpton were sold to Sir George St. Leger, whose son sold them to Thomas Risdon, by whom they were divided up and disposed of to tenants and others. The manor went to the Hillersdens, and from them to the Sweets.

33. Bickleigh and Walkhampton, and the lands of Hele and Rynmore, and those in Shaugh and Sheepstor, were purchased by John Slanning, September 24th, 1546, through whose descendants, by the marriage of daughters, they passed to the Heywoods, and from them, by purchase, to Sir Manasseh Massey Lopes, and are now held by his grandson Sir Massey Lopes.

34. The manor of Buckland, with the advowson of the church, was sold, 12th April, 1546, to a London haberdasher, Richard Crymes and his wife, for £1,451. Their descendants continued in the neighbourhood for some time, and intermarried with the Coplestones, Prideauxes, Drakes, Glanvilles, and other Devonshire families. About 1620, on, I suppose, the death of William Crymes, large portions of the property were sold, long leases being granted; but the manor was retained for some years later. In 1660, however, this was also disposed of to the Slannings, and from them, on the

* Exch. Queen's Rem., T. G. 6211 N. ¾.
† Appendix I. Drake pedigree.

marriage of daughters, it descended to the Heywoods in the same way as the Bickleigh and Walkhampton properties, and like them is now held by Sir Massey Lopes. The patronage of the vicarage was held by the Crymes family until a comparatively late period. It now belongs to the Hayne family.

35. Where the houses in Saltash and Exeter were situated I cannot ascertain, nor how or to whom they were disposed of.

36. In conclusion I have to describe the remains of the Abbey buildings as they now exist, but I must first observe that I cannot vouch for the absolute correctness of every statement I may make, inasmuch as the alterations, removals, and additions have been so extensive as to prevent absolute certainty of identification. Although I suspect that Sir Richard Grenville destroyed the greater part of the buildings, reserving only such as were useful for the purposes of his new house, yet much was left, portions of which appear to have been removed in recent years.

37. The earliest drawing that I can find,—although it is very rough, is interesting and suggestive, and to some extent valuable,—is in the ancient map of the Forest of Dartmoor, brought under the notice of our society at the last Exeter meeting by Mr. C. Spence Bate. In that map the Abbey Church of Buckland is represented much as we should have expected to find it—a long church with choir, nave, and central tower. It is always pleasant to overthrow the theory of another, and I am able to do so with respect to Mr. Bate's theory, that the map is of the date 1240 or thereabout. But at this time the Abbey Church could not have been there, for the Abbey was not founded or thought of for nearly forty years after. I think that the map is two centuries later than the date Mr. Bate assigns to it. You will notice the long cruciform building with low central tower,* no aisles, and south transept. The chancel longer than the nave is, I believe, the draughtsman's error, for the choir was always short, and there was no lady chapel, the whole church being dedicated to the Blessed Virgin. If there were aisles, I think they would have been shown, as the drawing is the largest of any on the map, and in the representations of much smaller churches, aisles are distinctly to be seen. The lines indicating buildings beyond, do not, I am of opinion, represent the parish church of Buckland Monachorum, but the Abbey buildings, and if so, here again the substantial

" * Turres lapideæ ad campanas non fiant, nec ligneæ altitudinis immoderatæ, quæ ordinis dedeceant simplicitatem."—*Nom. Cist.*

accuracy of the map is proved. One thing in the drawing I do not understand, the door-way shown in the transept. As a general rule the conventual buildings of the Cistercians were on the south side of the church, but occasionally, when the nature of the ground prevented their being so placed, we find the buildings on the north, and so it was at Buckland. The Cistercians, and indeed nearly all monks, loved the valleys, and they preferred shelter to the *lex non scripta* of the order. Here, on the south side of the church, the ground rises somewhat suddenly, and without a good deal of excavation sites for the buildings could not have been obtained. To the north, therefore, the monks went, and I think we may conclude that the chapter-house, the refectory, and the bulk of the buildings were on the north side of the cloister.

Leland only just refers to the Abbey, and no further information is attainable with reference to the buildings until we come to Buck's view, published in 1734, in which, although as to the surrounding scenery, and also in the drawing of some portions of the remains, there is a considerable amount of romance, it shows, that various alterations have been made, and some buildings altogether removed. Nearly fifty years later we have a plan of the house and its surroundings, to which the same remarks apply, many erections being there shown which cannot now be found. None of these help us in fixing the site of the conventual buildings; nor will the three important buildings still remaining, to a great extent intact—the church, the porter's lodge (after which I put a query), or the barn—render us much assistance.

38. On visiting the house (for Abbey now is a misnomer), after passing down one of the noble avenues leading thereto, and resting on the high ground to the north to admire the magnificent view of the country, on the banks of the Tamar and Tavy, stretching far away towards the sea, we shall find ourselves in a narrow valley shut in on the north, south, and east, with the ground gently sloping towards the west, until the little stream we cannot fail to notice falls into the river some short distance below. A spot more suitable for the Cistercian could not be found. Far from the busy town and haunts of men, and yet sufficiently near for the sale of wool, and for disposing of the produce of their farms, the monks settled down to their varied tasks, and praying and labouring, quickly made their little valley fertile, and caused it to become the centre of a new life.

39. Before the monks from Quarr could take possession, it was necessary that a church, or at least an oratory, for wor-

ship should be provided, with a refectory and dormitory for the monks, a guest-room for strangers, and a porter's lodge. With these the little community started; and soon the more stately church began to rise, with the domestic and farm buildings, the fratry, the scriptorium, the long building for the conversi, with sleeping-rooms above, and the great barn. The little stream was diverted into various channels, and used in different ways. One channel was the common sewer of the monastery, another, carefully banked and tended, led to the fish-ponds, important sources of supply in a Cistercian house. And so the Abbey of Buckland grew, and with their home-barton of nearly 800 acres, besides a large extent of moorland and pasture, with outlying farms, the little band had soon work enough to occupy their time and thoughts. And so they worked until the crash came, and they were sent forth to live as best they might on the pensions allowed them.

40. There has been found on the south side some little building rubbish, but there is nothing to lead us to suppose that there was anything of consequence on this side. The cloister was probably on the north-east. Just inside the gate of the garden is an old wall, shown in Buck's view, running almost from north to south. At the extreme south end on the western side is a recess with a stone seat, and this wall may be the eastern wall of the cloister. West of this is a building, which I think may be the porter's lodge, and perhaps a part of the entrance gate. It is now used with the stables. The window in front is really a blocked-up door-way, opening into a little hall or porch, lighted with a window on the north. Below is a cellar, with a window west, and opposite the window an entrance (now blocked up) to some place beyond. Over the little hall is a small room, reached by a newel staircase in the turret, and over this a platform. The platform on the top of the turret is reached by the continuation of the staircase. The whole appears to be late fourteenth century work; but in the arch in the cellar, and in the archway of the entrance, from what I have called the little hall, to the building beyond, whatever it might have been, the character of the earlier work in the church is imitated. This building is always called the bell turret, which it certainly never was. It is shown in Buck's view, and on the plan of 1769, but then apparently connected with the church.

41. Opposite this building, on the last-mentioned plan, are shown various erections not now to be found, but probably represented by a group of buildings which either formed

part of the monastery, or which were constructed with the old materials; more especially a large door-way facing west may be mentioned, and traces of other buildings extending upwards towards the north may be seen. Nothing certain is known as to the situation of the churchyard, or of any of the important buildings; but I have no doubt that the foundations of the latter are below the surface, and if excavation was permitted, considerable information with reference to many important matters, of which we are now entirely ignorant, might be obtained.

42. The orchards, now as formerly, are on the north side, west of the monastery, with a south aspect. The remains of three fish-ponds are easily made out, portions of the banks and traps remaining. The grand barn, upwards of 100 feet in length, with its fine door-way, remains externally much as the monks left it. Useful to their successors, the barn was spared the destruction and mutilation suffered by its neighbours.

43. The noble yews and cedars will not fail to attract the notice of the visitor as he approaches the house, otherwise the church, which we now come to. I think we may safely conclude that the present walls are those of the original church, and we have a plan at once simple and unusual,[*] consisting, as I have mentioned, of chancel, nave, and south transept. The present building is about 130 feet long and 33 broad. The chancel is 24 feet long. The breadth of the transept is 24 feet, and the depth from north to south probably the same, consisting of two bays, the column dividing them still remaining on the east side. The south wall of the transept is gone, and the bay of the tower leading into it is walled up. The capitals of the columns at the junction of the tower and transept are clearly distinguishable, as well as the corbels, drawings of which I have here. These are very interesting, and if they are, as I believe them to be, Early English, Mr. Sharpe tells me that they are the earliest known in Cistercian architecture.

44. Built into a wall over a door-way in the grounds is a large boss of great interest, from which shafts are seen spreading off, and which has evidently been the centre of a groined ceiling. When I first saw it I thought it was a mitred head, but it is clearly the head of a female. The upper pointed part is the head-dress, and below is a coronet, and whether the work is early or late, I have little doubt but that it is intended to represent the features of the

[*] The plan of Grey Abbey, County Down, Ireland, is similar.

foundress of the abbey, the widowed Countess Amicia. From what part of the abbey it came it is impossible to say, and it is equally impossible to assign a reason for its preservation.

45. On entering the house we shall find that it has been divided into a series of floors, and although somewhat intricate in its arrangements, it makes a very commodious and comfortable residence. It has, however, been so interfered with and so covered with plaster and battened throughout, that an investigation of architectural details is difficult, and in many places impossible. The string course on either side of the nave can be traced here and there from end to end as far as the tower. The tower appears to be perfect. It has been divided into floors. In the second from the top the great arches over the crossing can be traced. On the south and west these are perfect, the latter especially so, the whole of the stonework being uncovered and as sharp as when the workmen left it five hundred years ago. The southern arch is partly built into and plastered, but no doubt perfect. The eastern one is entirely covered up; but I think it is of a different character, being one of construction only, and not of ornament as well. The northern archway is formed of rubble masonry, and is of a different pitch, and I believe that there was a window here. The springers of the vaulting shafts remain, but I am inclined to think that the stone vaulting was never completed. Below the eastern arch we find north and south, parts of the columns, with their capitals, at the commencement of the chancel. The chancel arch was much lower than those of the nave and transept, but of the same character; and there seems to have been another arch of a similar size on the north side of the choir. On the north side of the nave is a very curious and beautifully vaulted little chamber, apparently opening from the tower, and with openings also on the east and west, with a window on the north. I think this must have been a porch or passage leading into the cloister, or in connection with the monks' dormitory, affording from thence easy access to the church. The church is not truly oriented, being situated E.N.E. The Cistercians do not seem to have been particular as to this matter. I have only briefly mentioned these points in connection with the ancient buildings in order to draw attention to them, and in the hope that some one more skilled in working out the details of ancient buildings may take up the subject and give us a full architectural history of the Abbey Church of Buckland.

46. Pass we now to the more modern house into which the

Cistercian Church was converted. The hall is a fine room, decorated with panels and Jacobean carvings in oak, said to have been brought from the manor-houses of Callisham and Durance, in the parish of Meavy, by the Drakes. Some of the figures are beautifully carved, but unfortunately the whole has been painted over. Over the chimney-piece is the date MCCCCCLXXVI. Assuming this date to be genuine, and as it is in plaster and corresponds with the rest of the plasterwork of the hall, I think there is no reason to doubt it, it shows that the conversion was accomplished during the ownership of the Grenvilles, and thus Risdon's statement that Sir Richard Grenville built a fair new house, which certainly he did not, is explained. There is no doubt, I think, that he destroyed the greater part of the monastic buildings, completed the house, and laid out the surrounding land in pleasure-grounds and gardens.

47. Sir Francis Drake has left no traces of his possession of the abbey, but the old bowling-green is shown on the map of 1769. In the staircase is a portrait of Don Pedro de Valdez, one of the vice-admirals of the Spanish Armada, who was taken prisoner by Drake, and kept by him at Buckland Abbey until his friends had paid the round sum which Drake doubtless required as his ransom; although, as Speed says, "Sir Francis his souldiers had well paid themselves with the spoile of the shippe, wherein were 55,000 ducats in gold, which they shared merrily among them."* The rest of the officers and men were detained in Plymouth for eighteen months until the ransoms arrived, and no doubt the Don spent the same length of time with his captor. His portrait shows him to have been every inch a Spanish cavalier—a noble figure, with handsome features, presenting a strange contrast to the portrait of Drake, whose appearance is the direct opposite in every respect.

48. In one of the floors of the tower, the second, is a mantel-piece with the shield, crest, and motto of Sir Francis in plaster. On the left side or flank is a shield bearing the ancient arms of the Drakes—a wyvern displayed, quartered with the new grant of a fess-wavy between two polar stars. Below is the date 1655 and the letters R. N. Sir Francis Drake, the second baronet, the great nephew of the Sir Francis, whose portrait is also at Buckland Abbey, was at this time in possession of the estates, but I cannot explain

* Barrow's *Life of Drake*, p. 131. The ship was the *St. Francis*, a galleon of 50 guns, and with a crew of 500 men. See *English Mercurie*, No. 50, July 23rd, 1588.

the meaning of the letters R. N. On the right flank of the chimney-piece are two shields, the first apparently a bird naiant, and the second three mullets within as many in crescents 2 and 1, with an acorn as a crest. Dr. Drake has suggested to me that the former may be a canting cont—a duck or drake swimming upon water. The second shield is that of Gregorie,* of Plympton St. Mary. Elizabeth Gregorie married first John Elford, of Sheepstor, and secondly Thomas Drake, the brother and heir of Sir Francis.

49. As every guide-book says, relics of the great navigator (these words seem indispensable) are to be found at the abbey. His drum (really there are two), and his Bible, sword, and shield, the two latter, most unlike what he would probably have used, are to be seen. In the dining-room is the well-known portrait of Sir Francis, and in the staircase, besides those of Don Pedro de Valdez and the second baronet, are two other family portraits, and a painting, apparently an allegorical subject, supposed to refer to some incident in the history of the Drake family. The other portraits are those of Charles II. in armour, and his queen, and Nell Gwynne.

50. The translations in the Appendix of some of the documents relating to the abbey will be found of interest. The names of places have not much changed, and the boundaries of the properties can be approximately ascertained.

DOCUMENTS.

A.

The following documents relating to Buckland Abbey will be found as under :—

Carta Regis Edwardi Primi. (Called "Edwardi Secundi" in Dugdale.)—Ibid; Dugdale, vol. v. p. 714; Oliver, p. 384.

Carta fundationis per Amiciam Comitissam Devoniæ. Cart. 8 Ed. I. n. 85.—Dugdale, vol. v. p. 712; Oliver, p. 382; trans. App. (C).

Carta Amiciæ Comitissæ Devoniæ, &c.—Ibid; Dugdale, vol. v. p. 714; Oliver, p. 384.

Carta Walteri Exon Episcopi.—*Reg. Exon. Epis.*, f. 96; Dugdale, vol. v. p. 713; Oliver, p. 383; Oliver, *Hist. Col.*, p. 71.

Carta alia Walteri Episcopi.—*Reg. Bronesc.*, f. 97; Dugdale, vol. v. p. 713; Oliver, p. 383; Oliver, *Hist. Col.*, p. 72.

Carta Isabellæ de Fortibus Comitissæ Albemarlæ.—Pat 9, Hen. IV. p. ii. m. 18; Dugdale, vol. v. p. 713; Oliver, p. 383.

De Libertatibus Abbatis de Bocland.—Oliver, p. 384.

* Az. within three in crescents or, as many mullets ar.

De Damno facto abbati de Bocland per minerarios et custodes mineræ regis.—Oliver, p. 385.

Compositio inter abbatem et conventu de Bocland et abbatem et conventu de Ford de secta hominem de Tale ad hundredum de Harige.—Oliver, p. 385.

Indulgentia pro adjuvantibus ad fabricum Ecclesiæ Cathedralis Exoniæ consummandum.—Oliver, p. 386.

Taxatio et ordinatio vicariæ de Walkhampton.—Oliver, p. 386.

Conventio inter abbatem de Buclond et quendam Belworthi pro sectâ ad hundredum de Rowborough.—Oliver, p. 386.

Ordinatio vicariæ de Bickleigh et visitatio ibidem.—Oliver, p. 387.

Appropriatio ecclesiæ parochialis de Baunton, taxatio vicariæ ibidem, et diversæ facultates factæ et concessæ per literas papales. —Oliver, p. 388.

B.

CONFIRMATION BY THE KING OF THE GIFT TO AMICIA.

Edward, by the grace of God, King of England, Lord of Ireland, and Duke of Aquitaine. To all to whom this writing shall come, greeting. Know ye that we have conceded and confirmed to Amicia, Countess of Devon, the manor of Buckland, with the hamlets of Columpton, Walkhampton, and Bickeley, together with all and singular their appurtenances wheresoever situate; To have and to hold to the same Amicia, according to the form and tenor of the deeds which she had from the gift of Isabella de Fortibus, Countess of Albemarle, her daughter; And if it shall happen that the said Amicia should wish to give and to assign the said manor and hamlets with all their appurtenances whatsoever to religious men, and with them to found a new religious house, know ye that we for ourselves and for our heirs, will consider and accept that gift as acceptable, provided that the said house, after the decease of the said Amicia, shall be held of us and our heirs *in capite*. And we faithfully promise to confirm it, when founded or appointed, in pure and perpetual alms. In witness, &c. Witness myself at Odiham, 8th day of August, in the 4th year of our reign.

C.

THE DEED OF FOUNDATION.

In the name of the most glorious and undivided Trinity, the Father, the Son, and the Holy Ghost, Amen, and by the favour of the most Blessed Virgin Mary and of the Blessed Benedict, we, Amicia Countess of Devon and Lady of the

Isle, trusting in the goodness of the Supreme Maker of all good things, who disposes the wills of both men and women at his pleasure, and faithfully directs them though unseen, and sustains our hope by the revelation of His mind if we offer anything in perpetual memory to the honour of His name; We found the Abbey, which we desire should be called or entitled St. Benedicts of Buckland, which is in our manor of Buckland, for the perpetual maintenance of abbots and monks of St. Benedict of the Cistercian order there to dwell, for the health of the souls of the Lord Henry, formerly King of England, the noble Queen Dame Eleanor his wife, and their children, of the Lord Edward, our illustrious King of England, the son of the same Henry, the noble Queen Dame Eleanor his wife, and the children of the same, and for the health of the souls of the Lord Gilbert of Clare, formerly Count of Gloucester and Hertford, our father, and the Countess Isabella, our mother, and the souls of Baldwin, Earl of Devon, our husband, and Isabella our daughter, Countess of Devon and Albemarle, and Margaret, our daughter, nun of Lacock, and for the souls of all our ancestors and descendants, and of all to whom we are bound for any kindness, we set apart, and give, concede, and have assigned as an abode and abbey for the aforesaid abbots and monks, and we decree that abbots and monks of the aforesaid order shall dwell for ever in the same abbey. And to this abbey, to Brother Robert, the abbot, and for the support of the monks dwelling in the same house, which have been bought by us from Quarr Abbey, and to their successors, for ever in honour of God and of the most Blessed Mary, Mother of God, and the Blessed Benedict; we give and we grant the same our manor of Bocland, and our manors of Columpton, Bykeley, and Walkampton, with the advowsons of the churches, and with the hundred of Rugheberewe, with all service, as well of free-tenants, villiens, as of others belonging to the said hundred, with all their appurtenances, as in demesnes and seigniories, military service, services of freed men, villeins and villanages, with their chattels suits, reliefs, aids, rents, heriots, heirships, escheats, aids of every kind, meadows, pasturages, pastures, ways, paths, woods, arable land, mills, waters, fisheries, moors, heaths, turbaries, together with all liberties and free customs acquired by us for the same abbey, with all other appurtenances, named and not named, which belong to the said manors and hundred, or which can in any way belong by whatever name they may be known, without any reservation by us, or by our heirs, and we have confirmed the same by this present charter to the said abbot and convent and their successors, to be held in free and full alms for ever, freely, quietly, well and peaceably for ever, without any contradiction or impediment by us or our heirs.

And we, the said Amicia and our heirs, will warrant, and acquit, and for ever defend the said abbot and convent and their successors to the manor, with the advowson of the churches and with the said hundred together with all liberties and free customs, and other appurtenances, named and not named, which to the said manor and the said hundred in any way belong or can belong in holy, pure, and perpetual alms, as aforesaid, against all Nations, whether Christians or Jews. And that this my gift, concession, and confirmation of this my present deed may remain firm and binding, we have caused this our seal to be placed unto this deed. Witnesses Hugo Peverell, William of Bikells, Thomas of Pyn, Warren of Secchevill, Reginald de Ferrars, Knights, John of Valletort, Richard Meavy, Ralph of Lenham, Stephen of Stoyll, Baldwin the Bastard, Humphrey of Doncsterre, and others.

D.

DEED OF AMICIA COUNTESS OF DEVON.

Know all men, now and to come, that we Amicia Countess of Devon and Lady of the Isle [in our lawful widowhood] with the thought of God and for the health of the souls of Lord Henry, formerly King of England, and the noble Queen Dame Eleanor, his wife and their children, and of the Lord Henry, formerly King of England, son of the same King Henry and the noble Queen Dame Eleanor, his wife and their children, and for the health of the souls of Lord Gilbert of Clare, formerly Earl of Gloucester and Hertford, our father, and the Countess Isabella, our mother, and Baldwin, Earl of Devon, our husband, and for the health of our souls and the souls of Baldwin, our son, formerly Earl of Devon, and Isabella, our daughter, Countess of Devon and Albemarle, our daughter, nun of Lacock, and of all our ancestors and successors, and of all to whom we are bound by any favours, and of others who do or shall bestow alms or any favours have given and granted, and confirm by this present writing to God, and the Blessed Mary, and St. Benedict, and to Brother Robert and his convent taken from Quarr, and their successors of the Cistercian order in holy, free, pure, and per-

petual alms, for building and perpetually supporting an
abbey in honour of Mary, most blessed Mother of God, and
the blessed Benedict, the manors of Buckland, Bickley, and
Walkhampton according to their metes and bounds; that is
to say, from the Lobbapilla, on the western part of Bocland
towards the north and east, through the middle of the water
of Tavy, and from Walkhampton to the boundaries of Dartmoor, on the northern part of Mistor, and thence towards the
south by the boundaries of the Verderers (regardorum) of
Dartmoor, that is to say, by Mistorhead (Mistor panna), and
by Hysfochres, and by Siwards Cross and Gyllesburgh and
Plymcrundla to the Plym, and thence by the Plym towards
the west to Yaddabrook, and so by the bounds which surround Rydemore and Smalacumba, that is to say, by the old
ditch to the angle of the ditch of Yllalonde, and thence by
Hurtwallen to Smalacumbacrosse and Smalacumbalak, and
by the water course of Meavy to Olyak, and by the ditch to
the road which leads from Plympton to Schitestor, and so by
the stone bounds to Biricombaford and by Crewecumba, and
Denebrok, and [along] the course of the river Meavy to
Schollaford, and so by the old boundaries to Yanedonecross,
and thence by the bounds to Stoford and Lake and Churcheford, and by the divisions between Elleford and Crosseton to
Elfordlak and to the course of the river Meavy, and so to the
place where the Meavy falls into the Plym, and along the
Plym towards the divisions of Hescombe, and to the cross
roads beyond Purpris, and thence by passing along the way
which leads from Cadaworth bridge to Plympton through
the land of the Schagh towards the east as far as Shitaburgh,
and thence by old bound-stones to Haneketorr, and thence
towards the west and north through the land of Farnhill to
Maynstonktown and Maynstoncross and Horingbrook and to
Writewillak, and thence by a certain footpath to Pudehel,
including Southpudehel, and so along the bounds towards
the east to Horsford, and thence along the ancient metes to
Writewille and Horyngbrok, and so to the Plym and to
Wolewillebroke and to Wolewille Cross, and thence by the
road which leads from Sutton to Tavistock at Copriscrosse,
and thence towards the north along the ancient ditch to
Bycacumbayoneda, and so along the ancient bounds to
Lobbapilla.

And the lands and villeins of Tor at Shitestorr, lying near
to the manor of Bickleigh, with the appurtenances and with
their villanages and chattels and belongings, and the hundred
of Roborough, and with all profits thence arising with all

suits of freemen and bondmen, and with everything which belongs or may belong to the said hundred.

We have also given, granted, and confirmed to the same abbot and convent and their successors the lands and villeins of Torr at Schitestor, adjoining the manor of Buckeleye, with their chattells and suits.

We also have given, granted, and confirmed, to the same abbey and convent and their successors the hundred of Roborough with all profits thence arising, with all suits of freemen and villains, and with all liberties, free customs, or whatever things belong to the hundred or can accrue or belong in any way to the same.

We also have given, granted, and confirmed to the same abbot and convent and their successors the manor of Colunipton, according to its bounds, that is to say, from Colump by the land of St. Nicholas of Exeter to Smalabrok, and by the outer bounds of the land of la Brok to the road which leads to Padokbrok, and thence by Lutteskeskell and Ponteford, and by the boundaries from Hillesdon to Burn, and by Linor and Sweton, and Morston and Burn to Culump, and so by la Nyweloud to Rotherford Bridge, and a certain piece of land on the eastern part of that water near Kyngesmill, and thence by Stonweya, Crundla, Waterleta, Halstrewa, Westerhays, and Lattemere, to Cliffbrigg, with the lands of Halsholte, and the meadows and woods of Swenham, and with the advowsons of the churches of Boclond, Walkampton, and Bykelie, with the chapel of Schitestorr, with all that to the same manor and lands, and to the same hundred belong, whether in suit of court, demesnes, seignories, knight's fees, homage, scutage, service of free men, &c., without any reservation by us or our heirs. To have and to hold freely of the lord the king and his heirs to the same abbey and convent, and their successors, the same manor and lands, with the advowsons of the churches of Boclond, Walkampton, and Byklie, and the chapels of Schitestorr, and with the aforesaid hundred, with all their appurtenances whatsoever in holy, free, pure, and perpetual alms, free, &c. These being witnesses, Sir Henry of Chaumbernon, Oliver de Denham, Hugo Peverell, &c.

E.

CHARTER OF ISABELLA DE FORTIBUS WITH METES AND BOUNDS.

To all the faithful in Christ to whom this present writing shall come, Isabella de Fortibus, Countess of Albemarle and Devon and Lady of the Isle, health in the Lord; Know ye that we have granted and confirmed and by this present writing quit claim for ourselves and our heirs, to God and the monastery of the Blessed Mary and the Blessed Benedict of Buckland, and to the Abbot and Convent, and to their successors of the Cistercian order serving God in the same monastery, and to all those who shall hereafter serve him (there), all gifts and grants which the noble woman, our dearest mother Lady Amicia, formerly Countess of Devon and Lady of the Isle, obtained and gave to the same, namely, the manors of Boclond, Bykelie, and Walkampton, according to their metes and divisions, that is to say, from the Lobbapilla, on the western part of Bocland towards the north and east, through the middle of the water of Tavy, and from Walkhampton to the boundaries of Dartmoor, on the northern part of Mistor, and thence towards the south by the boundaries of the Verderers (regardorum) of Dartmoor, that is to say, by Mistorhead (Mistor panna), and by Hysfochres, and by Siwards Cross and Gyllesburgh and Plymcrundla to the Plym, and thence by the Plym towards the west to Yaddabrook, and so by the bounds which surround Rydemore and Smalacumba, that is to say, by the old ditch to the angle of the ditch of Yllalonde, and thence by Hurtwallen to Smalacumbacrosse and Smalacumbalak, and by the water course of Meavy to Olyak, and by the ditch to the road which leads from Plympton to Schitestorr, and so by the stone bounds to Biricombaford and by Crewecumba, and Denebrok, and [along] the course of the river Meavy to Schollaford, and so by the old boundaries to Yanedonecross, and thence by the bounds to Stoford and Lake and Churcheford, and by the divisions between Elleford and Crosseton to Elfordlak and to to the course of the river Meavy, and so to the place where the Meavy falls into the Plym, and along the Plym towards the divisions of Hescombe, and to the cross roads beyond Purpris, and thence by passing along the way which leads from Cadaworth bridge to Plympton through the land of the Schagh towards the east as far as Shitaburgh, and thence by old bound-stones to Hanekctorr, and thence towards the west and north through the land of Farnhill to Maynstonktown and Maynstoncross and Horingbrook and to Writewillak, and thence by a certain footpath to Pudehel, including Southpudehel, and so along the bounds towards the east to Horsford, and thence along the antient metes to Writewille and Horyngbrok, and so to the Plym and to Wolewillebroke and to Wolewille Cross, and thence by the road which leads from Sutton to Tavistock at Copriscrosse, and thence towards the north along the ancient ditch to Bycacumbayoneda, and so along the ancient bounds to Lobbapilla.

And the lands and villeins of Tor at Shitestorr, lying near to the manor of Bykelie, with the appurtenances and with their villanages and chattels and belongings, and the hundred of Roborough, and with all profits thence arising with all suits of freemen and bondmen, and with everything which belongs or may belong to the said hundred.

And the manor of Columpton according to its bounds, that is to say from Colump by the land of St. Nicholas of Exeter to Smalabrok, and by the outer bounds of the land of la Brok to the road which leads to Padokbrok, and thence by Lutteskeskell and Ponteford, and by the boundaries from Hillesdon to Burn, and by Linor and Sweton, and Morston and Burn to Culump, and so by la Nywelond to Rotherford Bridge, and a certain piece of land on the eastern part of that water near Kyngesmill, and thence by Stonweya, Crundla, Waterleta, Halstrewa, Westerhayes, and Lattemere, to Clifbrigg, with the lands of Halsholte, and the meadows and woods of Swenham and their appurtenances. And the land of Lygh with its appurtenances in Sampford Spiny. And the advowsons of the churches of Bocland Walkampton and Bykelie with the Chapel of Scitestorr. And all things which belong to the aforesaid manors and lands, and to the aforesaid hundred whether in suits of courts, rights, seignories, military service, homage, scutage, services of freemen, bondmen, with their services, chattels and suits, wards, marriage rights, reliefs, aids, rents, heriots, and escheats of all kinds, with meadows, pastures, pasturages, ways, paths, woods, arable land, mills with their dams and tolls, dove cotes, waters, fisheries, fish ponds, alder beds, moors, wastes, heaths, turbaries, strays, waifs, together with all liberties and free customs, and all other things, and appurtenances named and not named, which belong to the said manor and land, and to the said hundred or which from them to us, or to our heirs may accrue without any reservation or demand; to have and to hold the aforesaid manors, lands, hundred and advowsons of churches, and the aforesaid chapel with all their liberties, possessions, and appurtenances, by whatever name known, of our lord the king and his heirs, to the aforesaid abbot and convent, and to their successors of the aforesaid order, freely, quietly, entirely, absolutely, well, and in peace, without any exaction or demand, actions, or hindrance from us or of our heirs, in free and pure alms for ever.

And we the said Isabella will for ever acquit and defend

to the said abbot and convent, and their successors, the said manors and lands, advowsons of churches, and the said chapel, and the aforesaid hundred with all their liberties, things, and appurtenances, named and not named, against all nations, Jews or Christians. In witness whereof we have affixed our seal to the present charter with these witnesses, Brother Richard, prior of Christ Church, Twynham; Brother Thomas, prior of Brommor; Sir Richard, Fitz John, Richard of Affeton; Hugo of Peverell; Gilbert of Knovile; Reginald of Ferrers Knights; Ralph of Lynham; Stephen Stoil; William of Stapeldon; Simon of Travailesworth; William of Budekeside; Robert of Coleford; and others. Given at Brommor, the Feast of St. Edmund, King and Martyr, 1291.

F.

AWARD OF THE PRIOR OF PLYMPTON AND JAMES CHUDLEIGH.

THE PRIOR OF PLYMPTON, ETC.

To all the faithful in Christ to whom the present letters indented shall come. We, William the Prior of Plympton and James Chudleigh, Esq., send greeting in the Lord everlasting. Whereas divers suits and discords have been moved between William the Abbot of the House and Church of the blessed Mary of Bokelond of the one part, and James Derneford, Esq., of the other part, at length, by the intervention of friends between the parties aforesaid, peace hath been obtained in this manner; viz., that the parties aforesaid have submitted themselves to stand our judgment, ordinance, and award in the premisses, whereupon the aforesaid abbot by his council hath declared to us that whereas he and his predecessors from time to time, to the contrary whereof the memory of man is not, have held, and of right ought to have, the hundred of Roweborgh and a court of view of frankpledge, to be holden three times in the year at Roweborgh, and all which to view of frankpledge pertains, and also chattles of felons, fugitives, and escapes, of thieves, tumbrel, gallows, and pillory, with all the suit of free men and villeins, and with all liberties, free customs, or whatsoever things which to the hundred do pertain, or in any manner may accrue or pertain, as of the right of his church aforesaid. Nevertheless the aforesaid James Derneford hath caused to be set up a certain pillory and tumbrel at Estonhouse, and hath caused a certain court to be holden at Estonhous, within the precinct of the hundred aforesaid, and there hath caused to be presented in his court aforesaid by his ministers the assize of bread and ale there levied, and effusion of blood and of arms and injuries done against the peace, and other articles which ought to be presented in the view of frankpledge at the hundred aforesaid; and hath refused the bailiffs and ministers of the said abbot to levy amerciaments and distress at Estonhous of himself and his tenants there, and hath caused such and so many injuries to them that they are greatly impeded about the business of the said abbot in exercising his office there, so that the same abbot hath lost the profit of his hundred aforesaid for five years past, which he ought to have received within the precinct of his visne of the manor of Estonhous aforesaid during the same time; whereupon the aforesaid J. Derneford being summoned before us, the aforesaid arbitrators says that he does not claim any right in the premises, or any parcel thereof, as against him is declared, nor hereafter intends to claim, but supposeth himself to be thereof not guilty. Therefore we the arbitrators taking upon ourselves the burthen of the arbitration, having heard the proofs thereof and mature deliberation thereupon had, do arbitrate, order, and adjudge on Thursday next after the feast of Saint Barnabas the apostle, in the 26th year of the reign of King Henry VI. at Boklond Monochorum, that the aforesaid pillory and tumbrel and every of them, together with appurtenances and supports, before Thursday next coming, shall be deposed, destroyed, and removed, and thereafter not erected, nor the same or any other be there used by the aforesaid James Derneford, his heirs, or assignes, or by any other by his procurement. Also we arbitrate, order, and adjudge that the aforesaid James Derneford and his heirs shall not hereafter hold any court with view to frankpledge at Estonhouse aforesaid, nor on any manner intromit himself, nor delay the said abbot and his successors concerning any articles which to view of frankpledge pertain, and he and his heirs shall permit the bailiffs and ministers of the said abbot and his successors at Estonhous aforesaid to collect, levy, and distrain the amerciaments, fines, executions, and other emoluments whatsoever which in the court of the hundred aforesaid so come, or in anywise hereafter may come, and to make summonses and executions, and also distresses and attachments there, and the distresses and attachments to there made to lead, drive, and carry away, and to retain in their custody without the contradiction, inpediment, or disturbance of the aforesaid James Derneford and his heirs, tenants, servants, ministers, or other whomsoever by his abatement or procurement in any manner. Also we arbitrate, order, and adjudge that the aforesaid James Derneford shall pay to the aforesaid abbot and his successors, before the feast of St. Michael the archangel next coming after the date of presents, £20 for his costs and expenses which he hath sustained against the said James Derneford by occasion of the disturbance of the ministers of the said abbot in exercising his office in Estonshous aforesaid, and by reason of the execution and levying of the pillory and tumbrel aforesaid to be paid in favor of the said abbot by our award. Also we arbitrate, order, and adjudge that the security of this our award may for ever remain secure and be unbroken and be also secured in law as by the advice and counsel of Henry Fortescue and Wm. Hyndeston before the feast of St. Michael the archangel next coming shall and may be desired. In witness whereof we the aforesaid prior and James Chudleigh to these indentures have set our seals, dated the day, year, and place above said, and hereupon the aforesaid Henry Fortescue and Wm. Hyndeston on Thursday in the feast of the beheading of St. John the Baptist, in the 26th year of the reign of King Henry VI., at Bokelond Monachorum, have advised and given council upon the award, order, and judgment aforesaid that the aforesaid abbot, or some one of his successors of the house and church aforesaid do, or ought to, prosecute against the aforesaid James Derneford, Esq., an action of trespass according as the law on that behalf demands and requires concerning the matters whereof the aforesaid award, order, and judgment are by the aforesaid arbitrators made and rendered. And the aforesaid James Derneford, in his proper person or by his attorney, in the same action ought to plead, have, and defend himself according to the advice and counsel of the aforesaid abbot or his successors, at the costs and expenses of the said abbot or his successors; so that after judgment in the action aforesaid given, the damages, costs, and expenses by the said abbot or his successors recorded to the aforesaid James his attorney, be released, and in nowise levied.

G.

LIST OF THE ABBOTS OF BUCKLAND.

Name.	Approx. Date.	Authorities.
1. Robert.	1281?	Pleadings in Gyroband's complaint.
2. William.	1288	Named in grant by Margaret de Ripariis.
3. Geoffry.	1305	Rolls of Parliament.
4. Thomas.	1311	Proceedings in claim upon the Priory of Plympton.
5. William.		Agreement with Ralph de Bellworthy.
6. Thomas Wappelogh.	1356	Oliver.
7. John Bryton.	1385	Oliver.
8. Walter.	1392	Oliver.
9. John.	1442	Lease to William Pomeroy and others.
10. William Rolff.	1448	Proceedings against Derneford. Epis. Reg.
11. John Spore.	1449	Oliver.
12. John Hylle.	1454	Episcopal Registers.
13. Thomas Olyver.	1463	Episcopal Registers.
14. John Brundon.	1508?	Oliver.
15. Thomas Whyte.	1511	Leases. Agreement with Derkeham.
16. John Toker.	1528	Episcopal Registers, &c.

H.
PEDIGREE OF THE REDVERS FAMILY.
Abridged from Oliver and Pitman Jones' Pedigrees of the Courtenay Families.

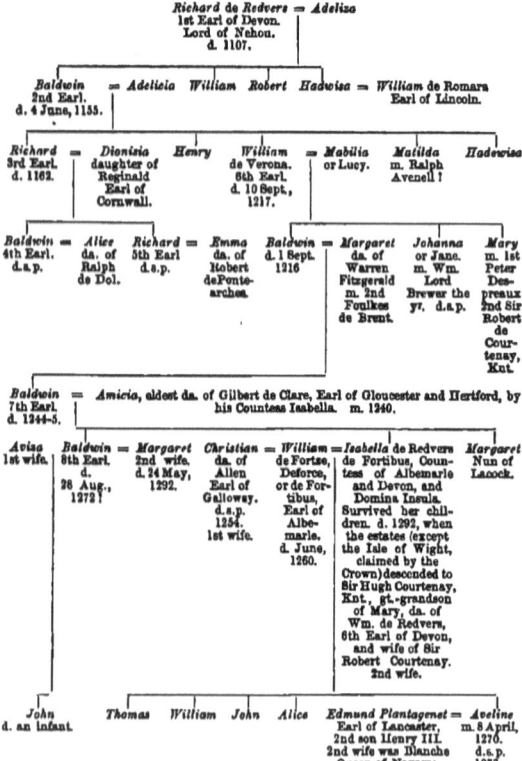

I.—DRAKE PEDIGREE.

NOTE.—The earlier pedigree and the connection of Sir Francis Drake with the Drakes of Ash is being worked out by Dr. Drake.—See *Arch. Journ.*, vol. xxx. p. 359.

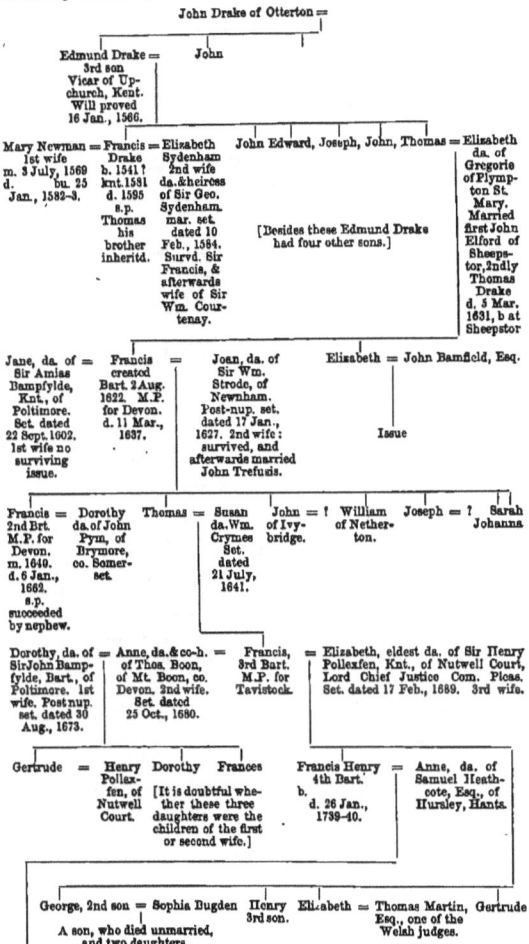

A

- **Francis Henry**, 5th Bart. b. 26 Aug. 1722, d. 19 Feb. 1794, when the estates passed to his nephew, the 2nd Lord Heathfield.
- **Francis William** of Hillingdon, co. Middlesex. Vice-adm. of the Red. bapt. 22 Aug., 1724. d. = **Elisabeth**, da. of Sir Wm. Heathcote, Bart. m. 1763. — Two daughters.
- **Francis Samuel**, Rear-adm. m. 1788. Created bart. 12 Aug. 1782. d. 1789. s.p. = **Pooley** da. Geo. Onslow, Esq.

Anne Pollexfen = **Sir George Augustus Heathfield**, created Baron Heathfield 6 July, 1787. d. 1790.

- **Francis Augustus Eliott**, 2nd Lord Heathfield. d. 26 Jan., 1813, and the title became extinct. Succeeded to the Drake estates on the death of his uncle, Sir Francis Henry Drake, the 4th Bart., 19 Feb., 1794.
- **Anne Eliott** = **John Trayton Fuller** of Ashdown House, Sussex.

Children of John Trayton Fuller and Anne Eliott:

- **Augustus Eliott Fuller** b. 7 May, 1777. m. 1801. d. 1857. s. & h.
- **Clara**, eld. da. & co-h. O. P. Meyrick, of Bodorgan, Anglesea. Issue
- **Francis John** Capt. 20th Dragoons. d. unmarrd. 2nd son.
- **Thomas Trayton** 3rd son. Assumed surname and arms of Eliott and Drake. Created Bart. 22 Aug., 1821, with rem. failure male issue to his brothers William Stephen and Rose-Henry. b. 8 Feb., 1785. m. 5 Aug., 1819. d. 6 June, 1870. s.p. Succeeded by his nephew, the present Bart. Became entd. under set. made by Sir Francis Henry Drake, 5 Bart.
- = **Eleanor** only da. of Jas. Halford, Esq., of Laleham, Middlesex. d. 18 Sept. 1841.

Children of Augustus Eliott Fuller:

- **William Stephen** 4th son. Capt. R.N. d. 10 Sept., 1815. s.p.
- **Rose-Henry** Capt. R.N. b. 1789. m. 1831. d. 1860. 5th son. = **Margaretta** da. of Sir Robert Sheffield, Bart.
- **Robert Fitzherbert** In holy orders. 6th son. = **Ursula**, da. of Sir Robert Sheffield, Bart. Issue
  1. Elisa = Jno Hamilton
  2. Sarah Maria
  3. Cordelia Eleanora
  4. Louisa
  5. Charlotte

Francis George Augustus Fuller Eliott Drake b. 24 Dec., 1839. m. 1861. Succeeded his uncle as second Bart. new creation, 6 June, 1870. Late Capt. Royal Horse Guards. Took by royal license, 3 Oct., 1870, additional surnames and arms of Eliott and Drake. = **Elizabeth**, daughter of Sir Robert Douglas, Bart., of Glenbervie.

- **Jane Eliza Anne Pollexfen** eld. da. m. 3 April, 1866. = **Rev. Robert Briscoe**, D.D., Rector of Nutfield, Surrey.
- **Eleanor Halford** m. 7 Aug., 1856. d. 21 Oct., 1858. s.p. 2nd da. = **Charles Eales** Esq., of Eastdon, Devon.

Son born 15 Oct., 1867.

Son born 3rd Nov., 1871. d. 1873.   Elizabeth Beatrice.

DESCRIPTION OF PLATES.

I. *a* Plan from Aislabie's map of the estate, hanging in the upper corridor at Buckland Abbey, referred to par. 37.
   b Ground-plan of the remains of the Church (approximate).
II. *a* and *b* Door-ways in the Turret of the building (plate VI.), described in par. 40.
   c The Abbey Church from the Perambulation Map, slightly enlarged, par. 37. See also *Transactions Devonshire Association*, vol. v. p. 512.
III. *c* Capitals of columns.
IV. Western Arch of Tower, showing springer of the Vaulting shafts.
V. *a* Boss Head of the Countess Amice (?) par. 43.
   b and *c* Corbels in Transept.
VI. West elevation of building referred to in par. 40.
VII. Seals and Arms of the Abbey, described par. 27.
VIII. Plaster Chimney-piece in the second floor of the Tower, with the arms of Sir Francis Drake, granted him 20 June, 1581, and the double motto. On the flanks, are the shields mentioned in par. 50.

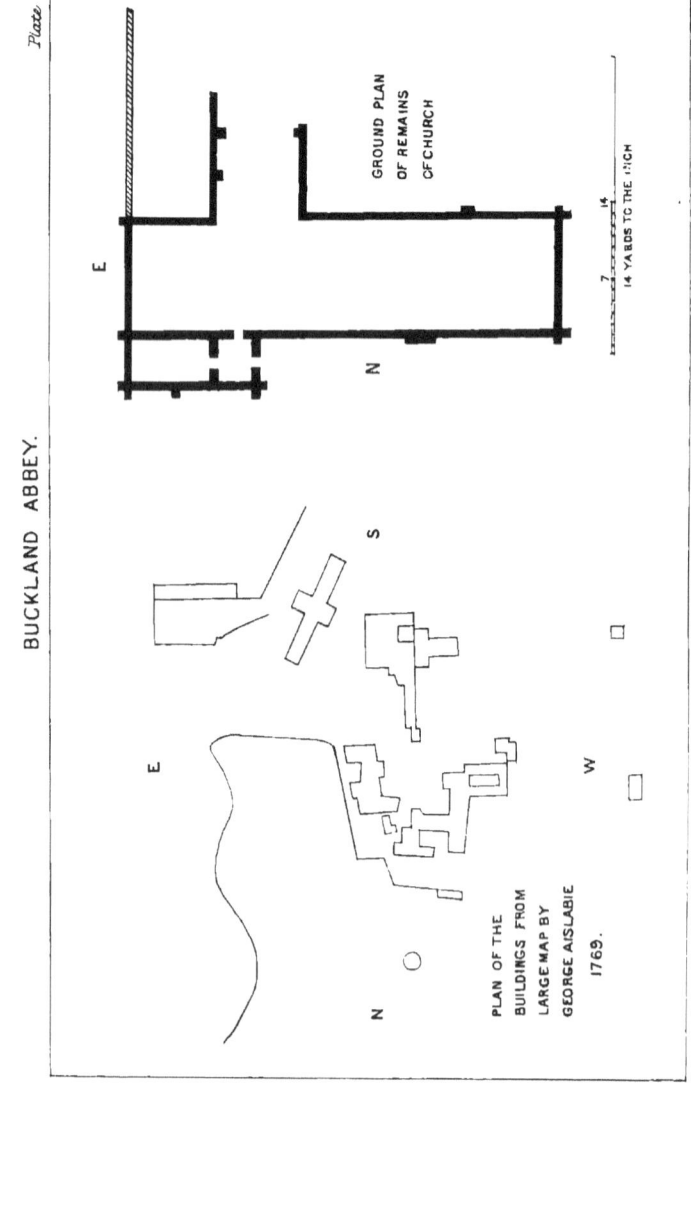

BUCKLAND ABBEY.

DOOR-WAY LEADING TO TURRET.

DOOR-WAY IN ROOM IN TURRET.

ABBEY CHURCH FROM DARTMOOR PERAMBULATION MAP.

BUCKLAND ABBEY.

Plate 3

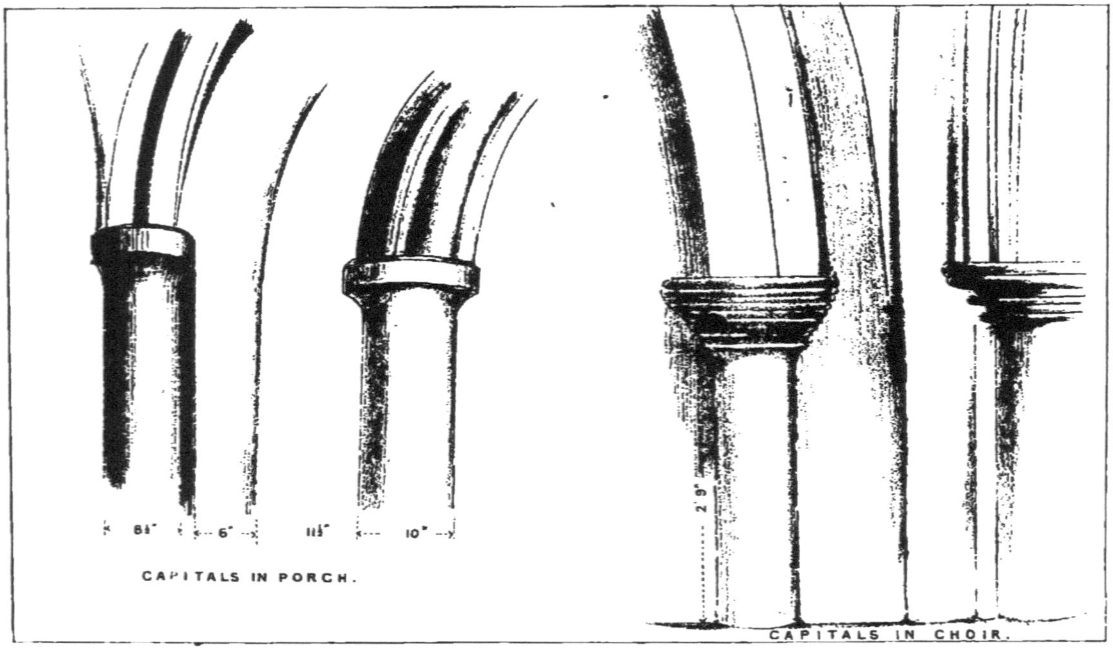

CAPITALS IN CHOIR.

CAPITALS IN PORCH.

Plate 4.

BUCKLAND ABBEY.

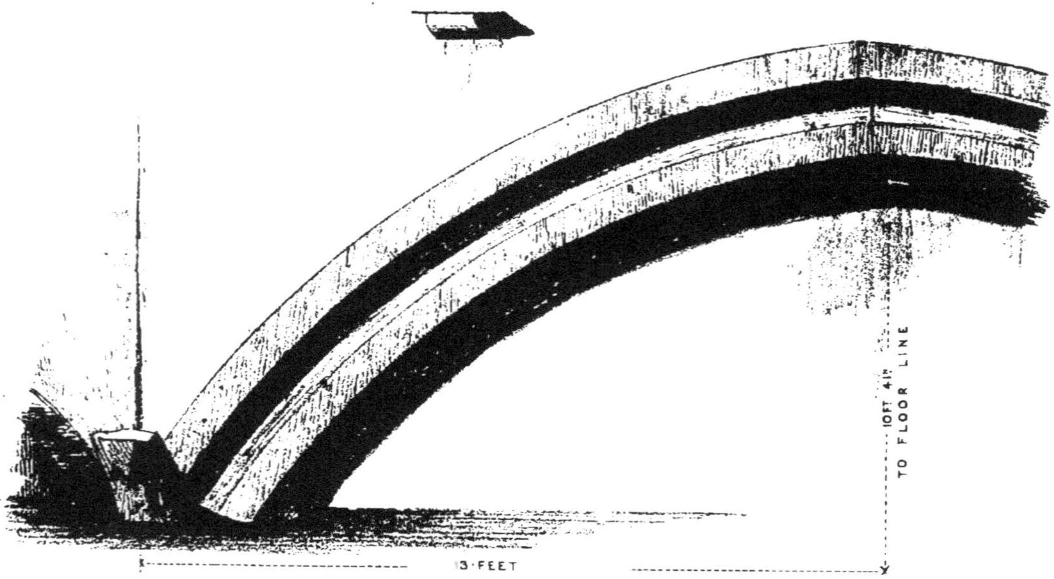

WESTERN ARCH OF TOWER

13-FEET

TO FLOOR LINE
10FT 4IN

BUCKLAND ABBEY.

BOSS.

CORBEL IN TRANSEPT.

CORBEL IN TRANSEPT.

BUCKLAND ABBEY. Plate 6

LODGE.

BUCKLAND ABBEY. Plate 7.

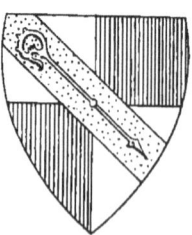

SEALS & ARMS.

BUCKLAND ABBEY. *Plate 8.*

CHIMNEY-PIECE ON SECOND-FLOOR OF TOWER.

THE

CISTERCIAN HOUSES OF DEVON.

II.

BUCKLAND—Concluded.

THE
CISTERCIAN HOUSES OF DEVON.

BUCKLAND.—CONCLUDED.

51. In my search for documents connected with Buckfast Abbey, I have met with a few relating to Buckland, which may as well be given, with a few additional quotations and notes, as a supplement to my former paper.

52. First as to the Abbey of Quarr, Quarrera, or Quarreria, in the Isle of Wight, from which Buckland was colonised, see par. 17. The pedigree of Buckland was as under:—

Savigny,
|
Quarr,
|
Buckland.

Quarr in the oldest deeds is called Quarraria, probably from the neighbouring stone-quarries. It was one of the first monasteries of the Cistercian order founded in England, and was, as I have before shown, begun by Baldwin, Earl of Devon, who, in the 32nd year of the reign of Henry I. gave the Manor of Arreton to Geoffry, Abbot of Savigny, for its building. The earliest charter now remaining is that of Engler de Bohun, who bestowed Haseley upon the monks, probably soon after Baldwin's donation. This deed was executed in Normandy and witnessed by Serlo, Abbot Geoffry's successor, and other Norman Bishops and Abbots. This, with other benefactions to the abbey, was confirmed by Richard son of Baldwin, whose deed without date must have been executed in the reign of Henry II. Most of the lands of the abbey appear to have been given in the reign of Stephen. There is also a grant from Henry, Duke of Normandy, of a place called Locwelle, in Normandy, for the monks of Quarr to build an abbey there, and a grant of confirmation from the

G

same Henry as King of England. This, Sir Richard Worsley conjectures to have been an act of gratitude in Henry to Earl Baldwin for espousing the cause of Matilda. Among the persons of consequence known to have been buried here are Earl Baldwin the founder, Adeliza his countess, and their son Henry. William de Vernun bequeathed £300 for the erection of a tomb here for himself and his father; the chapel also contained a monument to the Lady Cicely, second daughter of King Edward IV. (See *Dugdale's Monasticon, Hist. Isle of Wight,* p. 177, note.)

53. In the foundation deed of Amicia Countess of Devon mention is made of her daughter Margaret, described as a nun of Lacock. Lacock Abbey was in Wiltshire, founded in 1232 by Ella daughter of William Earl of Salisbury and widow of William Longspee, a natural son of Henry II. by fair Rosamond, and, in right of his wife, Earl of Salisbury. To this abbey Amicia gave the manor of Shorewell in the Isle of Wight, and also her heart. In all probability the body of Amicia was buried at Buckland, and her heart certainly was at Lacock. Her obit was kept at the latter place, on the Feast of St. Andrew, down to the Dissolution, and in the Valor is an entry:—"To money distributed to the poor on the feast of St. Andrew the Apostle for the soul of Amicia Countess of Devon, four bushels of corn worth 2s. 8d., and on the eve and day of that feast to three poor persons in bread drink and meat to each of them daily 2d. worth. 3s. 8d."

54. Of the documents, the first is from the Roll, Placita de Quo Waranto, Edw. I., whereby it appears that Amicia was called upon to show by what authority she held the hundreds of Wonford, Tiverton, Harrige, Roborough, and Axminster, and view of frankpledge, &c. in Tiverton, Collumpton, and Exminster, without licence, &c.

Amica Comitissa Devon' sum' fuit ad respond' dño Regi de p̃tito quo war̃'to tenet hundr̃a de WONFORD TYVERTON HAR-RIGG' RUBERGG & AXEMENISTRE que ad Coronam dñi Regis p̃tinent, Et quo waranto clam' h̃re visum francipleg' furcas emendas assis' panis & c'vis fracte in TYVERTON, COLUMP-TON' & EXEMINISTRE sine licentia, &c.

Et Amicia p' attor' suū venit, Et dicit q̃d non debet dño Regi ad hoc b̃re respond̃e quia dicit q̃d non tenet integre p̃dc̃a hundr̃a eo q̃d Abbas de Bocland tenet inde hundr̃a de HARRIGG & RUBERGG' et petit jud̃m de b̃ri.

Et Will's de Gyselh°m qui sequit̃ ͟dño Rege dicit q̃d licet p̃dc̃us Abbas teneat p̃dc̃a hundr̃a p̃dc̃ta Amicia tenetur responde dño Regi de tenancia suo quo ad alia hundřa et nisi inde respondeat petit judiciū de ip'a tanqᵃm de indefensa. Dies dat' est ei coram dño R'a die Pasch̃ in unū mensem ubicumq' &c. de audo judo suo &c.—Rot. 37. (Placita de Quo Waranto Edw. I. Ed: Rec. Com. fol 1818, p. 168.)

55. The next is from the Assize Roll, 1281: Robert of Buckland, who was the first abbot, is charged with unjustly dispossessing the Prior of Plympton of certain land:— At Exeter, Octave of St. Martin, 9-10 Edward I. A.D. 1281.

§ Assisa venit recogñ si Robs Abbas eccĩe sc̃i Benedc̃i de Boclaund frat̃ Rog̃us Iverlesboclond Witts le Forest̃ Thom̃ de Wythye Gilbs le Brewer̃ Witts de Wyrkᵃm Waltus de Eckeworth Robtus Gosce Rics de Crowet Witts de Elleswitt Rog̃us de Fylechᵃm Rog̃us Semer̃ Waltus le Provost Witts Russet Robs de Alwistoñ Rog̃us Upperig̃ Witts le Knyht Rics de Legh Rog̃us Orig' Gilbs de la Bure Thom̃ de Colewitt Thom̃ le Fotur Gilbs de Crewile Witts Altwy Waltus Uppehutt Ric̃us Bulymer Walterus Webbe Witts le Pyl Galfrs Aylmer Edwardus de Uptoñ Petr de Wobhutt Robs de la Yo Gilbs le Rede Robs de la Hole Ric̃us Berey Rog̃us Lond Godef'rs de Bikecumb et Rog̃us de Hamme injuste &c. disseis̃ Priorẽ de Plumptoñ de libo teñ suo in Plympton post p̃m ?c. Et unde querʳ q̃d diss̃ eum de quinq'ginta acr̃ tre cum ptiñ. Et Prior veñ et re' se de bři suo Ido p̃dc̃us Abbas et alii inde sine die Et Prior et p̃t sui de p̃s in mĩa scilt Galfrs le Frere et G'vas̃ de Crymel Postea c̃ovenit int̃ eos q̃d p̃dc̃s Abbas cogñ p̃dc̃as quinq̃ginta acr̃ tre cū ptiñ in Hetfeld juxa Pudele c̃o jus p̃dc̃i Prioris et ecc̃ie sue de Plympton et illas ei redd tenend p̃dc̃o Priori et succ̃ suis impet̃ Et p hac ?c. p̃dc̃s Prior c̃oc̃essit q̃d tenẽtos ip̃ius Abbis in Pudet̃ hcant communā in eisdem teñ tempe apto ad omnimoda avia etc. (Assize Roll, M. 1, 34.—1 Momb' 29d.)

56. The next is from the De Banco Roll, William charging Thomas the Abbot, and Brother John Bryton, monk of the abbey, and John Spenser, with breaking into the house of the said William at Collumpton and carrying off goods and chattels to the value of £10. The defendants did not appear, and we do not know the result.

Will's Couta p att̃ suū op' se iiijᵗᵒ die ṽsus Thomā Abbem de Bokland et frem Johem Brytoñ c̃omonacū eiusdē Abbis et Johem Spenser de ptito quare vi et armis domū ip̃ius Witti apud Colomptoñ freg̃unt et bona et cat̃ sua ad valenciā decẽ libraȝ ibidm invenī cēpunt et asptavunt et alia cnormia ci intulerunt ad gᵃve dampnū ipius Wiħi et cont⁻ pacē Reğ etc. Et ipe non veñ Et ħueř inde diē vsqȝ ad hunc diē scitt a die Pasche in tres septīas p essoñ suū postqam attacħ etc. I'o preē est viē q̄d distř eos p oñies ťr etc. Et q̄d de exiť etc. Et q̄d habet corpa eoȝ hīc a die sēi Micħis in xv dies etc. (De Banco Roll. East, 38 Edward III.)

57. In the Taxation of Pope Nicholas, 1291, we find some of the Abbey property mentioned:—

		£	s	d
Abbas de Bokland h't Man'ria de	Bokland q'd tax'	16	2	8
	Bikeley q'd tax'	16	2	8
	Walhampton & in Dertemore, q'd tax'	6	10	8
	Colompton q'd tax'	9	15	4
	Item apud Bikecumbe q'd tax'		13	4
S'mᵘ⁻		39	13	5
Decᵘ⁻		3	19	4½

(Pp. 146-153.)

There arc also two or three other scattered references.

58. The next, in Norman-French, from the White Book of Tenures in Cornwall, is a direction, that in consequence of the poverty of the Abbey it should be relieved from the payment of charges connected with the Forest of Dartmoor :—

Pur la maison de Bocklond. (fo. 61 b.)

Cornewaille. ffeᵛer Marȝ. Ian Dengť xxx E. etc. A ñre ch̄ vadlet Roƀt de Eleforď ñro señ de Corñ et Deveneš saluȝ. Porceqȝ noˢ avons entenduz q̄ la poure maison de ñre dame de Bokland est durement mult aninentie p̄ la charge et ȝvenue des forests de ñre foreste de Dertemore Sur quei noˢ desirrantȝ la relevacion de la dite maison Vous maundons q̄ vous mcismes ȝveicȝ q̄ ele ne soit chargee ou grevee p' les ditȝ forests ou auťs autrement q̄ ele ne doit estre de reson, et ne soeffrez q̄ labbe de la dite maison ou ses gentȝ et tenantȝ soient empeschieȝ ou endamageȝ p les ditȝ forests autrement q̄ nad estee vsee cinz ces heures ou q̄ ils deyvent estre de bon foi. Doñ etc. a lonďs le xiij iour de ffeᵛer Ian etc. p̄ ť levesqȝ de Wynē.

White Book of Tenures in Cornwall.—25-39 Edw. III.

59. The last document is a complete copy of the Ministers' accounts, 31-32 Henry VIII., so far as they relate to Buckland, carefully transcribed from the original. It gives full details as to the property of the abbey at the time, the rental, and the names of the various tenants.

BUCKLAND ABBEY, co. Devon.

Comp'a Oĩm et singuloȝ Balliuoȝ ꝑpoȝ Cott firmaꞃ et aꞇ nup'Monaster' Ministroȝ Computabiꞇ Oĩm et Singloȝ Dñioȝ Mañioȝ Terꞃ ot de Buckelande. tenꞇ Rectoꞃ poucoñ et porcoñ quaȝcumqᷓ tam Sp̄uaꞇ qam Tempaꞇ Dñi Regꝫ Dc̄o nup Moñ ptineñ sive spectañ viz. a ffesto sc̄i Michis Archi Anno Regni Henꞃ viijⁿ Deī gr̄a Angꞇ et ffraunc̄ Rꝫ fidei Defens Dñi hib̄n ac in terꞃ supmi Capiꞇꝫ Ecctie Augꞇ xxxjᵐᵒ vsqȝ iđm fb̄m sc̄i Michis Archi Anno eiusđm Dni Rꝫ extunc pxim̄ sequeñ sc̄iꞇ p vnū annū Integꞃ put inferius p̄t.

Comp'us Georgij Pollerde firmaꞃ ib̄m p tempus   Sciꞇ' d'ci nup' Mon' cū terr
p̄đcm.   D'nical' eid'm p'tinen'.

Nuꞇꞇ put in pede vltimi Comp̄i Anni px̄ p̄cedeñ plenius Arrerag. contꞃ.

Smᵘˢ—nuꞇꞇ.

Sed r̄ de—xxiij li. iij s. v d. de firm̄ Sciꞇ ib̄m cū Orꞇ pomaꞃ ffirm'. Gardiñ terꞃ praꞇ pasc̄ & pastuꞃ voc̄ Calses pke Barne pke Dedeh"m Quarry pke cū duobȝ pvis praꞇ eiđm Annex le Conyger Wyndemyll pke long pke cū 1 pvo praꞇ adiac̄ Longland Vyntens Oxenh"m Southefelde Penm)she pke Ookewell Higher Byckh"m Lower Byckeh"m Haylebolle Longpke Ruggomyll pke Cansey mede & Shepowayssho cū ȝ ptiñ eiđm sciꞇ ptiñ sive spectañ sic dim̄ p̄fato Comput ꝯ t̄mio xxj Annoȝ p Indeñ Dñi Rꝫ sub Sigiꞇꞇ Cuꞃ Augmeñ Reveñ coroñ ȝ ut asȝiꞇꞃ sot ad festa Annūc̄ b̄te Marie virginis & sc̄i Michis Archi equatr viz. p ij hmoi festis infra temp⁹ hui⁹ Comp̄i accideñ ut supra.

Smᵘˢ—xxiij li. iij s. v d.

Smᵘˢ Totlis firm̄ p̄đce—xxiij li. iij s. v d. q̄ libavit Thome Arundell Miliꞇ Rec̄ Dñi Rꝫ ib̄m de exiꞇ firme p̄đce huius Anni sine billa sed tm ex Recognicicoñ sua sup hunc comp̄m.

Comp'us Robti Toker Batt ib̄m p tempus p̄đcm.   Man'iū de
Nuꞇꞇ put in pede vltimi Comp̄i Anni px̄ p̄cedeñ plenius Colomptoñ cū
contꞃ.   cert' terr' in
                                                   Exoñ.
Smᵘˢ—nuꞇꞇ.   Arrerag.'

Sed r̄ de—ciiij s. vj d. de toto Redđ liboȝ Teneñ ib̄m p Redd' lib'o' Annū soꞇ ad fm sc̄i Michis Arch tm put p̄ Compm de Anno Tenen'. px̄ p̄cedeñ sup hunc Comp̄m exeunꞇ.

Smᵘˢ—ciiij s. vj d.

46 THE CISTERCIAN HOUSES OF DEVON.

Redd' Cust' Tenen'.   Et de—lvj li. vij s. xj d. de toto Redd Custum Tenen ibm p Annu cu xvj s. vj d. re int Tenen ibm p quodm redd voc loȝ guldage rent p Annu sot ad iiij⁰ʳ Anni tmios principat equis porcion put in Compo de Anno px pcedeñ ad larg annotat pleni⁹ contʳ.
Smᵘ—lvj li, xij s. xj d.

Terr' in Exoñ.   Et de—xxvj s. viij d. de Redd 1 Teñ infra Civitat Exoñ in tenuʳ Johᵃnne Chubbe vid p Annu sot ad tmios pdcos.
Smᵘ—xxvj s. viij d.

p'quis' Cur'.   Et de—x s. ix d. de pquis cuʳ ibm hoc Anno tent put p Rotlas eaȝdm sup hunc Compm ostens et examiat ultra xlj s. v d. de divs Amciam illevabit et pdonat tone Act pliam de goñali pdonac Dñi Re inde odit et pvis.
Smᵘ—x s. ix d.
Smᵘ Totlis Rec.—lxiij l. xiiij s. x d.
D quibȝ.

ffeod' et vad'.   Idm comput in food sive vad sui ipius compuᵗ Batt ibm ad lxvj s. viij d. p Annu sic sibi concess ac Wittmo & Hugoñ fit s p tmio vite coȝ p tras pateñ Dat sub sigillo nup conventuat ibm xxᵐᵒ die ffebruarij Anno ʳʳ Henrici viij˒ᵛⁱ xxv⁰ sot ad fest Annuc bte Marie virginis & sci Michis Archi equis porcion put in eisdm tris pateñ pleni⁹ contʳ viz. in Altone hmoi virtute traȝ pdict p hoc anno—lxvj s. viij d. Et in feod Johis Edmond Degennaʳ Manhij pdci ad xx s. p annu sic sibi silit Concess p tmio vite s p tras pateñ dci nup Abbis ʇ convent ibm dat xxᵐᵒ die Aprit Anno xxixⁿᵒ Re pdci sot ad fm sci Michis Archi tm viz in Altone hmoi virtute eaȝdm traȝ pateñ p hoc anno—xx s. Et in feod Anthonij Harvye subscñ Manhij pdci Ac Manhij de Bauntoñ ad xxvj s. viij d. p Annu sic sibi concess p tmio vite s p tras pateñ dci nup prioʳ & convent dat vj⁰ die Octobʳ anno xxxᵐᵒ Dñi Re pdci sot ad fest pdcm viz. in Altone hmoi Virtute traȝ pdcaȝ p hoc anno xxvj s. viij d. Et in Stipend ctici Auditoʳ scribeñ hunc compm put Cticis Audit Dñ Re Ducat s lancastʳ Allocaʳ Cons viz. in Altone hmoi put Alloc est in Annis pcedoñ—ij s.
Smᵘ—cxv s. iiij d.

Expen' Sen'.   Et in Expeñ Sent Ctici Cuʳ & At Officiaʳ ibm existeñ p cuʳ supᵃdict hoc anno tenend put p Rotut eaȝdm sup hunc compm ostens & examiat—xx s. ij d.
Smᵘ—xx s. ij d.

BUCKLAND ABBEY.

Et iu Denaȓ p dcm comp{a}nt̄ libat̄ Thome \
Arundell Milit̄ Recept̄ Dn̄i Rᵱ ibm do exit̄ } lvj l. xix s. iiij d. \
offic̄ ꝝ huius Anni sinc bitt sed t̄m ex \
Recognic̄ ꝝ sup hunc compm . . . . \
     Sm{ᵘ} Alloc̄ et libac̄ p̄dict̄—lxiij. li xiiij s. x d. \
Quo quidm Sm{ᵘ} correspondet sume Tot̄lis Rc{t} p̄dcc. \
             Et sic Eq.

Lib'ac' denar' \
r' Rec'.

COMP'US Walt̄i Langesforde Batt   Bucklond' Man'iū cu' hundred' de Rowburgh \
ibm p tempus p̄dcm.   Hayle Walkeh{a}mpton Shittistor & Rynmore cū \
                                   cert' terr' in Saultcaysshe. \
Nutt. put in pede vltimi compi Anni px̄ p̄cedeñ pleni? Arrerag'. cont{r}.
             Sm{ᵘ}—nutt.

Sed r̄ de—lix l. xij s. xj d. ob de toto Redd t{a}m liboȝ q{a}m Redd' Assis' \
custum̄ Teneñ ibm p Annū sot ad iiij{or} Anni t̄mios principat in Bucklond'. \
equis porc̄ put in compo de Anno px̄ p̄cedeñ ad larḡ Annotat̄ \
pleni{s} cont{r}. \
             Sm{ᵘ}—lix l. xij s. xj d. ob.

Et de—viij l. de Redd Assis in Hayle cū xx{a} de Redd Rowburgh & \
cuiusdm Coi̇e de Rowburgh p̄dca sot ad t̄mios p̄dict̄ put p Hayle. \
dcm compm de Anno px̄ p̄cedeñ. \
             Sm{ᵘ}—viij l.

Et de xxj l. xiiij s. viij d. ob de Redd Assis Custum̄ Teneñ Walkeh{a}m- \
cū iiij s. jd. ob. de Redd Guldaḡ ibm p Annū put pȝ p compm ton'. \
p̄dcm. \
             Sm{ᵘ}—xxj l. xiij s. viij d. ob.

Et de lxij s. xj d. de toto Redd Assis Teneñ ibm p Annū Shittistor & \
sot ut suṗ put pȝ p comp̄ p̄dcm.   Rynmore. \
             Sm{ᵘ}—lxij s. xj d.

Et de viij s. de Redd j Toñ ibm p Annū sot ut suṗ pȝ p Salteaysshe. \
compm p̄dcm. \
             Sm{ᵘ}—viij s.

Et de—xxiiij s. ix d. de p̄quis cur̄ ibm hoc Anno tent̄ cū P'quis' cur'. \
xxj s. de quod{a}m redd voc̄ Measure wheighte & watche sot p \
xiiij{d} decennar̄ ibm ex Antiq̄ cons put pȝ Rotul caȝd sup \
hunc Compm ostens & examiat̄ ultra xlviij s. iiij d. de divs \
Amciam̄ illevabit & p̄donat̄ r̄one Act̄ pliam̄ de geñali p̄donac̄ \
Dn̄i Rᵱ inde edit̄ & p̄vis. \
             Sm{ᵘ}—xxiiij s. ix d. \
    Sm{ᵘ} Tot̄lis Rct̄—iiij{li} xiiij l{r} ij s. iiij d. \
                    D quibȝ.

ffeod' & vad' cū Expen' Sen".

Iđm Comput in feođ sive Regarđ sui ipius Compute Baīt ibm ad xl s. p Annū sic sibi concesš p ỹmio vite š p tras pateñ dat sub Sigitt nup Conventuat ibm xxvj^to die Aprit Anno Frp Henric viij xxx^mo sot ad fm sci Michis Archi tm put in eisđm tris pateñ ad larğ rro^t pleni⁹ Apparet viz. in Attone ħmoi Virtute traʒ p̃dict p hoc Anno—xl s.

Et in Stipenđ Cħci Auditor scribeñ hunc compm put Alloc est in Ann pcedeñ—ij s.

Et in Expeñ Sen¹ Ctic Cur & at Officiar ibm existeñ p cur sup^adict hoc anno tenenđ put pʒ Rotut eaʒđm sup hunc compm . ostenš & examiat—iiij s. iij d.

Sm^us—xlvj s. iij d.

Decas' Redd'.

Et in defect Redđ j Teñ in Salteaysshe sup oħat in titlo p se ad viij s. p. Annū & duoʒ Teñ nup in te^a Joħis v^s Holdm^a & Joħis Broke iiij s. xj d. supius oħat in titlo redđ

sic dimiss' p' discrec' Auditor' & Recept'.

Assis Mañlij p̃dci infra Sumñam lviij l. xiiij s. x d. ob ad ix s. xj d. p annū. Et qđ dict Teñ totlr in decaš sunt & exist vac ac in nulli⁹ te^a p totū temp⁹ hui⁹ compi ex sacro dci compute viʒ. in defect ħmoi Redđ p temp⁹ p̃dcm xvij s. xj d.

Sm^us—xvij s. xj d.

lib'ac' Denar' r' Rec'.

Et in denar p Compntp libat Thome Arundell Milit Rec Dñi Rp ibm de exit officij š huius Anni sine bitt sed tm ex Recognic š sup hunc Compm } iiij^xx x l. v s. iiij d. [?]

Sm^us Alloc et libac p̃dict—iiij^xx xij li. ix s. vj d.

Et debt xxxij s. x d. q̃ Allo^r ei ut de tot Dcñ p ipm solut p divš Repac fact & impoit sup Divš Teñ & Cotag infra Mañiū p̃dcm hoc Anno maxie Ruinos ut in empcioñ Tegut finđ Clav Calc & areñ ac at ad hec necessar put p bitt de pticlis inde sup hunc compm ostenš & examiat.

Et Eq.

Byckeleigh & Shagh p'cell' Man'ij' de Buckland' p'dict' Arrerag.

Comp'us Joħis Stepħyñ Batti bm p tempus p̃dcm.

Nuīt put in pede Vltimi Compi Anni pʒ p̃cedeñ pleni⁹ cont^r.

Sm^us—nutt.

Redd' Assis'.

Sed r̃ de xxiiij l. iiij s. vij d. de toto Redđ t^a m liboʒ q^a m Custuñ Tenenc ibm p Annū sot ad iiij^or Anni tmios principat equis porc put in Compo de Anno pʒ p̃cedeñ ad larğ Annotat plenius cont^r.

Sm^us—xxiiij li. iiij s. vij d.

Et de iiij l. vj s. viij d. de firm̄ j Molend̄ ibm p Annū sic firm' Molen d.
dim̄ Thome Boreman̄ p Inden̄ ut Ass⁹it' sol ad festa p̄dca ut de Byckeleig h
pȝ in Comp̄o de Anno p̄x p̄ceden̄.
    Smᵃ—iiij l. vj s. viij d.

Et de xxvij s. vij d. de p̄quis xiij᪽ cur̄ ibm hoc anno tent P'quis' Cur'.
cū ixᵃ de h̄iett vij s. v d. de Redd̄ cens̄ ⁊ xj s. ij d. de At
p̄quiś put pȝ Rotul eaȝdm sup hunc comp̄m ostens̄ ⁊ examiat̄
ultᵘ xxix s. v d. de div̄s Am̄ciam̄ illevabit ⁊ p̄donat̄ r̄one Act
p̄liam̄ de gen̄ali p̄donac̄ Dn̄i Regȩ inde edit̄ ⁊ p̄vis.
    Smᵃ—xxvij s. vij d.

    Smᵃ Totlis Reᵗ—xxix li. xviij s. x d.
                       D quibȝ.

Idm Comput̄ in food̄ sive Regard̄ sui ip̄ius computᵗ Balł ffeod' & Vad'.
oīm & singloȝ Dn̄ioȝ Man̄ioȝ Terr̄ & Ten̄ cū om̄ibȝ eoȝ Membris in Byckleigh Abbottesrowe & Shagh ac vis fr̃ᵃunc̄ pleḡ
Man̄ij de Buckelond voc̄ Holme Baliff ad xxvj s. viij d. p
Annū sic sibi concess̄ p t̄mio vite s̄ p tras paton̄ dat̄ sub
Sigillo nup conventual ibm ixⁿᵒ die Aprił Anno r̄rȩ Henrici
viij ᵛⁱ xxxᵐᵒ sol ad f'm s̄ci Mich̄is Archi tantū put in eisdem
tris paten̄ ad larḡ rroᵗ plen̄i⁹ liquet viz. in Aƚƚone h̄moi virtute traȝ p̄dictᵗ p tempus huius comp̄i—xxvj s. viij d. Et in
food̄ sive Regard̄ cuiusdᵃm Simon Lawry Decennar̄ oīm &
singloȝ Dn̄ioȝ sive Man̄ioȝ p̄dict̄ ad vj s. viij d. p Annū viz.
in Aƚƚono h̄moi cauś excic̄ offic̄ȩ huius Anni put Alloc̄ est in
An̄n̄ p̄ceden̄—vj s. viij d. Et in Stipend̄ Clici Auditor̄ scriben̄
hunc comp̄m put Alloc̄ est in An̄n̄ p̄ceden̄—ij s.
    Smᵃ—xxxv s. iiij d.

Et in Denar̄ p dem computᵗᵉ solut̄ p expen̄ sen' Clici Cur̄ & Expen' Sen'.
Ał Officiar̄ ibm existen̄ ad Cur̄ supᵃdict̄ hoc Anno tenend̄
put pȝ Rotul eaȝdm sup hunc comp̄m ostens̄ & examiat̄—
xlj s. j d.
    Smᵃ—xlj s. j d.

Et in Denar̄ p dem computᵗ libat̄ Thome   ⎫   lib'ac̄' Denar'.
Arundell Milit̄ Rec̄ Dn̄i Rȩ ibm de exit̄   ⎪
offic̄ sui huius Anni sine bill sed r̄m ex   ⎬ xxiiij l. xix s. iiij d.
Recognic̄ s̄ sup hunc comp̄m   .   .   ⎭   r' Rec'.
    Smᵃ Allocac̄ et libac̄ p̄dict̄—xxviij l. xv s. ix d.

Et Debt—xxiij s. j d. q̄ Allor ei ut de tot den̄ p nov̄ fcurˢ
j pinfald̄ Dn̄i Regȩ ibm p Salv̄ Custod̄ Catall p dco Dn̄o
Rege district in eodm pinfald̄ ponend̄ hoc Anno sine bill sed
tm ex sacr̄o dci computᵗᵉ   Et Eqȝ.

Buckelonde Rector'. Arrerag'.

Comp'us Robti Tooker firmar ibm p tempus pdcm.
Idm oʳ do—xviij li. de arr̄ vltimi compi Anni px pcedeñ put ibm pleni⁹ contʳ.
Smᵘ—Pȝ.

ffirm' Rector'.

Sed r̄ de—xviij l. de firm̄ oïm Decim̄ Garb Rect p̄dict cū Om̄ibȝ At Com̄od eidm p̱tiñ sic dim̄ p̄fat Computᵗ Wittmo & Hugoñ fit ȝ de quinqueñ in quinquenniū durañ t̄mio lx Anñ p̱ Indeñ Dat quinto Die Octobr̄ Anno r̄rę Henrici viijᵛⁱ xxvijᵐᵒ sot ad fm sci Andree t̄m put in eadm Indeñ ad larḡ irroᵗ plenius contʳ.
Smᵘ—xviij l.

r' Rec'.

Smᵘ Totlis ffirme p̄dict cū Arr̄—xxxvj li. De qibȝ libavit Thome Arundell Milit Rec Dñi Rę ibm de exit firm̄ ȝ p̄dict hoc Anno sine bitt sed t̄m ex Recognic ȝ sup hunc Compm— xviij l. Et debt—xviij li. . . . . . Totū.

Sup'.

Ipm Computᵉ de Arr̄ firm̄ ȝ huius Anni eo q̄d het Diē Soluc inde uxsq, fm sci Andree px futur̄ post Claus hui⁹ Compi put p Indeñ dci firmar̄ . . . . xviij l.

Rect de Walkhᵉmton & Shittistor'. Arrerag,.

Comp'us dci Robti Tooker firmar̄ ibm p tempus p̄dcm.
Idm oʳ de—vij l. x s. de Arr̄ Vltimi Compi Anni px pcedeñ pleni⁹ contʳ.
Smᵘ—Pȝ.

ffirm' Rect'.

Sed r̄ de—vij l. x s. de firm̄ decim̄ Garb eiusdm Rectoʳ ac de iijᵇᵘˢ Teñ in Byckleigh cū om̄ibȝ at Com̄odit eidm Rectoʳ p̱tiñ sic dim̄ p̄fat Compi Wittmo & Hugoñ fit ȝ p t̄mio lx Annoȝ p̱ lndeñ supius in Compo px pceden specific sot ad fm sci Andree p̄dict put p Indeñ p̄dict.
Smᵘ—vij l. x s.

Smᵘ Totlis ffirme p̄dict—xv li. q̄ libavit Thome Arundell Milit Rec Dñi Rę ibm de exit firm̄ p̄dict hoc Anno sine bitt sed t̄m ex Recognic ȝ sup hunc Compm—vij li. x s. Et debt—vij l. x s.

Sup Ipm Computᵉ de Arr̄ firm ȝ hui⁹ Anni. Eo q̄d het Diē ut sup̄—vij l x s.

Rect' de Bampton'. Arrerag'.

Comp'us supᵉdci Robti Tooker firmar̄ ibm p tempus p̄dcm.
Nutt put in pede Vltimi Compi Anni px pceden plenius contʳ.
Smᵘ—nutt.

Sed r̄ de—xl li. de firm̃ Rector ib̃m cū Manc̃ dom̃ Clausur̄ ffirm'. ter̄r̃ Teñ necnon fruct̃ decim̃ oblacioñ & At pfic̃ quibuscūq̃ eid̃m Rect̃ ptiñ sic dim̃ p̃fat̃ Comput de qūinqueñ in quinqueñ durañ t̃nio lxt Anno₂ p̃ Indeñ dat̃ xxiiijto die Julij Anno r̃rc̃ Henrici viijvi xxvjto sot ad ffest̃ Pasche & Nat̃ Dñi p̃ equat̃ porcioñ cū xx l. p̃ penc̃ Vicar̄ ib̃m xl s. sot Ep̄o Exoñ & Decañ & Capit̃lo ib̃m p̃ pencioñ s̃ Ac xv s. ix d. sot Archno Exoñ p̃ Sinod̃ & pcur̄ Om̃ib; At ob̃ib; pochiat & Capell sci Luce put in eadem Indeñ ad larg̃ irrot plenius cont̃r.

Sm̃ᵘˢ—xl li.
Sm̃ᵘˢ Tot̃lis ffirme p̃dict̃—xl li.

D quib;.

Id̃m Comput̃ in Denar̄ solut̃ Vicar̄ ib̃m p̃ pencioñ s̃ ad P'enc' & Porc' xx l. p̃ Annū sic sibi & Succ̃ suis concess̃ p̃ quand̃m Compos ᶜᵘ Sinod' & inde int̃ dict̃ Vicar̄ ac nup̃ Ab̃b̃em & Convent̃ ib̃m confect̃ viz. ᵖ'ᶜᵘʳᵃᶜ' in Alt̃one h̃moi p̃ tempus huius comp̃i—xx l. Et in Consīlib; pencioñ Anntˡ sot Ep̄o ˣˡˢ & Decano ˣˡˢ & Capit̃lo Exoñ ᵛⁱᵈᵉⁿᵗʳᶜᵒⁿᶜᵉˢˢ. exeunt̃ exᵃ Rector̃ p̃dict̃ ad xl s. p̃ Annū viz. in Alt̃one h̃moi p̃ tempus huius Comp̃i put ab Antīq̃ Allocar̄ Cons̃ in Añ p̃cedeñ—xl s. Et in Denar̄ solut̃ Archno Exoñ p̃ Sinod̃ & pcurac̃ p̃ Annū put om̃ino Allocar̄ Cons̃—xv s. ix d.

Sm̃ᵘˢ—xxij l. xv s. ix d.

Et in Denar̄ p̃ p̃dcm computˡᵉ lib̃at̃ ⎫ lib'ac' denar'.
Thome Arundell Miᵗ Rec̃ Dñi Rc̃ ib̃m de ⎬
exit̃ firm̃ p̃dce sine bit̃ sed t̄m ex Recognic̃ ⎭ xvij l. iiij s. iij d. r. Rec'.
s̃ sup hunc comp̃m .

Sm̃ᵘˢ Allocac̃ et lib̃ac̃ p̃dict̃—xl l. Que quid̃m Sm̃ᵘˢ correspond sum̃e Tot̃lis firm̃ p̃dict̃.

60. In 1553 we find the following monks still alive and enjoying their pensions:—

John Tooker, Abbot . .	60	0 0
John West . . .	5	0 0
Thomas Hooper . .	5	0 0
William Gye . . .	5	0 0
William Alford . . .	5	0 0
Benedict Lonege . .	4	13 4
William Milford . .	4	0 0
William Ebsworth . .	3	6 8
John Jordayne . . .	3	6 8

Thomas Maynard, Robert Troope, Hugo Harvey, and Simon Rugeway having died in the meantime.

61. The enlargement from the old Dartmoor Perambulation

Map accompanying my first paper is incorrectly engraved. On reference, I find my drawing is right, but the lithographer has taken liberties, and on the right-hand side of the tower and transept has inserted an upper row of windows, giving the appearance of a clerestory, which is altogether wrong. The engraver has also made the buildings above, more distinct than they are in the original drawing.

61. In connection with Sir Francis Drake, I may mention that after our last meeting Captain Swann, of Honiton, was good enough to write me, asking if I had met with any boxes on which were carved or engraved the arms of Sir Francis Drake, and describing one in his possession. Curiously enough, his letter reminded me of a box which I had seen, which, as far as I could recollect, corresponded with the description given by Captain Swann. Of course, when wanted, the box could not be found, and it was supposed to have been altogether lost. Fortunately, within the last few weeks it has been recovered. It bears the inscription, John Brisset fecit, 1712. The arms of Drake appear in a shield, *A fess wavy between two polar stars;* above is a helmet and the crest, *a ship under ruff, drawn round a terrestrial globe with a cable rope by a hand out of the clouds.* The letters A. D. stand for the crest motto. The motto, *sic parvis magna*, is below the shield. At the top are the words " Sir Francis Drake," and below the ship the words, " The Adventure—Europe, America [? Hispania], Asia, Africa." The mantling is very good and the work delicate.

There is a box similar to this in the British Museum, and I have heard of others, and it would seem that there are many in existence of various sizes.

THE
CISTERCIAN HOUSES OF DEVON.

III.
BUCKFAST.

THE

CISTERCIAN HOUSES OF DEVON.

BUCKFAST.

62. The Abbey of Bulfestra, the name by which we find it called when we first learn of its existence, occupies a site—within the hundred of Stanborough, the Deanery of Totnes, and the parish of Buckfastleigh—which is not so typical of a Cistercian selection, nor so secluded, as are many of the houses of the White Monks. It is situated, it is true, in the deep valley, close by the river, selected originally more for use than pleasure, with the hills surrounding the retreat, and protecting the pasture land; but still, beautiful as the position is, and charming as is the scenery (and those who know Turner's exquisite engraving will not say that the painter has exaggerated its loveliness), there is not that sense of repose, that feeling which comes over the visitor of distance and apparent estrangement from the world without, which is so characteristic of many abbeys of the Cistercians. I must assume my hearers to be acquainted with the facts relating to the general history of the order contained in my first paper, pars. 1 to 14.

63. Throughout this paper I shall use the convenient word "Buckfast" in speaking of the abbey. We find the spelling varying from time to time in the different documents relating to the house—Bulfestra, Bulfestre, Bugfasta, Bocfasta, Bussestre, and Buckfestria, are instances. In the earlier deeds the last syllable has ordinarily the "r," which was dropped as time went on. The spelling Bussestre is evidently a mistake of the scribe or copyist mistaking the letter "f" for a long "s."

64. Unlike the abbey to which my two preceding chapters have been devoted, which was one of the latest mediæval monastic foundations in England, the early history of the Abbey of Buckfast is lost in remote antiquity.

65. It is one of the common errors, which, like the vulgar belief that all monks were and are priests, I suppose will never be eradicated from the mind of the ordinary Englishman, that monasteries had their rise in and only flourished during the middle ages. In spite of all that has been written and said, it is forgotten by many, that from the first institution of Christianity, to say nothing of the earlier dispensation, lives of seclusion were found necessary for the welfare of many souls whose lots were cast in the midst of a world steeped in heathen wickedness. And Britain from the first had monks, and the fury of the English vented itself upon them, and upon their priests, their altars, and their churches. The story of the massacre of the monks of Bangor will recur to everyone, and scattered throughout the pages of the earliest chroniclers are references to places which, if not monasteries in the sense in which we use the word, were places of retirement and religious asceticism. If these facts are forgotten, it is not much to be wondered at that the early history of the Abbey of Buckfast should have been lost sight of by the casual reader.

66. In all probability the abbey was in existence before the coming of the North-man, and it is an unquestionable fact that monks were settled in the pleasant spot on the banks of the Dart long before the Norman Conquest. The account will therefore carry us far back through the story of England's history.

67. There appears to be no good reason for doubting the claim, rather proudly put forward by the Buckfast monks in the reign of Edward I., where the jurors affirm that they, the monks, said that the Abbey held a certain manor called Sele Monachorum, by the gift of King Cnut,—
"*Dicunt quod Abbas Bucffestrie tenet quoddam manerium quod vocatur Sele monachorum in perpetuam elemosinam de dono regis Cnud.*"—Rotuli Hundredorum, Edw. I.

There can be little question that that sagacious monarch was interested in some way in this part of his kingdom of Wessex. You will recollect Lyfing was his companion on his pilgrimage to Rome, and to him, the then Abbot of Tavistock, afterwards the famous Bishop, the King entrusted that remarkable letter to his English people which contains so much kingly wisdom, and shows so much anxiety for the welfare of his subjects. Cnut, during his reign, did much for religion, and conferred many a gift upon the monks, and Ely and St. Edmundsbury, Glastonbury and Winchester, among other places, benefited by his bounty, and long cherished his memory, and the Church, during the years of peace which he gave to the country, fostered literature, art, and, to some extent, science, and spread throughout the land "great buildings and busy schools."

68. From the list of their possessions after the Conquest, it is not rash to assume that the monks of Buckfast received something more than the manor of Sele from the Danish King. In the possession of the Dean and Chapter of Exeter is a charter of Cnut, conferring land upon Burhwold, the Bishop of St. Germans, in which I think may be recognised the names of places in Devon, and on the death of Burhwold the King assented to the request of Lyfing, who was then Bishop of Crediton, that the sees of St. Germans and Crediton might be united, and to this king and the once Abbot of Tavistock, and to his successor Leofric, the establishment of the see of Exeter, as we now have it, is due. It is in our time, after a union of nearly nine hundred years, that the ancient sees of Devon and Cornwall are again to be separated.

69. From the death of Cnut, 1035, to the date of the Domesday Survey is but fifty years or thereabouts, and in the Great Survey we find clear evidence of the existence, and a list of the possessions, of Buckfast Abbey. Whatever the foundation of the Abbey might have been, Domesday Book shows us that at the time of the Survey Abbot Alwine and his monks were not only settled at Buckfast, which was the head of the abbacy, but had considerable possessions in land and other property in the county. The entries are interesting and valuable, and further on will be found translations which I have made from the Exeter and Exchequer books. The former, belonging to the Dean and Chapter, is supposed to have been the groundwork of the Exchequer book (the one intended to be preserved as the permanent record), and, as is apparent on comparing the two, much more full in its information. Thus, in 1086 it is clear that there was a religious house at a place called Bulfestra, that it had considerable property, and was apparently in a flourishing condition. There can be no question that this place was Buckfast Abbey.

70. It has been always stated, that in some way or other this house was dissolved after the Conquest, its possessions confiscated, its inmates scattered, that this was probably the work of the Conqueror, and that the land was given to the Pomeroys. But this could not, I think, have been the case. Because, to a great extent, the troubles of the Con-

quest were over, the land had been apportioned, William had rewarded his companions, and among the great lords whose lands are enumerated in Domesday the Abbey of Buckfast appears with Baldwin de Redvers, William de Pomeroy, and others, as holding large domains Domesday Book was completed only a short time before William met his death in the streets of Mantes, and yet within fifty years the abbey is said to have been dissolved, its possessions divided, and a new house founded in the same place. If such were the case, how did it happen, and what were the reasons for such a spoliation? A conjecture might be hazarded that the Red King found the abbey lands conveniently near his hunting-grounds in the Forest of the Dartmoors, and took possession of them with the usual disregard of the rights of the Church shown by him, but there is no evidence to support such a theory, and I think, although the contrary has always been stated, that I shall be able to adduce good grounds for believing that the monks of Buckfast continued to hold the lands that belonged to them at the time of the Great Survey uninterruptedly for five centuries after.

71. The only evidence as to the supposed dissolution and re-foundation of the Abbey is the unsupported statement of Leland, who says that *Ethelwardus filius Gul. Pomerey erat primus fundator.* Coll. Hearne, vol. i. p. 80, ed. 1770. Dugdale, with more caution, following him, says, that Ethelward is said to have been its founder, and Pole, Westcote, and Risdon, wishing to convey the same information, but making utter confusion of it and copying one another, tell us in the calmest way, that Duke Alford erected a fair abbey of the Order of Cistercians, Pole and Risdon saying that this happened before the Conquest. It is, I think, evident that the Duke Alford of the last mentioned writers is the Ethelward of Leland and Dugdale. It is also very evident that the additional statement of Pole and Risdon, "before the Conquest," cannot be true, simply because it is certain that there were no Cistercians in existence anywhere for more than thirty years after the Conquest, and that there was no Cistercian house in England until the year 1128.

72. An examination of the case with reference to Ethelward also induces us to believe that the claim made for him that he was the founder rests on no substantial foundation. His name is not mentioned in any deed or charter relating to the Abbey, and he is not in any way referred to in the royal confirmations of Henry and Richard, which are dated not long after 1137, the date of the alleged foundation. Again, the

greater part, if not the whole, of the lands mentioned in Domesday can be traced as being in the possession of the abbey at the end of the twelfth and the beginning of the thirteenth centuries; and even supposing that they had in some mysterious way, scattered as they were throughout the county, come as a whole into the hands of Ethelward de Pomeroy, it is not likely that they would have been granted in their entirety to the monks of Buckfast. But there is another fact of greater weight. In the deed of King Henry, which I shall refer to presently, and which was given before 1161, all the lands and tenements, and so on, belonging to the Abbey were confirmed to the monks, as they held them, "*avi mei.*" Henry died in 1135, two years before the alleged foundation by Ethelward. We have therefore to suppose that the land continued in the possession of the Abbey from the date of Domesday until some time in the reign of Henry I. and then it passed somehow to Ethelward, who in course of time established the monks afresh in the same locality, and endowed them with the same lands. In the unsettled state of the country during the reign of Stephen, the monks did not, as far as we know, trouble themselves to obtain a confirmation from that monarch; but, as soon as Henry's kingdom was firmly established, a charter confirming them in their possessions was obtained from the king.

73. Doubtless Ethelward was a benefactor to the Abbey, and on this account he and his descendants were held in grateful remembrance by the monks for many a long year, and on several parts of the ruined buildings, before their final destruction, the crest or badge of the Pomeroys, the red lion rampant, was to be seen, and there can be little question but that the story of Ethelward being the founder of the abbey arose from this fact.

74. I think, therefore, we may conclude, as far as the evidence goes at present, that there was no dissolution of the Abbey, and that Ethelward was not the first founder.

75. We have no clue whatever as to what the original foundation of the Abbey was, but in all probability it was Benedictine, and we know that it became a daughter house of Savigny, which sprang from the hermitage, afterwards the abbey, founded by Raoul de Fugeres and John de Landere in 1112, and which in 1148 was united to the Cistercian Order. Whether Buckfast became Cistercian at the time that Savigny and many others did, cannot be ascertained; probably it did not, as the confirmation charter of Henry II. about 1161, speaks of the monks "*que sunt ordine Savigny,*"

which seem to show that Buckfast did not pass in 1148, when the fourth Abbot of Savigny surrendered his house and its dependencies into the hands of St. Bernard. Leland says, "*Cænobium de Bukfest olim incepit per fratres quos appellabunt Grysæos, deinde admisit Bernardinos.*" *Collectanea*, vol. 3 (4) p. 152, ed. 1770.

76. Here he says that the monastery of Buckfast was commenced by brethren called "Grysæos," afterwards admitted Bernardines. "Grysæos" stands for the "grisei monachi," the monks of the order of Savigny. This extract from Leland I have never seen quoted; perhaps, from the sentence being curiously inserted in a list of manuscripts belonging to the Abbey, it has been overlooked. Leland's statement is confirmed by that in the charter of Henry II., to which I have just referred, "*monachis de Bugfasta qui sunt de ordine de Savineio.*"

77. What led Dr. Oliver to make the statement that Buckfast was colonized from Waverley I cannot imagine. There is not the slightest evidence, so far as I am aware, of there having been any connection between Waverley and Buckfast. Dr. Oliver seems also to have been confused as to Waverley itself, for he says that it was a daughter of the Abbey of St. Mary at Savigny, the fact being that it was a daughter of L'Aumone.

78. There is no foundation charter of the Abbey. The earliest document I can find relating to it, after Domesday, is the patent of Henry II., of which I have before spoken, confirming to the monks of Bugfast the church and abbey of Bugfasta and all the lands and tenements, &c., belonging to them, as they held them in the time of King Henry, "avi mei." The deed contains no names of places, or particulars as to the property of the Abbey; but it is interesting, and must have been granted some time before April, 1161, as among the witnesses are Theobald the Archbishop and Thomas the Chancellor, the famous Thomas Becket.

> Henry King of England and Duke of Normandy and Aquitaine and Count of Anjou. To the Archbishops &c. health. Know that I have granted in perpetual alms to the Monks of Bugfast, who are of the order of Savigny, the Church and Abbey of Bugfast, with all lands and tenements and churches and other possessions to the said church belonging, so well and in peace, &c. as if the aforesaid abbacy over, &c. held in

the time of King Henry my grandfather, &c. These being witnesses :
THEOBALD, Archbishop of Canterbury.
THOMAS, Chancellor.
HUMPHREY OF BOHUN, Steward.
ROGER DE NOVANT.
WARREN son of GERALD, Chamberlaine, &
WILLIAM the son of HAMO.
At Worcester.
(Patent Rolls, 1 Edw. IV., p. 2, m. 4.)

79. I have also obtained another copy of a charter, which is apparently the same as this, but differing slightly in the wording, and more full and precise in the description of the benefits conferred. It speaks of the monks of Buckfast as of the order of Cistercium (at least the word appears to be this) instead of Savigny, as in the other. The charter is nearly illegible at the edges, and many of the words are obliterated.

H. [illegible] Sciatis me p di amore & p salute anie mee & p aniabȝ ōnium antecessorᵃ ṁoȝ ꝯcessisse & in ppetuam Elemosinā c'firmasse đo & Monachis de Bugfasta de or.line de Custerc̄ ōnes ṫras & Tenuras suas q's Racionabilit̃ habnt libe tenendis cū socha & sacha & Thol & Them & Infangenet & cū ōnibȝ aliis libtatibȝ & libis c'suetudinibȝ [Q″re?] volo & [firmit̃?] pcipio q̇d ipi & hedes coȝ hant in pace libtates suas & quietancias de Scyr̄ & hundr̄ & placitis & querel & Murdr̄ & hidagiis & Scutagiis & Geldis & Danegeldis [illegible] & c'suetudinibȝ de Moris & ōni sec̄lari ȝvic̄o & exaccōe sic̄ mea Elemosina pp'a.
T. Thom̃ Canc̄: etc. (Cartæ Antiquæ. Y.)

80. But before the date of this charter, we have mentioned, in 1143, the Abbot of Buckfast, Eustachius, who was witness to an agreement between the abbot of St. Martin's-in-the-Fields and the Chapter of the Cathedral of Exeter in that year. This is the first Abbot of whom mention is made, after the English abbot Alwaine or Alcuin, whose name occurs in Domesday Book.

81. There is also a deed, which may possibly be earlier than the confirmation deed of Henry II., being a grant to the church of Buckfast by Henry de Novant, for the health of his soul and that of his wife Elizabeth, of the land of Scirhull, which he and his father granted to the monastery.

82. The date of this document is uncertain. If the grantor is Henry de Novant, son of Roger de Novant, to whom large

grants of land were made by Henry I., it is the earliest deed we have relating to the Abbey. There was a Roger, a grandson, and he had also a son called Henry, but Pole, Coll., p. 169, says, that the wife of this last-mentioned Henry was Isabel Bulbek, whereas the name of the wife of the Henry Novant of the deed is Elizabeth. It is to be noticed that, if the earlier date is the correct one, we have another piece of evidence against the destruction and resuscitation of the Abbey, after the Conquest, for it shows that in the reign of Henry I. it was flourishing.

Buckfast.   Notu sit õibus &c. q̃d ego Hen. de Nunant p salute anime mec et spouse mee Elizab' dedi et concessi Eccles' de Bokfasta omne ter' de Scirhull &c. quā pater meus Rog' et ego prius conces' Prædict. Monachis. Test. Will'o fil Stephani Johe Longo &c. H. 2, Pole's M.S., p. 182. (Add. MSS. (Brit. Mus) 28,649, p. 394.)

83. In 1189, Nov. 18, about two months after his accession, and not long before his departure for the Third Crusade, Richard I. confirms to the monks of Buckfast, by the hand of his newly nominated Chancellor, the famous Bishop of Ely, William Longchamps, the possessions which they then held, and apparently confers upon them further privileges. As in the former deeds, the words are general:—

Ricardus Dei gratia rex Angliæ, Dux Normannie et Aquitanie, comes Andegavie, archiepiscopus, etc. salutem. Sciatis nos pro Dei amore et pro salute anime nostre et omnium antecessorum et successorum nostrorum concessisse et presenti carta confirmasse Deo et ecclesie beate Marie de Bocfasta et monachis ibidem Deo servientibus omnes donationes que eis rationabiliter facte sunt in terris et tenuris et tenementis in liberam et puram et perpetuam elemosinam. Quare volumus et firmiter precipimus quod predicti monachi habeant et teneant omnes terras et tenuras et tenementa eis rationabiliter data in bosco et plano in viis et semitis in agnis et molendinis in vivariis et stagnis in pratis et pascuis in homagiis et serviciis et releviis in grangiis et virgulis infra burgum et extra cum soch et sach et thol et theam et infangenethef.

Concedimus etiam eis et hominibus suis quietanciam de theloneo et passagio et pontagio et de schiris ot hundredis et de omnibus placitis et querelis et de pecunia qne ad murdrum et latrocinium pertinet.

Preterea concedimus eis et hominibus suis quietanciam de heingwita et de flemeniswita et de blodwita et de girthwita et de hidagio et scutagio et geldis et danegeldis et de operacionibus castellorum et de essart et de wasto foreste et de rewardo et placitis foreste et de auxiliis vicecomitum et de misericordia comitatus et de omnibus auxiliis et de clifwardis et de consuetudinibus et de moris et de omni seculari servicio et exactione. Concedimus etiam eis pasturam in moris per totam annum ad omne genus pecudum suorum.

Prohibemus etiam ne quis predictos monachos gravet vel eis aliquam injuriam aut molestiam aut gravamen faciat, nec eos in placitum ponet de aliquo tenemento nisi coram nobis vel capitali justiciario nostro.

Testibus : Hugone Duñ, Johanne Norwic, Huberto Sarum episcopis. Rogero le Bigot, Waltero filio Roberti, Galfrido filio Petri.

Dat' apud S. Eadmundum, Nov. 18, per manum Willielmi Elien. electi, cancellarii nostri A. R. primo. (Cartæ Antiquæ, S. No. 19.)

84. We have another glimpse of the Abbey in 1196, when we find William, Abbot of Bukfestria, witnessing the execution of the foundation deed of the Promonstratensian Abbey of Tor by William Lord Bruiere, in that year.

85. Early in the thirteenth century we find Nicholas Abbot at Buckfast, he granting to John Lambrith lands and houses at Exeter, in what was then and still is the High Street there.

Omnibus fidelibus ad quos presens scriptum pervenerit NICHOLAUS, Abbas de Buckfesti, et ejusdem loci conventus, salutem in Domino

Noverit universitas vestra nos concessisse et dedisse Johanni Lambrith totam terram et domus nostras que fuerunt Ailmari Atlekin in Exon, scilicet duos sellas in regno vice cum introitu ejusdem domus versus magnum vicum Exonie, et omnes domos et terram retro, cum solario et pertinenciis sicud paries domus Ricardi Stukard' rectâ lineâ ducit in cimiterium sibi et illis quos inde heredes constituere voluerint, Tenendum de nobis inperpetuum jure heroditario libere et quiete reddendo inde annuatim nobis et successoribus nostris unam libram piperis ad pascha et domui hospitalis Sancti Johannis decem solidos per manu nostra ad quatuor annis terminos. Et nos tenemur warantizare predictas sellas et domos et terram predicto Johanni et heredibus suis adversus omnes homines.

Et si predicta tenementa prefato Johanni et heredibus suis warantizare non possumus faciemus sibi vel heredibus suis rationabile exscambium.

Pro hac autem concessione et donatione nostra dedit nobis predictus Johannes vigniti et quinque marcas argenti. Quod ut firmum permaneat sigillo nostro presenti scripto apposito confirmavimus.

Hiis Testibus :

 Magistro Willielmo Paz.
 Samsone et Rogero filiis Henrici tunc prepositis.
 Waltero filio Turberti.
 Willielmo Hastemend.
 Johanne Caperum.
 Martino Toton.
 Johanne Puddin.
 Johanne filio Walteri filii Tuberti.
 Roberto Tabernar.
 Waltero le Gyawe.
 Ilare et multis aliis.

Original in possession of the Dean and Chapter of Exeter. —(Oliver's Monast. Sup. pp. 33, 34.)

86. By this deed one pound of pepper is reserved annually to the abbot and his successors and 10s. to the house of the hospital of St. John, Exeter. That the Abbey of Buckfast was interested in, and helped to support this hospital, formerly that of St. Alexius, it is certain, but, so far, I have not been able to ascertain what the nature of the connection between them was. From an entry in the register of the hospital, now in possession of the Corporation of Exeter, Dr. Oliver thought that Abbot William granted an annuity of 30s. to the master and brethren of the old hospital, to issue from certain estates, the names of which are given as Lamenecote and Emilde, of which we know nothing now.

87. In 1207 a thirteenth part of the goods of the Church was demanded of the bishops and clergy by King John. The Cistercians were exempt from this demand, John being a friend of the order: "*Ad quam colligendam misit ministros suos per universos comitatus Angliæ; at hac exactione liber fuit ordo Cisterciensis.*"—(Annales de Waverleia Ann. Monast. ii. p. 258.)

88. About this same time we find the abbey received further gifts. Richard de Bauzan, whose pedigree I have not been able satisfactorily to make out, gives all his land of

Holne, with the appurtenances, to the abbot and convent of Buckfast.

Sciant presentes et futuri quod ego Ricardus Bausan dedi, concessi, et hac presenti carta mea confirmavi abbati et conventui de Bufestre, Deo et beate Marie servientibus, in puram et perpetuam elemosinam, pro animabus patris mei et matris mee et fratris mei Stephani Bauzan, totam terram meam de Holna cum omnibus pertinentiis suis ut in dominicis, villenagiis, boscis, turbariis, homagiis, et serviciis liberorum, videlicet Stephani Mugge, Michaelis Mugge, Wimundi Sele, Osberti Corbyn, et Warini de Budditone, et omnibus aliis pertinentiis tenendam et habendam dictis abbati et conventui et eorum successoribus vel cui eam assignare voluerint, de me et heredibus meis, libere, quiete, integre et pacifice jure hereditario imperpetuam in viis semitis, &c. faciendo inde mihi et heredibus meis ipsi et successores sui vel eorum assignati tricessimam partem feodi unius militis pro omni servicio, querela, demanda, acta et exactione.

Hiis testibus: Gilberto de Umfranvill, Hugone de Cardinan, Martino de Fisacre, Gilberto filio Stephani, Philippo de Bodrigan, Waltero Bernas, Nicholao de Ferariis, et aliis.

89. Lysons states that "the Manor of South Holne was given to the Abbey of Buckfastleigh by Reginald de Valletort, in the early part of the thirteenth century," Devon, p. 277, and goes by on to say that another manor of Holne was given them by Stephen Bauzun, which is manifestly a mistake. I have not been able to verify the statement that the Valletorts were donors to the abbey either of lands in Holne or elsewhere, and if, as seems to be the case from the deed I have just given, from the information given by the Hundred Roll, and from the fact of the arms of the Abbey being still to be seen upon the screen in the church, the monks held lands there, they must in some way have disposed of them before the Dissolution, for the ministers' accounts contain no mention whatever of property there. Of course the statement of Lysons, that the church of Holne was appropriated to the Abbey of Buckfast, is a mistake. It belonged to the see of Exeter, and was granted by Bishop Grandisson to St. John's Hospital in that city.

90. There is an order, dated in 1215, from King John to, among others, the Abbots of Ford and Buckfast, for the delivery of whatever vessels, jewels, &c. might be in their custody, handed them for safe keeping. This appears to be

one instance of the ordinary deposit of valuables with the officers of a religious house for their preservation, and not a deposit to secure the repayment of a loan due to the house, an instance of which we shall find further on.

91. In 1225, among the Feet of Fines, there is an entry of the final proceedings on the sale to the abbot of seven acres and a half of meadow land in Sele, which I give, as it enables me to add the name of Abbot Michael, the first of some abbots whose names have not hitherto been recorded, which I have the pleasure of adding to the list contained in the Monasticon.

Hec est finaƚ concordia fca in curio Dñi Reḡ apd Exoñ Die Sabƀi px^a post octaƀ trinitatis Anno Regñ Reḡ Henr̄ fiƚ Regis Joħis Duodeciɱ Coram Thoɱ de Muleƚ Robto de Lexinƚ Raɖo Musard & Jordañ Oliv̧ justic̄ Itiñantib; & aliis dñi Reḡ fidelib; tūc ibi p̄sentib; Inƚ Simonē Lampreie petētē & Michaelē Abƀm de Buffesƚr tenentē de Septem acris p^{a}ti & dimiɖ cū̧ ptiñ in Sele. Uñ assa mortis añcossor̄ sūmonita fuit inƚ eos in p̄fata curia Scilicet qɖ p̄dc̄us Siɱ remisit & quietū clamavit de se & ħedib; suis ip̄i Abƀi & successorib; suis & ecctie sue de Buffesƚr imppɱ totū jus & clamiū quod ħuit in toto p̄dc̄o p^{a}to cū ptiñ. Et p h^{a}c remissiōe quieta clamancia fine & cōcordia idem Abbas dedit p̄dc̄o Simoñ Septē marcas arḡnti.

Feet of Fines, Devon. Henry III. No. 107.

92. The friendship of John for the Cistercians did not last long. After his excommunication, he continued his exactions from the Church. The chronicler of Waverley tells us :—

Idem rex collecto multo exercitu in mense Junio transfretavit in Hiberniam, ubi hostibus ad votum subactis dimissis ibi episcopo Norwicensi, Johanne de Grai, et Willelmo Marescallo mense Septembri minus infestus omnibus viris Cisterciensis ordinis rediit. Convenerat enim eos antequam transfretaret, sicut et cæteros, de auxilio ipsi præstando contra iminicos suos; et quia idem Cistercienses pecuniam ei ad libitum suum contra libertatem ordinis sui dare noluerunt, in immensum eos afflixit, et a singulis domibus brevissimo temporis spatio indulto, multe valde causum ita ut summa xxxiii m et ccc marcatum collectio illa excederat, violenter extorsit. Ipsi vero per diversas domos monachorum et canonicorum dispersi sunt. Waverleia vero, omnibus facultatibus suis distractis et ablatis, facta similiter dispersione monachorum et conversorum circumquaque per Angliam, regis iram patienter sustinuit. Abbas ejusdem loci Johannes tertius timore regis peterritus, domum suum reliquit et de nocte latente aufugit. Acta sunt [hæc] circum festum beati Martini. Prohibuit etiam rex ut nullus de ordine Cisterciensi transfretaret, aut de alienis in Angliam veniret.

Annales de Waverleia. (Ann. Monast. vol. ii. p. 265.)

93. Letters resigning their property were also extorted from the Cistercians and others, and under Henry III. both monks and Jews suffered. In the year 1225, when the King confirmed the charters, a fifteenth of all movables in the kingdom was granted to him to enable him to recover the English possessions in France. The annalist from whom I have quoted says :—

"Monachi vero Cisterciensis ordinis, tam pro libertatibus quam pro gratia et benevolentia regis habenda, dederunt ei duo milia marcas argenti. Judæi autem existentes in Anglia dederunt ei eodem tempore quinque milia marcas argenti."— Ann. Waverleia ii., p. 300.

Were the Jews richer than the monks, or were they more patriotic?

94. In 1236 the abbot and monks became members of the Merchants' Gild of Totnes. On the back of a roll of the gild, in the possession of the Corporation of Totnes, is written a covenant between the abbot, probably Michael or Howell, and the Convent of Buffestleigh, 20 Henry III., and the burgesses of Totnes, to the effect that the latter have admitted the abbot and monks into the guild, so that they might make all their purchases in the same way as the burgesses, all sales, however, being excepted "nomine tabernæ" by way of trading. Third Report, Hist. MSS. Com. p. 343. To go forward a little, twenty-four years later, we find the Abbot of Buffestie second on the roll of the gild, then numbering about two hundred members, following the Abbot of Tor.

95. In 1243 we have entries on the Assize Rolls relating to disputes with the convent in respect to various properties.

Plac' Corone et Assise,
28 Hen. III. Devon.

Assa venit rec̄ Si Prior de Plumtoñ ini⁹te etc. diss Abb̄em de Buffestre de Communa paste sue i Walleworth que ptinet ad lib̄m teñ suū in ead villa p̄t p¹mā etc.

Et Prior veñ & nich dic q̄r assa remaneat.
Juȓ dnt qd p̄dcs Prior diss p̄dcm Abbem de p̄dca comuna ini⁹te etc. sic bre dic. Et io Consid est qd Abbs rec seis suam ꝯt Prior i m̄ia. p pt Walt'i de Bath.
Dampñ. ij s.

* * * * *

Wills Swenge & Isab vx ei⁹ potūt. Ꝟ Abbem de Buffestȓ dim̄ ferling tre cū ptiñ in Nyrifeud ut Jus & heditatem ip̄ius Isab & i quā idē Abbs nō ht ingȓm nⁱ p Robm de Waleworth qui nō nⁱ custodiam iñ huit dū p̄dca Isab fuᵗ infᵃ etatē & in custodia sua etc.
Et Abbs veñ & voc inde ad waȓ Henȓ de Altariis qui p̄scns est & ei waȓ & deffend Jus suū q̄n ꝯtē & tale ingȓm & dic qd huit ingȓm i cand trā p Willm frem frem* ip̄ius Henȓ. Et qd ita sit ponit se sup p̄riam. Et Wills & Isab sitr. Et ido fiat inde Jurata.
Juȓ dnt qd p̄dcs Abbs huit Ingȓm i p̄dcam ꝑram p p̄dcm Robm de Waleworth dū p̄dca Isablla fuit iſᵃ etatem & i custodia ip̄ius Robti Dicūt & qd p̄dcaꝉ carta qᵃ Abbs pfert de fcoffamento p̄dce tre fca fuit ptq̄ p̄dcs Robs eidc Abbi dimis p̄dcam trā. Et io cons est q̄d Wills & Isab rec seis suam. Et Henȓ· in m̄ia p pt Willm de Muthecumb & Robti de Avayngncs. Et fac escamh p̄dco Abbi ad vaīn p̄dce tre etc. Et Abbs in m̄ia p magna tᵃnsgȓ.

Plac' de Jur' Coron' &c.
33 Hen. III. Devon.

Ad de Broth qui tulit bre nove dissie v̄s⁹ Abbem de Bucfestȓ & alios in bȓi de Libo teñ suo in Tottoñ veñ & retᵃxit se. Io ip̄c & pleḡ sui de ps in m̄ia scitt Hugo de Corndoñ Rics Doulelegh de Brenta. Pleḡ Ad de m̄ia sua.

Assize Roll $\left.\begin{array}{c}M.\\1\\32\end{array}\right\}$ 1-2

96. The same year, on the Feet of Fines, we have an entry relating to another purchase by the convent of eight fꝯrlings of land in Engleburn in the parish of Harberton.

Hec est final concordia fca in Cuȓ Dn̄i Reḡ ap̄ Exoñ In cᵃstino Sce Trinitatis Anñ Regn̄ Reḡ Henȓ fiꝉ Reḡ Joh vicesimo octavo Corā Roḡo de Thurkelby Gilbto de P̄ston Johe Abbe de Shyleborñ & Robto de Bello cāpo Justic

* Sic. bis.
† It will be seen that no charter is *before* mentioned.

Itiñantibȝ & aliis dñi Regę fidelibȝ tūc ibi p̄sentibȝ Int̄ Abb̄em de Buffestr querī & Thoṁ de Reyny & Johannā ux ejus inpeđ de Octo f⁹ling t̄re cū ptiñ in Engeleburñ Unde plac̄ War carte suṁ fuit int̄ eos in endem cur Scitt qđ p̄c̄di Thoṁ ꝉ Johanna recognovūt totā p̄dc̄am t̄rā cū omibȝ ptiñ suis esse jus ip̄ius Abb̄is ꝉ Eccl̄ie sue de Buffestr ut illā q" idem Abbas ꝉ Ecctia p̄dc̄a ḣent de dono p̄dc̄oȝ Thoṁ ꝉ Joħe Habend ꝉ Tenend eidm Abb̄i ꝉ succ̄ suis ꝉ Eccl̄ie sue p̄dc̄e de p̄dc̄is Thoṁ ꝉ Johanna ꝉ ḣedibȝ ip̄ius Joħe in lib⁹am ꝉ ppetuā Elemosinā. Reddendo iñ p annū unū par Cyrothecarū albarū p̄cii sex denr̄ ꝉ sex denr̄ ad festū sc̄i Miċh et faciendo iñ forinsecū s̄vic̄ qđ ad p̄dc̄am t̄rā ptinet p ōi s̄vicō ꝉ exaccōc Et p̄dc̄i Thoṁ ꝉ Joħa ꝉ h⁹edes ip̄i⁹ Joħe Warantizabūt p̄dc̄o Abb̄i ꝉ succ̄ suis ꝉ Eccl̄ie sue p̄dc̄e totā p̄dc̄am t̄rā cū omnibȝ ptiñ suis in lib⁹am ꝉ ppetuā elemosinam suā p p̄dc̄m s̄vic̄ cont' oṁs homies inppetuū. Et p h'c recognicōe War finc ꝉ concordia Idem Abb̄s dedit p̄dc̄is Thoṁ ꝉ Joħe sexaginta ꝉ dec̄e marcas argenti.—(Pedes Finium Devon. Hen. III. No. 369.)

97. From the collections of Sir William Pole in the British Museum I have gleaned some little information relating to the Abbey, and some of its abbots. The first is dated the Feast of St. Lambert, 1246, and another William, hitherto unmentioned, is named in it.

Witt̄us Abbas de Bukfastr̄ et ejusd. Loci Convent̄ Salut̄ Nov̄ Cum aliquando mot̄ esset Placit̄ inter nos et Witt̄o de Sᵗᵒ Stephano de 24 Acris terre in La Dene una pax et concordia facta fuit in Curia Dñi Reḡ inter nos et idm [sic] Witt̄um de Sᵗᵒ Stephano Mañ suū de Dene Ded. Priori et Convent̄ de Plympton nos dictā conces. confirm̄. Test̄ Dño Tho: Arch. Tottoñ, Dⁿᵒ Witto de Widworthy et Galfrido de Pridens Milit̄. Galfrido de La Ya, Robto le Peyterin alijsꝗ. Dat̄ in festo sᵗⁱ Lamb̄ti 1246.—(Add. MSS. Brit. Mus. 28,649, p. 381.)

98. In 1247 Howell was abbot, and Durandus, Dr. Oliver says, was probably his successor, and in his time it is likely that those strange proceedings which occurred on the death of Bishop Blondy were investigated, and, as the abbot seems to have taken an important part in the inquiry, and as the inquiry was conducted in the chapter-house at Buckfast, I have thought it well to refer shortly to the matter. Bishop Blondy was consecrated Dec. 1st, 1245. He died 26 Dec.,

1257. He was a prelate of piety and learning, and conscientiously discharged the duty of his high office, but his biographers have confounded him with another of the same name, his opposite in every respect. Soon after his death his enemies traduced his memory and accused him of allowing his servants to forge collations for their personal benefit. This, of course, soon came to the knowledge of his successor, Walter Bronescombe, and on the 19th of March Walter of Loddeswell, the Chancellor, and Richard of Totnes, a notary, appeared before the Bishop and the Abbot of Buckfast in the chapter-house of Buckfast, and confessed to them that on the night of the late Bishop's death they entered his chamber and found several persons engaged in drawing up and signing letters for the disposal of benefices and the appropriation of the effects of the Bishop, who then, if not actually a corpse, was *in extremis*, and that after the parties were fully satisfied of the death of the Bishop many other letters were written and signed. Fuller details of the affair will be found in the extracts from Bishop Bronscombe's Register, given in the Lives of the Bishops by Dr. Oliver.[*]

99. In 1268 I can add the name of another new abbot, Henry, his name appearing in the following extract:—

A⁰ Regni Regis H. fit Johis 53 Facta fuit hæc concordia inter Honr̃ Abb̃m de Bukfast et ejus[d] Loci convent̃ et Rich filiũ Aluredi de Dodeworthy p cc̃muni pastura in Mañ de Brent. Test̃ D⁰⁰ Witto Probo [*i.e.* Prous] Johe de Niveton Johe de Boyvile Witto de Killbury Witto de Chiverston Johe de Davayly Petro de La Ya˙ et mult. alijs.—(Add. MSS. Brit. Mus. 28,649, p. 381.)

100. In the episcopal registers, where we frequently find similar entries, there is a record of Simon being blessed as abbot by the bishop on the Feast of the Nativity of St. John the Baptist, 1272.

101. The conveyance of the land in Holne parish by Richard Bauzan is said by Dr. Oliver to have been made in the time of this abbot. My impression is that it is of earlier date, but as I before said I have not been able satisfactorily to make out the Bauzan pedigree, and the learned doctor probably, although he does not give any evidence, satisfied himself as to the correctness of his statement.

102. I now come to the entries in the important documents known as the Hundred Rolls, which contain the results of

---

[*] Lives of the Bishops of Exeter, pp. 37, 38, and 39

the survey made by special commissioners appointed by Edward I. to ascertain the state of the demesne lands, the revenue of the crown, the various tenures by which lands were held, and so forth.

103. We find from the roll relating to Devon that the property of the Abbey had not much increased since Domesday. Curiously enough Holne, said to have been granted by Richard Bauzan only a year or so before, is mentioned as Sutholn, the gift to the Abbey of Richard Barcyn. The commissioners made their returns, and, as it was necessary for the Court of Exchequer to have in one view such parts of them as affected the crown and its rights, a selection from the fuller returns was made containing the entries relating to these matters. These latter rolls are called extracts, and they are valuable, as the fuller rolls of some counties are altogether lost. Fortunately both the rolls relating to Devon are in existence, and I give here the return of the commissioners, and the extract therefrom as well, relating to the land of Buckfast :—

Rotuli Hundredorum, Edward I. Printed ed. 1812. *Buckfast.*
Hoc e' vered'em xij jurator' Hundr'i forins' de Ermy'tone.
Jurati Walt' de Fenton Joh de la Porte Alvedr' de Ponte Wills de Karswitt Ric de Leg' Joh' de Collaton Ric de Colamor' Robt de Gudeford Rand' de Bahecumb' Robt' de Wonigwill Walt' de Longeh^{a}m Joh' de Bosco p' sac^{a}ment' suū dict.

It' BATTEKESBURNE HETFELL & ESSA *tenet^r fuer 'de d'nico coron'* de Reḡbȝ p̄decessorib; Reg' q^i ñc ē E in capite & tenet m^o abbas & dom^9 Bufestie in purā & p̄pet' elemosinā a q^o tp̄r ignorāt. p. 69.

It' abbas & dom^9 Bufestr' hnt' furcas in maner' de HETFELL & assis^{a}m servis' ibidm & ap' BATTEKESBUHR a q^o tp̄r' & q^o war' ignorat'. p. 69.

It' BACEKESBURHE HETFELL & ESSA fu^{o}nt de dnico corone Extract'. p̄dec R & tenet modo abbat Bufest^{i}e in pura & ppetuam elemosinā a quo tp̄e ignorant. p. 90.

It' abbas Bufestr' habet furc' in mañio de HETFELL & Extract'. ass^{a}m ćvisie ibidē & apud HATTEKESBURH a quo tp̄e & quo waranto ignorant. p. 91.

Vered'em Hundr' de Schefbeare.
Et Abbas de Bufest^{i}a het apud PAT^{d}CHSTOWE furcas assis^{a}m ćvis & alias libertates regias & het war' sed de quo Rege ignorant. p. 78.

Extract'.

Veredictu' xij
jur' de Hundr's
de Stanburg'.

[Churchtowe.]

& Abbas de Buffestria ħt apud PATRICHESTOWE furc' & assias c̣visie and alias libertat' regias & habet war' de quo' Rege ignorant. p. 94.

It' q' clamant ret'nu v̄l ext'ctū breviu & q', tenent placit' do naumeo vetito vl clamant here wreckū mar.

Dicūt qd 'nult sed . . . . & man'iu de BRENTE & man'ia de BUFFESTR' q' sūt abbat' de Buffest' . . . . & mañiu de THURESTOWE ten3 abbas de Buffest' & ħnt furcas & assis' pan' & s'vic & in q° mañio est novu' burg' q' respondet p' se p' vi. mr & tenent mcatu die Ven'is & teñet placit' assis' pan., & s'vis q° waranto ignorant. p. 79.

It' de his q' ħnt libtate p Reg. Angl' concessas.

Dicūt q^d abbas de Buffest' clam' here libtate q^d q'eti sint de hid' murdriis & aliis q'ib3 guldis quo warranto ignorant. p. 79.

It' de pprest'is feis.

Dicūt q^d abbas de Buffest' & convent' fecunt pprest'am de q°d magno wasto 9munis mora in aust'le pte de DERTEMORE ad nocumentu' toci' pat'e q' in tepē H. Reg' p'tis d'ni E' Reg' q' nūc est Howaldus abbas de Biffest' and convent' predic' wastu' sibi approp'aṽūt & teñt & vendūt carbon' t'b & past'as de anno in annū & capiūt inde redd' quo waranto ignorant ad dampm annuatim xl^s. p. 79.

It' dicut' q'd Rog's Mirabel tenuit t'ram de SCIREDON de d'no Reg' in capit' p' s'jantiam t'u sagitta3 quandocuq' d'ns Rex c'eret in foresta de DERTEMORE q' fec' feloniam p' q^d utlagiat' fuit & tuc' predcam t'ram accidit in man' dñi Reg. H. pat's dñi Reg' Ed q' dedit illam magro Walto Medico & modo ten3 Joh' de Boyvile & Dyonis' ux' sua fil & hes' predci Walti & ptea duo ferling' t're in KYNGDON ptin predce s'ganc de SCIREDON alienata est de novo tepe isti' Reg' p' Nichin de Kyngdon libe tenent' predce t're de KYNGDON q' dedit illam abbat' & convent' de Buffestre & val3 p' ann' x sol'. p. 79.

Veredictu' Hundri' de Teyngebrugg'.

Dicut & q' mañia de Kingdon Sekiredon & Hokneton fu°unt in manu' dni R. H. pat's dñi Reg' nuc tanq^a eschaet' sua p' fellon' cuj^adam felonis Rog]' Mirabel & illa mañia dedit Walto de Skiredon p s'vic' iij^s ad festū Sci Michis & t'um sagitta3 q^ando dñs R volūit venare in forestā de DERTEMORE. Que q'd mañia p mortem pdci Walti decendebant cuidam Dionis' filie sue q^am Johnes de Boyvile ht in ux' & idm tenent mañia p'dicta mañia de dño R p' s'vic p̄dem excepto uno ferlingo t're q' abbas Buffestr' m° ten3 p' alienacõne Nichi de Kingdon tenen^t dci Johnis de Boyvile q^am fec' eidm abbti & valent mañia p̄dicta p' annu xl^s unde KINGDON valet viij s.   p. 81.

D' hiis qui Clam' returnu' vel extract' breviu' &c.

Dnt qd qd Hugo de Ferrar' & Witts de Chiv'ston apud Thurleston, Gilbo de Cnovitt Lodeswell Abbas de Buffestria apud BRENTE & BUFFESTR' Johes de Boyvill apud Sciredon prior de Plimton apud DEN Abbas de Sco Donmel' apud RASTRIWE Nich^s fil Martini apud DERLINGTON Rog's de Mulés apud DUPEFORD et Johēs de Besillis apud ALFINGTON hūt furc' & assisas c'visie set [sed?] nesciūt quo waranto. It' Abbas Buffest^rie in man'io de Churestorwe habet fur' et assisas panis & c'visie in quo man'io est novo burg' qui respondit p' se p' vj jur' & tenēt m'cutu die Veñis & hnt assisas panis & c'visie s; nesciūt quo waranto.   p. 91.   *Hund' de Stanburg'. Extract.*

It de hiis qui h'nt libertate &c.

D'nt q'd abbas Buffestrie clam' hre lib' qd quiet' est de hidag' murdriis & aliis comūnib; gildis s; nesciūt quo war' & man'iū de DERTIGTON et Dupeford quiet' sint d'coīb; gildis & de turno vic' s; nesciūt quo war'.   Et sei^d q'd Nichs fil Martini tenet man'iu de DERTIGTON Rog's de Mules man'iu de DUPEFORD & Gilb' de Conevill man'iu de LODESWELL.   p. 91.   *Extract.*

It de hiis qui de novo appropriav'int chac' &c.

Dnt qd man'iu de DUPEFORD DERLINGTON and L . . . . . clam' hre warenna & hut s; a quo tpe vl quo waranto ignorant.

D'nt q'd abbas de Buffestria & convent' fec'int purprestura de quoda' magno vasto comun' more in australi p'te de DERTEMORE ad nocumentu' totius patrie q' in t'pe H. Reg' p'ris d'ni Reg' nūc (nup?) Hewaldus abbas Buffestrie & convent' p'dcs vastū sibi appropriav'ut & tenēt & vendūt carbones turbas & pasturas de anno in annu & capiunt inde redd quo waranto ignorāt ad dapnū annuali XL. sol.   p. 91.   *(Sic).*

Hund' de Colrig'.

D' feodis dni' Reg' & tenentibu; ejus &c.

D'nt q^d Rog's de Valle Torta tenuit baronium de Hurberton cū membr' de d'no Rege in capite p' s'viciū duo; militu' ad bellū quando dñs Rex h'uit necesse v'l q^atuor armigeru' & eadem baronia est nūc in manu d'ñi Reg' p' morte d'ci Rog'¡ de qua· baronia Abbas de Bufest'a tenet SUTHOLN p' donū

Rici' Bareyn qui feoffat' fuit de baronia de Hurberton et dedit eide abbati t'pe H. Reg' p'ris dñi R' nūc xl. q'nto.
It d'nt q'd abbas de Bufest'a tenet centu' acr' bosci apud Sutholn in man'io de Huberton quē boscū elemosinavit Rads de Valle Torta fra't dc̄i Rog'i nuper defuncti d'co abb'ti tp̄e ejusde' H. Reg' p'ris dñi R. nuc XL. sōdo. p. 89.

104. In consequence of the returns of the commissioners it is supposed that the statute of Gloucester was enacted, and various holders of land were called upon to answer "Quo Waranto" such things had or had not been done, and in the Rolls of the Pleadings in answer we find that the Abbot of Buckfast was called upon to defend the then possessions of the house, inasmuch as he claimed to have a view of frankpledge, assize of bread and beer, and free warren, and a gallows in Buckfast, Churstow, Heathfield, and Batteburg. The abbot by his attorney pleaded that he claimed no free warren, and that as to the gallows he produced the deed of Richard I., which gave him the rights he exercised, and as to the other matters he pleaded that the crown had no right to question him, for the places where they were exercised were within the precincts of the hundred of Roger de Moles and Richard, the Lords of the Manors of Stanborough and Ermington respectively. On behalf of the King it was alleged in reply, that privileges of that kind especially pertained to the King, and, as the abbot showed no warrant from the crown, judgment was demanded on its behalf. As far as I know there is no account of the termination of the case, which was tried at Exeter. It frequently happened that proceedings, up to a certain point, were carried on, and then dropped, either because the King's advisers knew they had a bad case, or because it was not thought worth while to disturb the holders, or, which perhaps happened as frequently as either of the others, that unmolested possession was retained by judicious bribes.

At Exeter. Octave of St. Martin. 9 10 Ed. I, A.D. 1281.

Abbas Buffestr̄ sum̄ fuit ad respond̄ dño Regi de pto quo War clam̄ hr̄e visum f^nci pleḡ emend̄ ass panis & c̄vis f^cte & furc̄ in Buffestr̄ Thorestowe Hecfeld & Batteberḡ & lib̄am Warenñ in dnicis tris suis ibid̄m sine licenc̄ etc.

Et Abbas p atorn̄ suū veñ Et quo ad lib̄am warenñ dic̄ q̃d nullam warenñ clam̄ in p̄dc̄is vit̄l Et quo ad furc̄ dic̄ q̃d dñs Ric̄s Rex concessit ei Infangenethef & Itfangenethef in omibȝ p̄dc̄is vit̄l p cartam suam q^am pft & hoc id̄m testat^r Ĭo inde sine die Et quo ad visum f^nci pleḡ emend̄ ass panis & c̄vis ᵱcte in Buffestr̄ & Thorestowe dic̄ q̄d sunt infra ᵱcinctum Hundr̄i Roḡi de Mooles de Stanberwe Et quo ad Hecfeld & Battebergh dic̄ qd sunt inf* ᵱcinctū Hundr̄i Ric̄i fil Stephi de Ermingtoñ in quibus Hundr̄ nich pot̄ accsc̄e dño Regi Et pet̄ jud̄m.

Here, in the later entry mentioned below, follows: "Et petit Jud̄m si d̄ns Rex accōem k̄eat ad p̄dcas libtates petendas que sunt in alienis Hundr̄is."

Et Wilt̄s de Gyselh*m qui sequit' etc. Dic̄ q̄d huj⁹ mod libtates s̄palit̄ ptinent ad Coroñ dn̄i Reḡ Et desic̄ nullū aliud ostend war Io ad jud̄m.

Dies dat⁹ est coram dño Rege a die. Pasch in unū m̄ensem ubicūq, etc. [de audo Judo etc Et Abbas po lo suo Walt̄m de ffyrsedoñ, added on the Roll in the note.]

Assize Roll. Devon $\left.\begin{array}{c} M \\ 1 \\ 34 \end{array}\right\}$ Memb. 20 d.

A similar entry in the Assize Roll $\left.\begin{array}{c} M \\ 1 \\ 33 \end{array}\right\}$ 3 on memb. 37,

with, here and there, a trifling variation in the Record. The names of places are written: "in Buffestre Thurescowe Hetfeld & Batteburḡ & libam warennam in d̄nicis suis ibidem sine licencia etc." This last-mentioned entry will also be found in the Placita Quo Waranto. ed. Record Com. fol. 1818, p. 168.

105. Of Robert, who was confirmed abbot in 1280, we have nothing to record. He did not, I think, continue abbot long, for I have found that Peter, whom Oliver mentions as occurring in 1306, was abbot at least as early as 1290, and his name appears again in 1295-6, as will be seen from the following extracts:—

A° Regis E. 19, facta convenc. inter Petrū Abtem de Buckfastre et ejusd Loci convent̄ ex vna p̄te et Johe de Hubernford ex alt̄. p terra in Brenta. Test. Wilt̄o de Kilberry Wilt̄o de Boyvill. P. 9. (P. 381.)

Convencio facta 24 E. inter Petr. Abb. de Buckfastr̄ etc. et Johm Welbrok p t̄ra in Brenta. Test. Pho de Boterford, Heñ le Norreis, Huḡ de Corndon, Ric̄o de la Forde, Ric̄o de la Forde, Ric̄o de Hubernford, 24 E. 1, p. 10. (Additional MSS. Brit. Mus. 28,649, p. 380.

106. In Abbot Peter's time the Survey for the Taxation of Pope Nicholas was taken. In 1288 this Pope gave to Edward I. the tenth of all the revenues of the churches in England,

L

Scotland, and Ireland, in aid of the war in the Holy Land. The survey was not made till 1291 and 1292, as the King did not immediately avail himself of the benevolence of the Church. The entries relating to this abbey are as follows :—

Decanat' de Cadebur.

	Taxatio.	Decima.
Abbas Buffestr' p'cipit de ecclia de Donne	2 0 0	0 4 0

Decanatus de Chamlegh.

| Abbas Buffestr' p'cipit de ecclia de Sele | 2 13 4 | 0 5 4 |

Decanatus de Totton.

Ecclia de Brenta,	6 13 4	0 13 4
Vicar' de eadem .	1 10 0	non ex
Ecclia de Birfestr'	5 6 8	0 10 8
Vicar' de eadem	1 0 0	non ex

Decanat' de Wodlegh.

| Pens' alibi bñfic { Abbas Bufestr' p'cipit de Ecclia de Thurstonde* } | 0 13 4 | 0 1 4 |

Archidiaconat' Totton'.

Abbas Buftr' hēt	Maniū de Brent q'd tax'^	9 15 4
	Maniū de Northon † q'd tax'	6 6 8
	Apud Donfestr' ‡ q'd tax'	3 14 4
	Apud Hedfelle § q'd tax'	4 8 0
	Apud Bankesburgh ‖ q'd tax'	2 13 4
	Apud Bodrikeston ¶ q'd tax'	2 4 8
	Apud Sele q'd tax'	2 9 4
	Apud Dymm' ** q'd tax'	3 10 0
	Apud Trisma q'd tax'	1 15 8
	Apud Robrok and Hyndon q'd tax'	0 8 0
	Sma	37 5 0
	Dec'	3 14 6

Taxatio Ecclesiastica, P. Nicholai, pp. 144, 146, 149, 151-153, fol. 1802.

107. In 1297, April 8, Edward I. visited the Abbey, probably on his way to Plympton Priory. He was in Devonshire fourteen years before, and spent some time at Exeter with Queen Eleanor, and the Court kept Yule-tide in the Bishop's palace.

108. Abbot Peter was one of the witnesses to a deed with the Abbot of Tavistock and the Priors of Plympton and

* Churchstow.
† Notone.
‡ Buckfastleigh.
§ Heathfield.
‖ Batisborough.
¶ Petrockstowe.
** Donne.

Totnes, which was an undertaking by the Burgesses of Ashburton to provide a maintenance for a priest and necessaries for divine worship for the Chapel of St. Laurence, at Ashburton. A transcript of this deed will be found in the Lives of the Bishops of Exeter, by Dr. Oliver, from the Registers of Bishop Stapledon, p. 69. Robert, Stephen, and John de Churstowe succeeded Peter, 1 Aug. 1316; 24 June, 1330; and 1 Nov. 1332. I have not found a single entry relating to acquisition of land, disputes leading to legal proceedings, or to any event in the history of the Abbey during the time of these three abbots.

109. William Giffard was confirmed 6th June, 1333, his predecessor having been abbot for only about eight months. He seems to have been more than once involved in controversy as to the rights of his Abbey. I have not been able to trace in the Year Books the particulars of the dispute between him and the Stoners, the then Lords of the Hundred and Manor of Ermington, mentioned by Dr. Oliver; and I have in other cases been unable to verify the learned doctor's references to public records, which in two or three instances I particularly regret.

110. On the death of William Giffard early in 1349, Philip was admitted, 21 May, 1349, and in the following year he obtained from the King, a grant to his Abbey of a weekly market at Buckfastleigh, and a yearly fair at Brent, the former on Tuesday, and the latter on the feast of St. Michael and the two preceding days, to be held on Brent Down. I believe this fair is now represented by the Brent September fair. How long the Buckfastleigh weekly market continued I do not know, but an unsuccessful attempt to revive it was made early in this century.

GRANT TO THE ABBEY OF BUCFASTE OF A WEEKLY MARKET AT BUCKFASTLEIGH AND OF A YEARLY FAIR AT BRENT.

R̃ eisdem* saltm. Sciatis nos de gra nra spali concessisse *Pro abb'e et* ⁊ hac carta nra confirmasse ditcis nob in xp̄o Abb̃i ⁊ Conventui *conuentu de* de Bucfast in Com̃ Devoñ q̃d ip̃i ⁊ successores sui imppetuũ *Bucfast.* heant vnũ m̃catũ sing̃lis septimanis p diem Martis apud Bucfastenlegh ⁊ vnam feriam sing̃lis annis apud Brente in quadam placea vocata Brentedoune p tres dies duraturam videlt in die sci Michis in mense Septembr̃ ⁊ p duos dies px̃ p̃cedentes nisi m̃catũ illud ⁊ feria illa sint ad nocumentũ

* Archiep'is Ep'is Ducib' Comitib' Baronibus Justic' vice commitib' prepositis Ministris et om'ibu' Ball's et fidelib' suis.

vicinoȝ m̃catoȝ τ vicinaȝ feriaȝ Quare volum⁹ τ fermit̃
p̄cipim⁹ p nob̃'τ heredibȝ ñris qd̃ p̄d̃ci Abbas τ Conventus τ
successores sui imppetuũ h̃eant d̃ca m̃catũ τ feriam apud
loca p̄d̃ca cum om̃ibȝ lib̃tatibȝ τ lib̃is consuetudinibȝ ad
huiusmodi m̃catũ τ feriam ptinentibȝ Nisi m̃catũ illud τ feria
illa sint ad nocumentũ vicinoȝ m̃catoȝ τ vicinaȝ feriaȝ sicut
p̄d̃cm est. Hiis testibȝ veñabilibȝ p̄ribȝ J. Archiep̄o Eboȝ
Angł Primate Cancellario ñro W. Ep̄o Wyntoñ Thes̃ ñro
Henr̄ Duce Lancastr̄ Witto de Bohun Norht̃ τ Thoma de
Bello Campo Wampo War̄r Comitibȝ Barttio de Burgherssh̃
seniore Jotie de Grey de Retherfeld̃ Seneseallo hospicij ñri
τ aliis. Dat̃ p manũ ñram apud Wyndesore xxiiij die Aprilis.

p ipm Rege nunc Witto Mugge.

(Charter Roll 25 to 27 Edw. III. m. 7.)

111. Philip was not abbot long. He was succeeded by Robert Simons, whose name I find frequently occurring in legal documents for nearly forty years. As early as 1358 he is mentioned, and as late as 1393. Whether it is that he was particularly litigious, or that his predecessors had been lax in their care of the rights of the Abbey, I do not know, but, besides the case of the Abbey against the Dean and Chapter of Exeter with reference to the fishery of the Dart,* I have found references to several other cases in the Assize and De Banco Rolls, some of which I give.

112. The first relates to a claim made against the abbot by Richard Avery, who complains that on the Thursday after the Feast of St. Dionysius in the 30th year of Edward III., the Abbot *vi et armis*, at Trusham, carried off the goods and chattels of the said Richard, labour horses [*jumenta*], oxen, cows, heifers, calves, pigs, and sheep, besides corn, hay, straw, and other things, and alleged that he was injured to the extent of £100. The abbot in person stated, in reply to the charge, that he ought not to be called upon to answer, inasmuch as Richard Avery was his villein, belonging to the Manor of Trusham, the property of his church of the Blessed Mary of Buckfast, and sought judgment accordingly. Richard said that he was a free man and not a villein, but the jury upon their oaths were satisfied that poor Richard was *nativus*, and the abbot had judgment. This document therefore is valuable, showing that at this time, 1358, the villein had no rights, at all events against the lord of the soil. Professor Stubbs eloquently describes the position of the *nativus* after the Con-

* Oliver's Monasticon, p. 371.

quest, and shows that, although it may seem a hard one to us at this time, it had many advantages. "Under a fairly good lord, under a monastery or a college, the villein enjoyed immunities and securities that might be envied by his superiors; he had a ready tribunal for his wrongs, a voice in the management of his village; he might with a little contrivance redeem his children and start them in a higher state of life. His lord had a peremptory claim on his earnings, but his lord had a lord, whose claims on him were as irresistible, if not as legally binding. He was excluded from juries and assizes touching property, but by that exemption he was freed from the risk of engaging in quarrels in which he would be crushed without pity by the more powerful neighbour against whom he might have to testify. If he was without political rights, so were also the great majority of his superiors."*

Robtus Simoñ Abbas de Buckfestre attachus fuit ad res- At Exeter. pondend̄ Riĉo Averay de ptito t*nsḡr p billam Et unde idem 32 Ed. III. Ricūs in ppria psona sua quer* qd̄ die Jovis px post fm̄ sc̄i Sept. 1358. Dionis anno regni Reḡ·E' nunc Ang̈t tricesimo vi ⁊ armis videlī glad̄ ⁊c̄ apud Trussume bona ⁊ catalla ipsius Rici scilt tria Jumenta p̄cii quadraginta solidoꝫ sex boves p̄cii quatuor libraꝫ quatuor vaccas p̄cii quadraginta solidorum duas Juventas p̄cii sexdecim solidoꝫ duos bovettos p̄cii di m*rc̄ tres vitulos p̄cii sex solidoꝫ quinque porcos p̄cii q̄ndecim solidoꝫ nonaginta bidentes p̄cii sex libr ⁊ sexdecim solidorum cepit ⁊ abduxit ⁊ quinq, qᵘʳtia fr septem quart̄ia siliḡis quatuor quart̄ia aveñ duodecim trusses de feno sexaginta trusses stramis quatuor coffr una carucā ⁊ ij hcias de ferro ⁊ viginti clayes p i fald ad valenciam decem libraꝫ cepit ⁊ asportavit cont* pacem ⁊c̄. unde dicit q̄d detioratus est ⁊ dampnū het ad valenciam centū libraꝫ. Et inde pducit sectam.

Et p̄dc̄us Robtus Abbas in pp'a psona sua venit ⁊ dicit q̄d p̄dc̄us Ricus responder non debet quia dicit qd̄ idem Ricus est nativus ipsius Abbt̄is de Mahlia suo de Trussume Et idem Abbas ⁊ p̄decessores sui Abbt̄es loci p̄dc̄i sēiti fuerunt de ipso Riĉo ⁊ antecessoribus suis ut de nativis suis Mahlii sui p̄dc̄i de jure eccte sue be Marie de Bokfast ⁊ petit judiciū etc. Et p̄dc̄us Ric̄us dicit q̄d ipse est liber homo ⁊ libe condicōis ⁊ non nativus ipsius Abbt̄is put idem Abbas v̄sus eū ptitando allegat ⁊ hoc petit qd̄ inquirat p̄ p̄riam. Et p̄dc̄us Robtus Abbas similiter. I'o prec̄ est vic̄ qd̄ venire fac̄ coram p̄fatis Justic̄ hic die M⁹ cuᵲ in prima septiā quadragesime xxiiijᵃ tam milites etc. Et qui nec etc. ad recogñ ⁊c. Quia tam ⁊c. idem dies datus

* Stubbs, Const. Hist. vol. i. p. 430.

est ptibus pdcis etc. Ad quem diem coram Justic hic veñ ptes pdce in ppriis psonis suis Et Jur veñ qui de consensu pdco Rica Averay t Robti Simoñ Abbtis ad hoc etci triati t Jur dicunt sup sacrm suum qd pdcus Ricus Averay est nativus ipius Robti Simoñ Abbtis de maniio suo pdco put idem Abbas supius allegat. I'o cons est qd pdcus Ricus nichil capet p billa sua set sit in mia p injusta queret sua Et pdcus Robtus Abbas quietus sine die.

Assize Roll. $\left.\begin{array}{l}M \\ 1 \\ 34\end{array}\right\}$ 8 Memb. 4[d]. Devon.

113. In 1364, in the White Book of Tenures in Cornwall, we have an order for the delivery of a tun of wine to the Abbot of Buckfast. The Carmelites of Plymouth at the same time obtained five tuns. I have printed this elsewhere.*

114. In 1366 there was a dispute with the Vicar of Harberton, and in 1367 the abbot had occasion to take proceedings against John Prestcote and Matthew Kelly, who had destroyed trees to the value of ten pounds.

Devon. Dies datus est Abbi de Buckfast quer p Johem Wonard att suum t Galfro vicar ecctie de Huberton p Johem Wilby att suu de ptito t'nsgr hic a die sce Trinitat in xv dies pce pciu sine essoñ tc. (De Banco Roll, 41 Edward III. Hilary, m. 424.)

Devon. Abbas de Bukfast p Johem Prestecote attorn suu op se iiij[to] die vsus Ricm Asshelegh t Matheu Kellygh de ptito quare vi t armis arbores ipius Abbis ad valenc decc libra apud Bukfast nup crescent combusserunt t alia enormia tc. Et ipi non veñ et pdcus Ricus fuit attach p Johem Ude t Johem Hert I'o ipi in mia Et pc est vic qd distr cum p omnes tras tc. et qd de excitib tc. Et qd heat corpus eius hic a die Pasche in tres septias p Justic tc. et de pdco Matheo mand vic qd nichil het tc. I'o pc est vic qd cap eum si tc. et salvo tc. Ita qd heat corpus eius hic ad pfatum tmiñ tc. (De Banco Roll, Hilary, 42 Edward III. m. 163d.)

115. The next document is from Rymer's Fœdera. It must not be supposed that John Beaumont was the Abbot of Buckfast in 1372. Doubtless this proclamation was issued in the time of trouble following the victory of the Spaniards over the English off Rochelle, when the Earl of Pembroke, the son-in-law of the King, was taken prisoner.

* Ecclesiastical Hist. Old Plymouth, Appendix, p. 88.

DE HOMINIBUS AD ARMA IN COMITATU DEVON' ARRAIANDIS.

A.D. 1372.
46 Edw. III.
Rot. Franc.
46 Edw. III. m. 27,
in Turr' Lond.

Rex venerabili in Christo patri Thomæ, eadem gratia episcopo Exon' ac dilectis et fidelibus suis Hugoni de Courtenay comiti Devon', Johanni de Cheverston, Theobaldo Grenevillo, Ricardo de Stapuldon, Johanni Beaumond abbati de Bukfast, Johanni Daumarle, Willielmo de Bykebury, et Martino Ferrers, salutem.

Sciatis quod nos, de fidelitate et circumspectione vestris pleniùs confidentes, assignavimus vos, conjunctim et divisim, ad omnes homines defensabiles comitatûs Devon', infra libertates et extra, exceptis nominibus, qui nobiscum in obsequium nostrum sunt profecturi, cum omni festatione arrairi, et ipsos, videlicet, quemlibet eorum juxta statum et facultates suas, armis competentibus muniri, faciendum: et ad ipsos, sic arraiatos et numitos, videlicet, illos qui terras vel tenementa juxta costeram maris habent, ad morandum super eisdem terris continuè cum totâ familiâ suâ, et alios, terras et tenementa super costeram prædictam non habentes, juxta præmunitionem vestram, et cujuslibet vestrum ad costeram prædictam quociens necesse fuerit, et periculum aliquod iminuerit, viis et modis quibus melius expedire videritis, venire compellandum, ibidem quamdiu indiguerit super salvâ custodiâ terræ maritimæ continuè moraturos, ad resistendum malitiæ inimicorum nostrorum, si qui regnum nostrum invadere præsumpserint.

Et ad omnes illos, quos in hac parte contrarios inveneritis seu rebelles, arestandum, et prisonis nostris mancipandum, in eisdem moraturos, quousque de eorum punitione aliter duxerimus ordinandum.

Et ideò vobis et cuilibet vestrûm districtiùs quo poterimus, mandamus, firmiter injungentes, quod circa præmissa, omnibus aliis prætermissis, cum omni diligentiâ et solicitudine quibus poteritis, effectualiter intendatis, et ea faciatis et exequamini in formâ prædictâ: et vos ipsi et qualibet vestrûm ad terras et tenementa vestra, costeræ prædictæ propinquiora, cum omni festinatione vos trahatis, ibidem super salvâ custodiâ terræ maritimæ, cum totâ familiâ vestrâ continuè moraturi.

Damus autem vicecomiti nostro comitatûs prædicti, ac universis et singulis aliis fidelibus nostris comitatûs prædicti, tam infra libertates quam extra, tenore præsentium in mandatis, quod vobis, et cuilibet vestrûm in præmissis

pareant, obediant et intendant, quociens et quando per vos, seu aliquem vestrûm, super hoc ex parte nostrâ fuerint præmuniti.
In cujus,
Teste Rege, apud Westm' xx die Julii
Per ipsum Regem et consilium.
[Rymer's Fœdera, vol. iii. p. 2, p. 956, ed. 1830.]

116. In the Year Book, 50 Edward III. 1375, is mentioned the case of the Abbot of Bukfast *versus* the Dean and Chapter of Exeter, John Wyllyot, and Robert Davy [see ff. 10b and 11], and in the Liber Assisarum, 47 Edw. III., the Dean and Chapter of Exeter and John Wiliot, clerk, were attached to answer to Robert, abbot of Bukfast, of the plea, "quare ipsi cum Thomas Bail de Staverton, etc. injuste & sine judicio levaverunt quendam gurgitem in Staverton ad nocument' liberi ten' sui in Bukfast post primam, &c." The abbot used to take fish to the value of 40*l.* per annum, and now cannot take more than to the value of 10*s.* a-year. Arguments upon verbal omissions and technicalities followed, but nothing apparently was done. The last words are "Et sur ceo adjornatur."

117. The following relate probably to the same matter, and are taken from the De Banco Roll :—

Devon. Jur^a in^r Abbem de Bukfast quer^r ꝝ Robtm Sumpter Decanū ecctie beati Petri Exoñ ꝝ Capitulum eiusdc ecctie ꝝ Joħem Wyliet cticum de eo si p̄dcus Abbas pendente b̄ri suo v̄sus ipos Decanū ꝝ Capitulū ꝝ Joħem impetrato supponendo q̄d ip̄i sim̄l cum Thoma Baillyf de Stav̄toñ iniuste ꝝ sine indico levaverunt quendam gurgitem in Stav̄toñ ad nocumentū libi toñ ip̄ius Abbis in Bukfast pstravit gurgitem p̄dcm p quod idem Abbas b̄re suū vltius v̄sus p̄dcm Joħm manutenere non debet sicut idem Joħes dicit vel non sicut p̄dcus Abbas dicit Et eciam si die impetracois b̄ris p̄dci Abbis sciīt decimo die Nov̄ anno regni Regis nunc Angł quadragesimo p̄dci Decanus ꝝ Capitulū fuerunt tenentes vt de libo teñ soli in Stav̄toñ vbi supponit^a nocumentū p̄dcm fieri ad nocumentū libi teñ p̄dci Abbis in Buckfast p q̄d ip̄i vt tenentes soli illius ad excepc̄oem allegand in Cassac̄oem b̄ris p̄dci admitti debeant sicut ijdem Decanus ꝝ Capitulū Dicunt vel non Immo p̄dco die impetrac̄ois b̄ris p̄fat̄ Joħes Willyet fuit tenens eiusdem soli vt de libo teñ sicut p̄dcus Abbas dicit ponit^{ur} in respc̄m hic vsq̄, a die Pasche in xv dies nisi Justic̄ d̄ni Regis ad assias in com̄ p̄dco capiend assigñ p formā statuti etc. die M^o cur̄ px̄ post fm

sči Mathic Apli apud Exoñ prius veñint p defcu Juř quia
nullus veñ. I'o vič ħeat corpa etc.—(De Banco Roll, 48 Edw.
III., Hilary m. 169 d.)

Jur⁴ inᵗ Jońem Welyet queř ꝇ Robtm Abbem de Bukfast Devon.
ꝇ fratrē Jońem Skyredoñ frem Radm Middelworthy frem
Robm Cok* ꝇ frem Walterum Morchard cōmonač eiusdē
Abbis de ptito t⁴nsgř ponit‴ in respectū hic vsqꝫ a die Pasche
in tres septīas p Justič nisi Justič dni Reǧ ad asšias in coñ
pdco capiend assigñ p formā statuti etc. die Mercuř px post
festū sči Mathic Apli apud Exoñ prius veñint p def'cu Juř
quia nullus veñ. I'o vič ħeat corpa etc. Ad quē diē veñ ptes
etc. Et vič non mis bre. I'o Jur⁴ pdca ponit‴ in respčm hic
vsqꝫ a die sče Trinitatis in xv dies p def'cu Juř quia nullus
veñ. I'o vič ħeat corpa ꝇc. Ad quē diē * *
   *   *   *   *   *

Further put in respite to Michaelmas, then to Hilary.
(Apparently here the Record stops, but the writing is so bad,
small, and close, that it is difficult to say positively).—*Ibid.*
m. 263.

118. In 1377 we again find Abbot Robert in legal mire,
prosecuting James Audeley for interfering with the river
Dart and the fishery at Dartington, Staverton, and Little
Hempston. No decision upon the case can be found. It is
repeated *de novo* in subsequent Rolls.

Jacobus de Audele Chivaler suñ fuit ad respondend Robto Devon
Abbti de Bukfast de ptito quare ipe injuste ꝇ sine judicio
levavit sex gurgites in Dertyngtoñ Stavertoñ ꝇ Hemmestoñ
Arondel ad nocumentū libi teñ ipius Abbtis in Bukfast ꝇ
Ayshpertoñ post p‴m ꝇč Et unde idem Abbas p Thomam
Spyrweye attorñ suū dič qd ubi idem Abbas ħet ꝇ ħere debet
ipcqꝫ ꝇ omēs pdecessores sui Abbtes loci pdči a tempe quo non
extat memoria ħuerunt in villis de Bukfast ꝇ Ayshpertoñ in
quadam aqua vocata Derte quendam gurgitem de quo quidem
gurgite pdča aqua de Derte currit usqꝫ ad pdčas villas de
Dertyngtoñ Stavertoñ Hemmestoñ Arondel ꝇ a pdčis villis
usqꝫ ad altum mare extra portum de Dertemouthe de quo
gurgito idem Abbas ħere debet ipcqꝫ ꝇ omēs pdecessores sui
Abbtes ejusdem loci a tempe cuj⁹ cont‴rii memoria non existit
ħuerunt quandam aperturam latitudinis sex pedū in aqua

Elsewhere (in previous Rolls) *Cooke.*

p̄dc̄a in medio majoris cursus ⁊ pfunditat̄ ejusdem aquo in
omib; locis ⁊ dn̄iis int̄ p̄dc̄as villas de Bukfast ⁊ Ayshperton
⁊ altū mare extra portū p̄dc̄m ex quacumq̨ p̄te ubi majorē
cursū ⁊ pfunditat̄ ejusdem aque in alneo suo fore contigit p
quam quidem apturam salmones trutes peles ⁊ alii pisces
maris natare solebant ⁊ potuerunt ab alto mari extra portū
p̄dc̄m usq̨ ad gurgitē ip̄ius Abb̄tis sup̄°dc̄am p̄dc̄us Jacobus
levavit p̄dc̄os sex gurgites ex t°nsv̄so ejusdem Aque ⁊ p̄dc̄e
apturo in eadem aqua de Derte in p̄dc̄is villis de Dertyngton
Staverton ⁊ Hemmeston Arondel int̄ gurgitē ip̄ius Abb̄tis
p̄dc̄m ⁊ altū mare ⁊ portū sup̄°dc̄m p quos quidem gurgites
in eisdem villis de Dertyngton Staverton ⁊ Hemmeston
Arondel sic levat̄ aptura p̄dc̄a est obstructa ita qd̄ pisces ⁊c̄
natare non possunt ab alto mari usq̨ ad gurgitem ip̄ius Abb̄tis
p̄dc̄m sicut solebant p quod ubi ip̄e Abbas solebat ⁊ potuit
cape pisces in gurgite suo p̄dc̄o ad valenciam quadraginta
librar; p annū ante levacōc̄m ⁊ obstruccōc̄m sup̄°dc̄as ⁊ modo
non potest cape pisces nisi ad valenc̄ decem solido; p annū
et sic ad nocumentū etc. unde dic̄ qd̄ deter̄ est ⁊ dampnū het
ad valenc̄ mille libra; Et inde pduc̄ sectam etc.

Et p̄dc̄us Jacobus p Johēm Bozoun att̄ suū veñ Et pet'
inde visū heat ⁊ Dies datus est eis hic a die sc̄i Michis in xv
dies p Justic̄ Et intim ⁊c.

De Banco Roll, Trinity,
Ric. II. m. 210.

119. In 1377 a brief somewhat similar to the one before
mentioned (par. 115) from the King and his Council, is
directed among others to the Abbot of Buckfast.

De mora facienda, super invasione Gallicorum.

A.D. 1377.
51 Edw. III.

Rot. Claus.
51 Edw. III. m. 8
in Turr. Lond.

Rex venerabili in Christo patri Th. eadem
gratiâ episcopo Exoniæ, salutem. Quia
pro certo intelleximus quod inimici nostri
Franciæ, et alii sibi adhærentes, magnam
multitudinem navium gallarum, et barge-
arum, cum homnibus ad arma et armatis, congregârunt, et
infra regnum nostrum Angliæ, ad citiùs quo poterunt, ap-
plicare, et nos, et dictum regnum nostrum, ac totam linguam
Anglicanam destruere et delere proponunt, nisi eorum
malitiæ manu forti resistatur:

Nos volentes hujusmodi dampnis et periculis, quæ nobis et
dicto regno nostro, ex subitis dictorum inimicorum nostrorum
aggressibus evenire possent præcavere, vobis, districtius quo

poterimus, firmiter injungendo mandamus, quod vos, cum omni festinatione, ad terras et tenementa vestra, villae de Dortmouth propinquins adjacentia, personaliter divertatis, ibidem, cum hominibus vestris, et tota familia vestra, fortiori modo quo poteritis, super defensione villæ prædictæ, et partium adjacentium, contra hostiles agressus, continue moraturi.

Et homines et tenentes vestros ibidem, videlicet, quemlibet eorum juxta statum et facultates suos, arraiari, et moram continuam ibidem, fortiori modo quo poterunt, hujusmodi periculis iminentibus, facere, et ipsos ad hoc celeriter faciendum, per districtiones bonorum et catallorum suorum, et alios vias et modos quibus poteritis, compelli et distringi faciatis indilatè; et hoc, sub periculo quod incumbit, nullatenus omittatis.

Teste Rege, apud West'm xiv die Maii. Per ipsum Regem et consilium. (Rymer's Fœdera, vol. iii., part 2, p. 1078, ed. 1830.

120. In the following extract, 1378, the abbot seeks to recover from John Suddon and Margaret his wife a messuage and land in Petrockstowe, which Robert Goding held of William Giffard, the former abbot, and which the then abbot claimed, as reverting to the Abbey on the death of Goding.

Robtus Abbas de Bukfast petit v̄sus Johem Suddoñ ⁊ Margiam uxorem ejus unū ferlingū t̄re ⁊ tres acras p̄ti cū p̄tiñ in Petrokystowe que Robtus Godyng⁹ tenuit de Witto Giffard nup Abbe de Bukfast p̄decessore nunc Abbis et que ad ip̄m nunc Abbem revti debent tanq"m escaeta sua eo qd p̄dc̄us Robtus Godyng⁹ obiit sine her ⁊c. Et unde idem Abbas p Thomā Spirwey att suū dicit qd p̄dc̄us Robtus Godyng⁹ fuit sc̄it⁹ de ten p̄dc̄is cū p̄tiñ in d̄nico suo ut de feodo ⁊ Jure tempe pacis tempe dñi E nup Reḡ Angl Avi dñi Rege nunc capiend inde explec̄ ad valenc̄ ⁊c. ⁊ ea tenuit de p̄dc̄o Witto p̄dc̄o ⁊c. p homaḡ ⁊ fidelit ⁊ scutagiū dñi Rege cū accederit ad quadraginta solidos decem solid qñ ad plus plus qñ ad minus minus ⁊c. ⁊ p ȝvicia sex solidoȝ p annū ad quatuor anni t̄mios principales solvend, vidett ad festa sc̄i Michis Natal Dñi Pasch ⁊ Natal sc̄i Johis Bapt de quibȝ ȝviciis idem p̄decessor ⁊c., fuit sc̄it⁹ ut in juro ecctie sue sc̄e Marie de Bukfast [blank] p manus p̄dc̄i Robti Godyng ut p manus veri tenentis sui vidett de p̄dc̄is homaḡ ⁊ fidelit ut de feodo ⁊ Jur ⁊ de p̄dc̄o redditu in d̄nico suo ut de feod o ⁊ Jure Et que ad p̄dc̄m nunc Abbem reverti debent tanq"m eschaeta sua eo

Devon.

memb. 28⁊d.

qd etc. Et inde pducit sectā etc. Et p̄dc̄i Joh̄es ⁊ Margeria p Joh̄em Coplestoñ att̄ suū veñ Et defend Jus suū quando etc. Et dicunt qd ip̄i nichil h̄ent in teñ p̄dc̄is nisi ex dimissione Joh̄is Hopere ad vitā ip̄o⁊ Joh̄is Suddoñ ⁊ Marg̃ie tantū rov̄sione inde ad p̄dc̄m Joh̄em Hopere ⁊ her̄ suos spectante sine quo non possunt p̄dc̄o Ab̄bi inde respondere ⁊ petunt auxiliū de ip̄o Joh̄e Hopere h̄eant eū hic in Crastino sc̄i Martini etc. Idem dies dat⁹ est p̄dc̄is ptib⁊ p attorñ suos p̄dc̄os hic ⁊c. ad quē diem p̄dc̄us Joh̄es Hoper sum̄ fecit se essoñ de malo venienđ v̄sus p̄dc̄m Ab̄bem ⁊ de p̄dc̄o p̄tito et h̄uit inde diē p Essoñ suū hic ad hunc diē scit̄t a die Pasche in tres septias extunc p̄x̄ seqñ put patet rot̄lo Essoñ sexto Idem dies dat⁹ fuit ptib⁊ p̄dc̄is hic ⁊c. Et modo ad hunc diē veñ tam p̄tes p̄dc̄e p attorñ suos p̄dc̄os q"m p̄dc̄us Joh̄es Hoper p Joh̄em Coplestoñ attorñ suū veñ Et idem Joh̄es Hoper se jungit p̄dc̄is Joh̄i Suddoñ ⁊ Marg̃ie iñ respondend v̄sus p̄dc̄m Ab̄bem de p̄dc̄o p̄tito etc. [Hereupon a day was given to the parties, as well yᵉ Abbot as John Suddon or Margery and John Hoper, now joined, from Michaelmas to fifteen days; at which day come the parties aforesaid from Hilary to fifteen days; at which day come the parties aforesaid from Trinity to fifteen days; at which day come the parties aforesaid to the morrow of St. Martin; at which day come the parties aforesaid from Easter to three weeks] in statu quo nunc salvis ptib⁊ etc.

De Banco Roll, Trinity, 1 and 2 Ric. II.

Here, too, the termination of the case does not appear on the Rolls. For some reason or other it would seem to have been dropped, a compromise being effected, or one of the parties not being sure of his success, allowing the other to take or retain possession of the land in dispute.

122. The next extract I have during Abbot Simon's time relates to his claim against Walter Rosere and William Buriman, whom he charged with carrying off his villeins, Christina Barry and John Barry, of Downe St. Mary, and the abbot claimed that he was injured to the extent of 20*l*.

Devon.

m. 175d. Abbas de Bukfast p Joh̄em Lacche att̄ suū op̄ se iiijᵗᵒ die v̄sus Walt̄um Rosere ⁊ Witt̄m Buriman de p̄tito quare vi ⁊ armis Cristinā Barry ⁊ Joh̄am Barry nativas ip̄ius Ab̄bis in v̄ico suo apud Scyntemarydoune existentes cepunt ⁊ abduxerunt p quod idem Abbas sviciū nativa⁊ sua⁊ p̄dc̄a⁊ p magnū tempus amisit ⁊ alia enorma ⁊c. ad dampnū ip̄ius

Abbis viginti libraȝ ⁊ conᵐ pace dñi E' nup Regis Angł avi ⁊c. Et ipi non veñ Et p̄c fuit vic̄ q̄d capet oos Et vic̄ nichil inde fecit nec b̄re misit. I'o sicut prius capiantʳ q̄d sint hic a die s̄ci Michis in xv dies p Justic̄.
De Banco Roll, 8 Rich. II. Trinity [1384].

123. In the next, of the date 1393, the abbot is the defendant, being called upon by William Beaumont to deliver to him a box, with writings and documents in it. It appears that the box, with its contents sealed up, was handed by John Beaumont the father of the claimant in his lifetime to John Warre, Episcopus Cumogensi, [? Le Mans] and that on the death of John Beaumont the same should have been handed to the son. And afterwards the bishop died at the Abbey of Buckfast, and the box with its contents came into the possession of the abbot, who would not give it up, by which William, the heir of John Beaumont, was much injured, and claimed redress and satisfaction. The bishop appeared by his attorney John Lack, to whom he must have been a good client, admitted having the box, and in effect stated that he was only desirous of doing what was right with it. He produced it in open court, and said that he had received it from the deceased bishop to take care of; that there was another claimant for the box, a certain John Brightricheston, and which was the right owner he did not know; and asked that John Brightricheston might be protected. The court thought it necessary under these circumstances to give John an opportunity of proving his right, and a day was fixed for him to appear. On the day named he did not come, and eventually the box with the deeds and muniments were handed over to the first claimant, the plaintiff William Beaumont. Here we have, among other interesting matter, the apparent fact that an Englishman was a bishop of a foreign see, if Le Mans is meant, and that he died, and was probably buried, at Buckfast Abbey.

Following this are three other extracts from the same roll, relating to litigation initiated by the abbot in respect of trespass committed on the abbey lands.

Robtus Abbas de Bukfestrie sum̄ fuit ad respondend̄ Wiłło Devon. Beaumount de ptito q̄d reddat ei quandam-pixidem cū cartis scriptis ⁊ aliis munimentis in eadem pixide contentis quam ei iniuste detinet ⁊c. Et vnde idem Wiłłs p Thomam Hertescote attorñ suū dic̄ q̄d cū quidam Johēs Beaumount pat̄ ipius Wiłłi cuius heř ipe est die lune px post fm sci Andř apli anno regnoȝ dñi Regis nunc quarto apud Exoñ libasset cuidam Johi Warre Epo Cumogensi* pixidem p̄dcam sigillatam cum cartis scriptis ⁊ alijs munimentis c̄ta ꝓras ⁊ teñ que eidem Witto post mortem p̄dci Johis Jure hereditar̄ descenderunt tangencia in eadem pixide contentis salvo custodiend̄ et eidem Johi vel her̄ suis cū inde requisitus fuisset reliband Ac postmodum p̄dcus Ep̄us in Abbia Bukfesrie obijt post cuius mortem pixis p̄dca cū cartis etc. ad manus p̄dci Abbis devenerunt. Idem tamen Abbas licet sepius requisitus pixidem p̄dcam p̄dco Johi Beaumount in vita sua nec eciam eidem Witto fit ⁊ her̄ p̄dci Johis Beaumount nondū libavit set illas ei huc usqȝ libare cont⁴dixit ⁊ adhuc cont⁴dicit vnde dic̄ q̄d deꝯioratus est ⁊ dampnum het ad valenciam centū libraȝ. Et inde pduc̄ sectam ⁊c.

Et p̄dcus Abbas p Johem Lacche attorñ suū veñ Et pfert hic in cur̄ pixidem p̄dcam cū cartis ⁊c. patam ad reddend cui cur̄ Regis hic consideravit dic̄ q̄d pixis illa cū cartis ⁊c. p p̄fatū Ep̄m eidem Abbi libatū fuit salvo custodiend̄ et cui de Jure libari debet deliband Et dic̄ q̄d quidam Johes Brightrichestoñ claim pixidem p̄dcam cū cartis ⁊c. eidem Johi Brightrichestoñ de Jure libari debe set an pixis p̄dca cū cartis ⁊c. p̄dco Johi Brightrichestoñ an p̄fato Witto de Jure libari debeat nec ne dic̄ q̄d ip̄e oīnio ignorat Et pet q̄d p̄dcus Johes Brightrichestoñ p̄muniatur ⁊c. I'o prec̄ est vic̄ q̄d p pbos ⁊c. scire fac̄ p̄fato Johi Brightrichestoñ q̄d sit hic in Octab̄ s̄ci Michis ostens si quid p se heat vel dic̄e sciat quare pixis p̄dca cū cartis ⁊c. p̄fato Witto libari non debeat si ⁊c. Idem dies datus est ptibȝ p̄dcis hic ⁊c. Ad quem diem veñ tam p̄dcus Wittus qᵃm p̄dcus Abbas p attorñ suos p̄dcos Et p̄dcus Johes Brightrichestoñ iiij¹ᵒ die pťiti solempniter exactus non veñ Et vic̄ modo mand̄ q̄d scire fecit eidem Johi Brightrichestoñ essend hic ad hunc diem ostens in forma p̄dca p Nichm More Johem Toune ⁊ Robm More Feryby I'o cons est q̄d p̄dcus Wittus heat libnc̄oem pixidis p̄dce cum cartis etc. extra possessionē p̄dci Abbis Et sup hoc p̄dcus Abbas pfert hic in cur̄ p̄dcam pixidē cum cartis ⁊c. paratā ad reddend p̄fato Witto quequidem pixis cū cartis etc. p̄fato Witto hic in cur̄ liberat⁴ I'o idem abbas de eadem pixide cū cartis ⁊c. exoñet⁴ ⁊c.—De Banco Roll, 17 Rich. II. Trinity.

Devon. Robtus Abbas de Bukfast ⁊ frater Edwardus Stele ⁊ frater
memb. 176 d. Henr̄ Haredoñ ⁊ frater Robtus Asshe ⁊ frater Stephus

* ? for *le Mans* in France.

Roulande cōmonacos eiusdem Abbis ⁊ Ricus Roke in m̄ia p plur̄ defalt̄.
Dies dat⁹ est Johanne que fuit p̄x⁹ Johis Jaycok quer̄ p Johem Jaycok attorñ suū Et p̄dcis Abbi Edwardo Henr̄ Robte Stepho ⁊ Rico p Johem Lacche attorñ suū de ptito t⁹nsgr̄ hic in Octab sci Hillar̄ p̄cepcium sine essoñ etc ad quē diē veñ ptes p̄dce ⁊c. Et sup hoc dies datus est eis hic a die Pasche in tres septias p̄ce p̄ciū sine essoñ ⁊c.
Mem.—On this Roll (230 d.) Robert, Abbot of B. v. "Johʼam que fuit vxor Johis Jaycok" who "clausa fregit" and cut down the abbot's trees, depastured lands, &c. She does not come. Sheriff ordered to distrain her through all, &c., and have her body here from Hilary to fifteen days. No writ. Order for Easter as before.—*Ibid*. 18 Rich. II. Mich.

The next two extracts refer, one to a defaulting bailiff of the Abbey at Battochsburgh, who was not to be found, and the second, to a claim for the recovery of land and houses at Buckfastleigh.

Robtus Abbas de Bukfast p Johem Lacche attorñ suum op' Devon'. se iiijᵗᵒ die v̄sus Johem Weryng de South lodebroke de plito q̄d reddat ei r̄onabilem compotū suū de tempe quo fuit ballivus suus in Battokysburgh ⁊ receptor denario꜠ ip̄ius Abbis Et ip̄e non veñ Et p̄cep̄t fuit vic̄ q̄d capet eū Et vic̄ modo mand̄ q̄d non est invent̄ ⁊c. Iʼo p̄cep̄t est vic̄ q̄d capiat eū si ⁊c. Et salvo ⁊c. Ita q̄d heat corpus eius hic in Octabis sci Hillar̄ ⁊c. —De Banco Roll, 18 Rich. II. Mich. m. 250.

Abbas de Bukfast p Johem Lacche attorñ suū pet v̄sus Devon'. Johnam Jaycok ⁊ Walt̄um Deghere vnū toftum cum ptiñ in Bukfastlegh Et v̄sus Johnam que fuit vxor Johis Jaycok septem mesuaḡ duas acr̄ t̄re ⁊ vnam acr̄ pʼti et dimid̄ cum ptiñ in eadem villa Et v̄sus Walt̄um Deghere de Bukfastlegh duo mesuaḡ vnam acr̄ t̄re ⁊ dimid̄ ⁊ vnam acr̄ pʼti cum ptiñ in eadem villa vt Jus ⁊c. p br̄e Regis de forma donacōis ⁊c. Et p̄dci Johna Jaycok Walt̄us Deghere Johna que fuit vxor Johis Jaycok ⁊ Walt̄us Deghere de Bukfastlegh p Johem Jaycok attorñ suū veñ Et sep̄atim petunt inde visum heant ⁊c. dies dat̄ est eis hic a die Pasche in quinq̄ septimanus Et int̄im ⁊c.—*Ibid*. m. 333 d.

124. I have not been able to find any account of the case referred to by Dr. Oliver which he calls the valuable cause of the fishery of the River Dart at Buckfastleigh against the Dean and Chapter at Exeter, but only a short reference to it.

In Hilary term, 1376, a verdict having already been given in favour of the Abbey, apparently at the assizes, the matter came before the Court of Common Pleas on demurrer. Davy, one of the defendants, had never once appeared. The words showing the finding are " Sur que quant a les autors " [Davy not having appeared] " qui averont pled' al enquest trove fuit p' nisi prius que le Dean & le Chapitre n'averont reens en le frank tenement, & auxi l'abbot n'avera abatu le Gorce pendant le brē, coē."

125. While hunting for the Dart case another important fishery case turned up, which is very fully set out in the De Banco Roll. It is too long to produce at length, but a friend who has helped me in transcribing documents for the purposes of this paper has prepared a full abstract of the proceedings. The dispute arose as to the right of fishery in the Brent River, the Avon, and the action was brought by the abbot, still Robert Simons, against Richard Knight, Vicar of Brent, and others. The case was tried, apparently, at Exeter, when a verdict was given in favour of the abbot. There was an appeal, and the verdict was reversed on technical grounds. I have given the judgment and some other parts of the proceedings as they appear on the Roll.

The King (Richard II.) issued a Writ of Mandamus to Walter Clopton and the Justices of the King's Bench, dated at Westm., 8 June, 22 R. 2 (1399); whereby he directed that the record and process relating to a plea of trespass between Robert, late Abbot of Buckfast, and Robert Knyght, Vicar of the Church of Brent, John Beare [and others as hereinafter], &c., being seen by them, a manifest error committed (as alleged) by the Justices of Common Pleas should be corrected. The Record and process mention in the said writ as follows:—

Buckfast.

Devon'.

Attorñ recept apud Westm̃ coram * * * Justič Dñi Reḡ de côi Banco de t̃mio Hillaŕ Anno regni Reḡ Riči sĕdi quartodecimo.

Robtus Knyght vicaŕ ecctie de Brente Joħes ffox Joħes Beare Witts ffenford Witts Pitman Witts Langedoñ Joħes Langedoñ Walt̃us Schaghe ⁊ Thomas Schaghe po lo suo Thomam Reymound vel Thomam Noreys v̄sus Robtm abbem de Bukfast de plito t̃"nsgr̄.

Plita apud Westm̃ coram Robto de Cherltoñ ⁊ soč suis Justič Dñi Regis de Banco de T')mio sčo Trinitatis anno regni Reḡ Riči sĕdi quintodecimo. Ro. cccvj.

Robtus Knyght vicar ecclie de Brente Johes ffox Johes Devon'. Beare Witts ffenford Witts Pitman Johes Langedoñ ⁊ Walt̄us Schago attach fuerunt ad respondend Robto Abbti de Bukfast de ptito quare ipi cū Witto Langedoñ ⁊ Johe Shaghe vi ⁊ armis clausi ipius Abbis apud Brenta fregunt ⁊ arbores suas ibm nup crescentes succiderunt ⁊ in sepali piscar̄ sua ibm piscati fuerunt ⁊ piscem inde ac arbores p̄dcas necnon alia bona ⁊ catalla sua ad valenc̄ viginti librą ac quingentos cuniclos suos p̄cij centum solidoą ibm inventa ceperunt et asportaverunt ⁊ blada ⁊ herbam suam ad valenc̄ centū solidoą ibm nup crescencia cum quibusdam averijs depasti fuerunt conculcaverunt ⁊ consumpserunt ⁊ alia enormia ei intulerunt ad grave Dampnum ipsius Abbis ⁊ cont⁻ pacem Regis Et vnde idem Abbas p Johem Lacche attorn̄ suū querit q̄d p̄dci Robtus Knyght Johes ⁊ Johes Witts Witts Johes ⁊ Walt̄us siml̄ etc. die Jovis px̄ post festū oīm scoą anno regnoą dn̄i Reḡ nunc nono vi ⁊ armis scitt glad archubą ⁊ sagittis claus ip̄ius Abbis apud Brenta fregunt ⁊ arbores suas vidett quadraginta quercus viginti fraxinos decem ulnos decem tremulos ⁊ viginti fabos ibm nup crescentes succiderunt ⁊ in sepali piscaria sua ibm piscati fuerunt ⁊ piscem inde vidett quadraginta salmones lupos aquaticos percheas tencheas anguillas ⁊ pelos ac arbores p̄dcas necnon alia bona ⁊ catalla sua vidett pannos lineos ⁊ laneos ad valenc̄ viginti librą ac quingentos cuniclos suos p̄cij centum solidoą ibm inventos ceperunt ⁊ asportaverunt ⁊ blada vidett frumentū ordeū fabas pisas ⁊ avenas ⁊ herbam suam ad valenc̄ etc. ibm nup crescenc̄ cū quibusd avijs vidett equis bobą vaccis affris bidentibus ⁊ porcis depasti fuerunt conculcaverunt ⁊ consumpserunt t⁻nsḡr p̄dcam quoad succisionem arboą piscac̄ōem ⁊ depastū bladoą ⁊ herbe p duos annos tunc px̄ seqn diversis vicibus continuandi et alia enormia etc. Et cont⁻ pacem etc. vnde diç q̄d detor est ⁊ dampnū het ad valenc centū librą ⁊ inde p̄duc sectam etc. Et p̄dci Robtus Knyght Johes ffox Johes Beare Witts ffenford Witts Pitman Johes Langedoñ ⁊ Walt̄us p Thomam Norreys Attorn̄ suū ven̄ ⁊ defend̄ vim ⁊ iniur̄ quando etc. Et quo ad venire vi ⁊ armis necnon fracc̄ōem clausi succisionē arboą ac asportac̄ōem bonoą ⁊ catalloą dic̄ q̄d ip̄i in nullo sunt inde culpables et de hoc poñ se sup priam Et p̄dcus Abbas simitr̄. Et eciam p̄dcus Johes ffox ⁊ om̄es alij p̄r p̄dem Robtm Knight quoad capc̄ōem cunicloą dic̄ sīlit̄ q̄d ip̄i in nullo sunt inde culpables Et eciam idm Robtus Knight quoad depastū bladoą ⁊ herbe p̄dcoą dic̄ q̄d ip̄e in nullo est inde culpabit Et inde sepatim poñ se sup priam Et p̄dcus Abbas similit̄ et quoad piscac̄ōem etc. pfatus Robtus Knyght

N

dic q̃d quidam Witts Gybbe circa f̄m Oīm s̄coȝ Anno regnoȝ
dni Regis nunc sexto cepit de p̃fato Abbe ad vs̄u ip̄ius Roƀti
ȝ p̃dci Witti Gybbe ac quoȝdam Jotis Brode ȝ Witti ffylyp̃
piscariam p̃dcam tenend̃ ad voluntatem ȝc. ad piscand̃ in
ead̃m p voluntate sua. Et dic q̃d id̃m Roƀtus occupavit
piscariam p̃dcam ȝ in ead̃m piscaȓ fuit absqȝ hoc q̃d ip̄e
aliquo alio tempe in ead̃m piscaria piscaȓ fuit et p̃dcus Jotes
ffox ȝ om̃es alij defend̃ dic q̃d ip̄i veneȓ in auxiliū ip̄ius Roƀti
ad piscand̃ in piscaria p̃dca p̃dcis Annis sexto ȝ septimo absqȝ
hoc q̃d ip̄e [aliquo] alio tempe in ead̃m piscaȓ piscaȓ fuerunt
Et hoc pati sunt sepatim ṽrificare vnde singillatim non intend̃
aliquam Iniuȓ in p̄sonis suis ea de causa assignari posse ȝc.
Et quo ad cap̃cōem cuniclōȝ etc. Roƀtus Knyght dic q̃d ip̄e
fuit capettus p̃dci Abbis ȝ cū eod̃m Abbe com̃orabat" ȝ p
p̃ceptū p̃dci Abbis Annis regnoȝ dni Regis nunc s̄cdo ȝ ȝcio
cepit duos cuniclos ad vs̄u eiusd̃m Abbis iƀm ȝ eos eid̃m Abbi
afferebat ȝ liƀavit absqȝ hoc q̃d ip̄e aliquo modo aliquos
cuniclos iƀm cepit Et hoc patus est ṽrificare vnde non intend̃
aliquam iniuȓ in hac p̃te in p̄sona sua assignari posse ȝc. Et
p̃dcus Jotes ffox ȝ om̃es alij defendentes p̃ p̃dem Roƀtm
Knyght quo ad depastū bladoȝ ȝ tibe etc. dic q̃d diṽsis viciƀȝ
p tempus in narracōe p̃dcis Abbis content̃ diṽsa aṽia sua in
bladis ȝ herba p̃dci Abbis capta ȝ imp̃cata fuerunt ȝ in diṽsis
cuȓ eiusd̃m Abbis p id̃m tempus iƀm p t"nsgȓ illis que sunt
ead̃m t"nsgȓ vnde id̃m Abbas querit" am̃ciati ȝ afforati fuerunt ȝ am̃eiamenta illa eid̃m Abbi de tempe in tempus sepatim
solverunt ȝ sic dic q̃d p̃dco Abbi p dampno p ip̄os in bladis ȝ
herba eiusd̃m Abbis vnde id̃m Abbas modo querit" in forma
p̃dca satisf̄em existit vnde non intend̃ q̃d ip̄i occone illa iȝum
molestari seu gᵃvari debeant etc. Et p̃dcus Abbas dic q̃d p̃dci
Roƀtus Knyght Jotes ffox Jotes Beare Witts ffenford Witts
Pitman Jotes Langetoñ ȝ Walȝus vi ȝ armis ȝ de iniuȓ sua
ppria p tempus in narracōe eiusd̃m Abbis content̃ in sepali
piscaȓ ip̄ius Abbis apud Brente piscati fuerunt ȝ piscem inde
ceperunt ȝ asportaveȓ cont" pacem Reḡ put p querelam ip̄ius
Abbis supponit" Et hoc peȓ q̃d inquirat" p p̃riam. Et p̃dcus
Roƀtus Knyght ȝ om̃es alij defendentes qui modo comp̃arent
siliȝ Et eciam id̃m Abbas dic q̃d Roƀtus Knyght p tempus
in narracōe ip̄ius Abbis specificaȓ vi ȝ armis ȝ de iniuȓ sua
ppria ȝ cont" pacem Reḡ cepit quingentos cuniclos suos iƀm
put idem Abbas querit" Et hoc similiȝ peȓ q̃d inquirat" p
p̃riam Et p̃dcus Roƀtus Knyght simitr Et quo ad depastū
bladoȝ ȝ herbe p̃dcoȝ id̃m Abbas dic q̃d p̃dci Jotes ffox Jotes
Beare Witts ffenford Witts Pitman Jotes Langedoñ ȝ Walȝus
blada ȝ herbam sua p̃dca p tempus in narracōe eiusd̃m Abbis

content depast fuer cont" pacem Reg absq; hoc q̃d ijdm Johes ffox Johes Beare Witts ffenford Witts Pitman Johes Langedoñ ɿ Walt̃us p t"nsgr̃ illis amiciati ɿ afferati fuerunt vel eidm Abb̃i inde p eisdm t"nsgr̃ satisfecerunt Et hoc pet q̃d inquirat" p priam Et p̃dci Johes ffox Johes Beare Witts ffenford Witts Pitman Johes Langedoñ ɿ Walt̃us silit̃. l'o pr̃ est vic̃ q̃d venire fac̃ hic a die sc̃i Michis in xv dies xij etc. p quos etc. et qui nec etc. Ad recogñ etc. Quia tam etc.

Afterwards the jury being placed in respite at York from Michmas day to three weeks 16 R. II. unless the justices, &c. come before to Exeter, &c. Afterwards on the day and at the place before Wm. Rykhill and Wm. Brenchell Justices assigned &c. in Co. Devon, come as well Robt Abbot of B as Robt Knyght, John Fox, John Beare, Wm. Fenford, Wm. Pitman, John Langedon, and Walt. Shaghe by y^{eir} att. and likewise the Jurors who &c. say on their oath That ye s^d John Fox, Wm. P. and John L. are not guilty of the trespass mentioned. And that the s^d Robt. K. John B. Wm. F. and Walter Shaghe as to breaking the close, cutting down and carrying away 12 oak trees are guilty; and as to cutting down and carrying away the residue of ye trees ment^d, also taking and carr^g away the goods and chattels ment^d they say that s^d Robt K. John B. Wm. F. and Walter S. are not guilty ; and as to fishing in ye sev^l fishery of ye Abbot and taking fish, that the s^d Robt. John, Wm. and Walt. with force and arms for the time contained in the Abbot's description fished at Brent and took and carried away 30 salmon as complained by the abbot; and as to taking the remaining fish mentioned that they (R. J. W. and W.) are not guilty; and as to ye taking of the rabbits, except twenty of them, that ye s^d Robt. John, Wm. and Walt. are not guilty; as to the 20 rabbits, they took and carried them away as compl^d by ye abbot; and as to the depasture that s^d Robt Knyght is guilty, and the s^d John Beare, Wm. Fenford and Walter Shaghe also depastured, &c. and they were not amerced, &c. And they assess the damages of the s^d abbot on acc^t of ye s^d trespasses at Ten Pounds So it is cons^d y^t ye s^d abbot sh^d recover agst ye said Robt. John, Wm. and Walter his s^d damages assessed at 10t. and ye s^d R. J. W. and W. be taken And ye s^d abbot in mercy for his false claim agst John Fox, Wm. Pitman, and John Langedon who are acquitted of ye s^d trespasses. And hereupon s^d abbot confesses " se nolle ulterius prosequi " agst Wm. Langedon and John Shaghe of plea afores^d. So ye s^d abbot may have exon, &c.

Afterw^{ds} viz. in octaves of S. Hil. 16 R. II. Robt Knyght, present here in Court, is committed to Flete prison (goale de ffiete) there to remain until &c.

The abbot by his s^d att^y offered himself on the 4th day v. s^d Wm. Langedon and John Shaghe And they do not come And the sheriff is ordered &c. The sheriff has not sent ye writ Adjourned to Trinity Term then to be at York on ye morrow of S. John Bapt. At wch day no writ from ye sheriff. To be at York in the octave of S. Michael &c.

(Pleas at Westm. de Banco Mich 15 R. II.) Robt. Abbot of B. plt. v. Robt. Knyght vicar of ch. of Brente, John Fox, John Beare, Wm. Fenford, Wm. Pitman, John Langedon and Walter Shage of a plea of trespass. Jury in respite. Adjourned to Hil. term when (no writ from ye sheriff) Jury in respite to Trin.* 16 R. II. Again respited to Michmas unless before &c. Jury to be before ye K.'s Justices at York &c.

Afterwards, *i.e.* in Mich term 1 Hen. IV. before ye King himself at Westm. at the suit of s^d Robt Knight, John Beare, Wm. Fenford and Walter appearing in person and ascertaining there was error in the record and process afores^d and in the delivery of the judgment aforesaid and because s^d Robt late abbot praying for a writ to summon Wm. now abbot of Bukfast to be before the King to hear s^d record and process. So the sheriff is ordered to let Wm. know, &c. The same day is given to s^d Robt. J. Wm. and Walt. At wch day come before the King at Westm s^d R. J. W. and W. in person, and the sheriff returns that he let Wm. now abbot know that he was to be at Westm. to hear &c. as required by ye K's writ by " With^m Lamelan, With^m Hamstede, Johem Coke ? Ricm More," &c. Which said Wm. now abbot, tho' warned and solemnly called on the fourth day, does not come. Hereupon ye s^d Robt. John, Wm. and Walter say that in the record and process and delivery of judgment there are divers errors, viz. :—

That whereas the s^d Robt late abbot prosecuted a writ of trespass agst ye s^d Robt. Knyght and other def^{ts} before ye s^d justices etc. and ye s^d def^{ts} by Thos. Norreys y^{eir} attorney wch said writ was quashed namely in Hilary Term 14 R. II.; and long afterw^{ds} *i.e.* 12 April 14 R. II. the s^d late abbot obtained that writ agst ye def^{ts} in wch Thos. Norreys as the attorney of ye def^{ts} (as contained in the said rec^d and proc.) whereas ye s^d Thos. had no warrant in that second writ " de

---

* Robert (abbot) " po. lo. suo Joh'm Lacche " in this Term.

quo totū pcessū p̃dcm warrantizat^{ur} ;" and so in this, that the s^d justices proceeded upon the said plea without any def^t appearing in his own pson or by att^y have erred And by writ as well Wm. Thirnyng Ch. Justice de Cōi Banco as Wm. Pountfreit keeper of the K's writs de Banco "ad certiorand etc." whether ye s^d Robt. John, Wm. and Walter made any att^y in the plea aforesaid, etc. The s^d Wm. Thirnyng to search the Rolls and the s^d Keeper to examine the writs of the terms and years afores^d and to certify w^{t}out delay. Afterw^{ds} 30 Jañy in that same term Wm. Thirnyng certified that the Rolls of ye s^d terms and years had been examined; and no attorney can be found of record in ye same. And ye s^d keeper certified that he had no Writ of Att^y for the terms and years aboves^d, and that the date of ye orig^l Writ in the dispute afores^d is 12 April 14 R. II. And ye s^d Robt. John, Wm. and Walter say, that there is manifest error as appears by ye s^d certificates. And in this, that whereas the s^d Robt. late abbot supposed that they depastured at Brent, and they, the def^{ts}, alleged that they were diverse times amerced and satisfied the abbot of those amercom^{ts}, and ye s^d abb^t alleged that they were not amerced, &c. Afterw^{ds} the Justices by Writ of Nisi Prius inquired if John Fox, Wm. Pytman and John Langecon were guilty of the s^d trespasses or not, whereas ye s^d J^{ces} ought to have inquired if ye s^d John, Wm. and John were amerced and satisfied the abbot for said trespasses or not. And, because the Justices inq^d if they were guilty or not of ye trespasses which the def^{ts} acknowledged, they erred. Also there is error in this, that whereas John Shaghe came not in his own person or by att^y and never pleaded, nevertheless ye Justices inquired if he were guilty or not of the s^d trespasses, they erred. Also in this, that whereas Walter Shaghe s^d that he was not guilty of taking ye s^d rabbits (conies) as alleged by ye abbot, the Justices did not inquire whether he was guilty or not, they erred. Also in this, that whereas ye s^d abbot supposed that s^d Robt Knyght and other def^{ts} fished in his several fishery at Brent and took fish, etc. the s^d Robt K. s^d y^t about ye Feast of All Saints 6. R II. one Wm. Gibbe took from the abbot to the use of the s^d Robt and others ye fishery aforesaid as tenant at will, etc. and said y^t said Robt occupied the s^d fishery and fished there: to wch plea ye s^d abbot made no answer but maintained his writ, and ye s^d Justices inq^d as to the justification of s^d Robt K. in s^d plea, wherens the abbot made no answer to the justif^n, they erred. Also in this, that whereas John Fox and other def^{ts} said in y^{eir} plea that they came to assist Robt Knyght to fish in the 6th and 7th years, etc. whereas no mention was made of any seventh year in the plea and ye s^d abbot by accepting that plea and answering thereto, whereas it is not the plea on which the parties joined issue (as appears in the Record) which issue the Justices accepted and inquired upon, they erred. Also in this, that whereas ye s^d abbot supposed that the trespass was done at Brente, "postea in replicac̃oe sua idm Abbas manutenuit d̄cam t̃nsḡr fieri apud Brente ⁊ sic non manutenuit t̃ngr̃ p̃dcam fieri in villa in narac̃oe sua contenta s; in alia villa et in hoc q̃d Justic̃ pcesserunt ad iudm sup t̃li p̃tito erraverunt." And they pray that the said judgment on acc^t of s^d errors and others in the Record and process aforesaid be reversed; and that the Court proceed to the exam^n of the said Record and process. Hereupon a day is given to ye said Robt Knyght and others from Easter to three weeks, at wch day came ye s^d Robt and others in person; and, the Court not being ready to deliver judgement, a day is given to s^d R. &c. to be before our Lord ye King wherever, &c. in term of Holy

Judgment. Trinity to hear judgment. Ad quem diem coram dno Rege apud Westm̃ ven̄ p̃dc̃i Robtus Knyght Johes Beare Wiltms Fenfford ⁊ Waltus in ppriis p̃son̄ suis Et vis̃ ⁊ diligent̃ examinatis recordo ⁊ pcessu p̃dc̃is videt^r cur̃ q̃d in hoc q̃d ubi p̃dc̃us Robtus nup Abbas etc. supposuit p b̃re ⁊ nar̃r sua q̃d p̃dc̃i Rob Knyght ⁊ alii defendent̃ etc. blada ⁊ herbam sua cū quibusdam av̄iis suis depasti fuerunt apud Brenta etc. p̃dc̃i Johes Fox Johes Beare Wiltms Fenfford Wiltms Pitman Johes Lang^edon ⁊ Walt̃ Shaghe allegar̃ q̃d p eisdm̃ t^ansgr̃ in Cur̃ ipius nup Abbtis apud Brenta div̄sis tempib; amciati ⁊ afforati fuc̃r ⁊ de eisdm̃ amciament eidm nup Abbti satisfecet̃ ad quod idm nup Abbas p̃titando allog̃ q̃d p̃dc̃i Johes Fox ⁊ alii defend̃ non fuer̃ amciati ⁊ afforati p eisdm t^ansgr̃ nec p eisdm t^ansgr̃ eidem nup Abbti satisfecer̃ Sup quo postea c̄tis die ⁊ loco put continet^r in recordo q̃d Justic̃ adinquir̃ de t^ansgr̃ p̃dc̃is p b̃re de Nisi Prius deputat̃ inquisivet̃ si p̃dc̃i Johes Fox Wiltms Pitman ⁊ Johes Langedon̄ fuc̃r culpables de t^ansgr̃ p̃dc̃is vel non ubi p̃dc̃i Justic̃ inquisivisse debuissent si p̃dc̃i Johes Fox Wiltms Pitman ⁊ Johes Langedon̄ p p̃dc̃is t^ansgr̃ amciati ⁊ afforati fuerunt ⁊ p eisdm̃ t^ansgr̃ eidm nup Abbti satisfecer̃ vel non put ip̃i p̃titando allegar̃ Et in hoc q̃d Justic̃ inquisiver̃ si ip̃i fuerunt culpables de t^ansgr̃ p̃dc̃is vel non ubi ip̃i p p̃titm suū p̃dc̃m cogñ t^ansgr̃ p̃dcum manifeste est err̃. I'o cons̃ est q̃d ob errorem p̃dc̃m ⁊ alios in recordo ⁊ pcessu p̃dc̃is comptos q̃d judm̃

Jud'm adnull. p̃dc̃m revocetur adnullet^r ⁊ penit^9 p nullo ĥeat^r Et q̃d p̃dc̃i

Robt⁹ Knyght Johes Beare Wilts Fenfford ? Walrus reheant dampna sua p̃dc̃a si que occ̃one p̃dc̃a p̃fato nup Abbti aut dc̃o nunc Abbti satisfec̃)int Et q̃d ĩpi eant inde sine die etc. (De Banco Roll, Hilary, 1 Henry IV.)

127. I have failed not only in verifying Dr. Oliver's authorities in the Dart fishery case, but also in ascertaining further particulars with reference to the placing of the arms of James and Thomas Audelay "in the window of the west end of the Conventual Church and in the window of the gable end in the Lady Chapel there." Although a careful search has been made, the entries have not turned up, and they are not where Dr. Oliver states they are. I much regret this, for I believe there is some mistake, inasmuch as Cistercian churches had no Lady Chapel, the whole church being dedicated to the Blessed Virgin [See Monasticon Cisterciense, cap. xviii.] I was in hopes also that the document might have contained some further references to the church, which might have enabled us to form some idea of its extent and appearance.

128. Robert Simons was evidently an abbot who had the interest of his house at heart, and did much for its worldly prosperity. He must have been abbot for upwards of thirty-five years, and was succeeded in his office by William Paderston, who was confirmed in September, 1395. He was not abbot long, and I have not been able to find anything relating to the abbey in which he was interested, except the Avon fishery case, which was finally decided in his time, and the following from the De Banco Roll 3 Henry IV., 1202.

Wm. abbot of Buckfast, Brother Wm. Beagh, and Brother Richard Gorwet, fellow monks of the said abbot, and Thomas Baker and Richard Helyere, the abbot's servants, were attached to answer to Thomas Knight, Vicar of the Church of Brent, of the plea "quare vi et armis in ipsum Robtm apud Brente insultum fecerunt, etc.," and detained him in prison there until he, Robert, paid 20l. for deliverance. The abbot denied his culpability, and alleged that Robert had diverted a water-course which ran through his, Robert's, lands, &c. All parties put themselves on the country, so the sheriff, to make come twelve, &c., from Michaelmas to fifteen days.

129. My next document is dated 18th May, 1414, when the learned William Slade had become abbot. He was a Devonshire man and educated at Exeter. Proceeding to Oxford, he acquired a good reputation, and about 1413 became abbot of Buckfast. As far as we know, with the

exception of the last abbot, he was the most distinguished man connected with the house. He was not only a scholar and a theologian, but an artist, and a spiritual guide to those over whom he was set, and to the parishioners of the churches belonging to the Abbey. He made many important additions to the conventual buildings, and I think it may be concluded that it is to his exertions that the people of Kingsbridge are indebted for the Chapel of St. Edmund, king and martyr, —consecrated by Bishop Stafford, 26th August, 1414, at which time the cemetery adjoining was also blessed—being made a parish church.

130. Kingsbridge was in the parish of Churchstow. Certainly, as early as 1333, 7 Edward III., the manors of Churchstow and Kingsbridge belonged to the abbey, but how it became possessed of them is not clear. In 1291, when the Survey for the Taxatio of Pope Nicholas was taken, Churchstow belonged to the Abbey, and, as appears from the entry paragraph 106, the value is entered at 13s. 4d., the tenth being 1s. 4d. Churchstow is two miles from Kingsbridge, and, as often happened, a particular part of the parish, as time passed on, became as important as, or more important than, the neighbourhood around the mother church; and we find from a deed without date, but probably late in the twelfth century, that provision was required for the spiritual wants of the people of Kingsbridge. The original deed is in the possession of the feoffees of the town lands of Kingsbridge, and a translation will be found in Hawkins's History of Kingsbridge, p. 122.

"Sciant præsentes et futuri quod ego M. de Litlecumba Rector Ecclesiæ de Chirchstowe concessi Abbati et Monachis de Bukfest edificare Ecclesiam in honore beati Edmundi Regis et Martiris in Dominio suo in Villa qua dicta Kingesbrig, ita quod omnes proventus illius Villæ ad Ecclesiam pertinentes cedant ad Sustentationem unius Capellani qui in prædicta Ecclesia Divina celebret imperpetuum, et omnes Homines in prædicta Villa manentes audiant divinum Servicium in prædicta Ecclesia Et omnia Ecclesiastica jura ibidem percipiant, ita cum quod Saltem semel in Anno insitent Matrem Ecclesiam scilicet Chirchstowe videlicet in Assumptione Beatæ Mariæ Virginis ut infra octavum oblationibus quibus infra limites Parochiæ prædicta villa consistet. Verum propterea Ecclesia de Chirchstowe de loco illo scilicet Kingesbrig nunquam aliquid percipere consuento et ideo libere istud concedo quam omnino est sine prejudicio Matris Ecclesiæ et Maximum opus Misericordiæ est Divinum inchoare servitium quod per omnibus Christi fidelibus unus et Defunctus Annuente Cristo in loco illo celebrabiter in perpetuam. Ut aut hæc concessio mea firma permaneat huic præsenti Scripto in Testimonum et Confirmationem Sigillum meum appono.

131. This deed was the consent of the rector of the mother church to the erection of a new church, but apparently the new building was not consecrated for some time after, for the consecration deed of Bishop Stafford speaks of the chapel which then and from time immemorial (the scribe did not trouble himself to make very careful inquiry, or he would have found that his "time immemorial" would have dwindled down to very few years) was erected, and magnificently built by sufficient and lawful authority, that the parish and parishioners were distinct from Churchstow, and that the rector was obliged to perform all divine services at the chapel for the people of Kingsbridge, except burial of the dead, which was accustomed to be done at Churchstow.

132. The chapel received assistance towards maintaining its independent character. John Cob, Vicar of Hennock, gave to the chapel of St. Edmund at Kingsbridge, and to the overseers of the chapel, a tenement and garden near the cemetery of the chapel. The deed conveying this is dated 23rd April, 1410, more than four years before the consecration, so that the cemetery although provided was not used.

Noverint universi per presentes me Johannem Cob Vicarium Ecclesiæ de Heanok remisisse relaxasse et omnino pro me et hærodibus meis imperpetuum quiesce clamasse Deo et Capellæ Sancte Edmundi Regis et Martiris de Kyngesbrigge et Hugoni Pocok et Roberto Fayrefot Custodibus instauri dictæ Capellæ et successoribus suis Custodibus dictæ Capellæ et instauri ejusdem totum jus et clameum quæ habeo in uno tenemento et gardino eidem tenementum adjacente situatis inter Cimiterium dictæ Capellæ ex parte australe et tenementum Thome Duer et Johanne uxoris suæ Filiæ Johannis Granute ex parte boreali Et ego vero prædictus Johannes et heredes mei totum prædictum tenementum et totum prædictum gardinum cum pertinentiis præfatis custodibus et successoribus suis contra omnes gentes warrantizabimus imperpetuum.

In cujus rei testimonium præsentibus sigillum meum apposui. Hiis testibus:

Thoma Duer tunc præposito Villæ prædictæ.
Johanne Jaycok.
Rogerus Degher.
Johanne Vele.
Willielmo Gormond.
Johanne Torryng.
Johanne Radeville et multis aliis.
Datis apud Kyngesbrygge Vicessimo tertio die Aprilis Anno Regni regis Henrici Quarti post Conquestum undecimo.

133. A copy of the sentence of consecration is, like the others to which I have referred, in the custody of the feoffees of the Kingsbridge Town lands, and a translation will be found in Hawkins's History of Kingsbridge, p. 123. Attached are six seals, those of the Bishop, the Archdeacon, probably, and the Abbot of Buckfast. In the fourth a double key is to be made out, which shows that it is the seal of the Prior or Priory of Plympton, the fifth seal is altogether gone, and the sixth is the seal of the Kingsbridge Feoffees. Entries relating to the consecration will also be found in Bishop Stafford's Registers.

134. It is clear therefore that, for the convenience of the inhabitants of Kingsbridge, the rector of Churchstow, with the consent of the abbot and convent, promoted the erection of what we should now call a chapel of ease, which very soon became or was considered, if not a parish, a district with certain parochial rights. The dead of Kingsbridge had still to be brought, as stated in the petition, from the chapel, on the low ground near the sea, to the church, founded on the summit of a high mountain, proceeding through a troublesome and tedious ascent of the said mountain. The rector of Churchstow had to provide for all the duty, and now Abbot Slade thought that the time had arrived when the new building should be consecrated. Kingsbridge was now becoming more important and required development, which the abbots of Buckfast as lords of the manor did their best to encourage.

135. William Slade did not devote the whole of his time to the temporal affairs of his Abbey. He was a student and author, and Leland has left us a list of his books which remained in the library of the Abbey, which I here give. It contains also the titles of other manuscripts belonging to the Abbey. In the middle of this list is the observation as to the origin of the house to which I have before referred :—

" *Cœnobium de Bukfast olim incepit per fratres quos appellabant Grysæos, deinde admisit Bernardinos.*"

CATALOGUE OF MANUSCRIPTS IN THE LIBRARY OF BUCKFAST ABBEY.

Trivet super tragædias Senecæ.
Triveti historia ab initio mundi usque ad nativitatem Christi ad Hugonum de Engolisma, atchidiaconum Cantuar.
Lectura Blencot super quartum Sententiarum.
Kilwardeby de conscientia et synderesi.
Quæstiones Johannis Sutton.
Quodlibeta Johannis Sutton.
Quæstiones Gaynesburg.
Quæstiones Gilberti Segrave.
Quolibeta ejusdem.
Universalia magistri Sharpe super libros Phisicorum.
Quæstiones Gulielmi Slade abbatis de Bukfest de anima.
Quæstiones ejusdem super 4^{or} libros Sententiarum Vixit tempore Ricardi 2^i.
Beda de nominibus regnorum.
Flores Moralium Gulielmi Slade.
Johannes abbas de Forda de contemporibus Mundi.
Stephanus Cantuar de benedictionibus et maledictionibus datis in monte Ebal.
Grostest super decem præcepta.

Antiquarii Collectanea, Johannis Lelandi.
Ed. 1770. Vol. iii. (iv.), p. 152.

136. If there was nothing else to show the great mistake made in dealing with the monasteries as they were dealt with at the Dissolution, the atrocious way in which the priceless libraries were dispersed and destroyed would be quite sufficient to convince the most sceptical. Even the fanatical Protestant Bale called the destruction wanton and shameful, and prophesied that it would be to England a most horrible infamy, "among the grave senyours of other nacyons."

137. From the Issue Roll it appears that the Dean and Chapter of Exeter, with the Abbot of Buckfast and others, lent moneys to the King, taking care to have security for the repayment.

18 May. To John Copelston, junior, and divers other persons coming from the county of Devon to London, with a certain sum of £573 6s. 8d. borrowed from the Dean and Chapter of the Cathedral Church of Exeter; the Mayor of the town of Exeter; the Abbot of Tavystock; the Prior of Lanceton;

the Abbot of Bukfast; Robert Gary, Prior of Plymton; Alexander Chambernoun, Mayor of the town of Plymouth; John Bonel and John Copelston. In money paid to the aforesaid John Copelston, junior, and his companions, for the safe conduct of certain of the King's jewels, valued at £800, delivered to the aforesaid persons as security for the said sums borrowed of them under conditions contained in certain indentures made between our lord the King and the said John and his companions, &c. By writ, &c.—£10.
Issue Roll, Easter, 3 Hen. V. 1414.

137. The assent to the consecration of the church at Kingsbridge must have been one of the latest acts of Slade's life, for in 1415, Sept. 8th, about twelve months afterwards, William Beaghe or Beagle was confirmed abbot. In the glories of Agincourt in the following month the Abbey participated, for William Beaghe contributed one hundred marks towards the expenses of the expedition.

138. It would seem from the De Banco Roll, 3 Henry IV. before quoted, par. 128, that William had been a monk of the house before his election in the time of Abbot Paverston.

139. The first of the three following extracts relates to a defaulting collector of some of the revenues; the second to a debt due; and the third to a trespass committed upon some property of the Abbey at Totnes.

Devon.

Abbas de Buckfast in ppria persona sua op' se iiij^{to} die versus Johem Torryng de Lostwythyell in com̃ Cornub m̃chant de p̃ito q̃d reddat ei r̃onabilem compotū suū de tempore quo fuit receptor denar̃ ip̃ius Abbis etc. Et ip̃e nō ven̄ Et prec̃ fuit vic̃ q̃d suñ eū etc. Et vic̃ modo mand̃ q̃d nichil h̃et etc. I'o capiat" q̃d sit hic a die sc̃e Trinitatis in xv dies etc.—(De Banco Roll, Easter, 8 Henry V. m. 251.)

Devon.

m. 159 d.

Witts Abbas de Buckfastro per Attorñ suū op' se iiij^{to} die ṽsus Johem Johan de Dodbroke in com̃ p̃dico Milward de p̃ito q̃d reddat ei sexaginta ℥ vndecim solidos ℥ octo denarios quos ei debet ℥ iniuste detinet etc. Et ip̃e non ven̄ Et prec̃ fuit vic̃ q̃d suñ eū etc. Et vic̃ modo mand̃ q̃d nichil h̃et etc. I'o capiat". Ita q̃d sit hic a die Pasche in tres septimanas etc.*—(De Banco Roll, Hilary, 8 Henry V. m. 159 d.)

Devon'.
m. 203.

Witts Abbas de Bukfast p attorñ suū op' se iiij^{to} die ṽersus Patriciū Mark de Tottoñ in com̃ p̃dco Crokker de p̃ito quare

* The same debt appears in the Roll Easter, 9 Henry V. [m. 355 d] and then order made to " have him here " from Trinity to fifteen days.

cū idem abbas in feodo suo apud Totoñ p consuetudinibȝ ꝗ
vicijs sibi debitis quedam catalla p Robtum Marchant
svientem suū capi fecisset idem Robtus catalla illa nōie
districcōis sċdm legem ꝗ consuetudinem regni Regis Angt
ibm detinere voluisset ṗdcus Patricius catalla illa eidem
Robto vi ꝗ armis abstulit et alia enormia ctc. ad gᵃve
dampnū etc. ꝗ contᵃ pacem Regis etc. Et iṗe non veñ
Et sicut prius preċ fuit viċ ꝗd capet cū etc. Et viċ modo
mand ꝗd non est inventus etc. Iᵒ sicut pluꝝ capiatᵃ. Ita
ꝗd sit hic a die Pasche in tres septimanus etc.—(De Banco
Roll, Hilary, 8 Henry V. m. 203).

140. During this abbot's rule the house had trouble, and six
years after his elevation things had become so bad that it was
found necessary to refer them to William, Abbot of Hayles,
and Brother Michael of Moreton. I have to thank Mr.
Edward Bishop for furnishing me with a transcript of a
notarial instrument published in the chapter-house at Buckfast 26 January, 1421. It is a most interesting document,
perhaps more so than any I have been able to include in this
paper.

141. The name of the notary is not given. In it the name
of the abbot is spelt Beagle. Oliver gives his name as Beaghe,
and in the extracts from the De Banco Rolls it is also so spelt.
I give a free outline of the contents.

After a preamble with the date of the year, the reign of
the Pope, and so on, the document goes on to say that the
abbot, Abbot William of Hayles, Brother Michael of Lang
Benynton, which was originally an English cell of Savigny,
Thomas Roger, Prior of Buckfast, with the whole assembly of
the monastery being present in the chapter-house, the
abbot of Hayles handed to the notary a paper, praying that
he would read the contents aloud, which he did to the following effect.

A subject of discord having arisen between that honourable
man the abbot and the convent, with regard to the government of the brethren within and without, which, by the wisdom, labour, and zeal of the Abbot of Hayles and Brother
Michael, was settled thus, that the abbot might entertain
according to the ancient and worthy and wonted usage of the
Abbey, might receive his guests and strangers, and that the
servants of the monastery might wait upon them according to
his instructions. That the abbot, being advanced to a considerable age and frequently crippled with bodily disease, was
often broken down with infirmity, so that things which,

according to the statutes of the order, should be fulfilled in person, he was unable to fulfil, and the monastery had suffered, and it was feared would suffer more in future, it was decreed that the abbot should not interfere in any way except when required to do so by the prior and brethren, and then that he should agree to their wishes. That the abbot should not obtain any privileges or exemptions from Rome, as such might tend to the curtailment of the statutes and privileges of the order. That the abbot should receive either 10*l.* or 40*l.* [which is uncertain, probably the latter,] per annum, paid quarterly, for his clothes and necessaries. That when the abbot was summoned or invited to take part in any ceremony, such as the installation of the Bishop of Exeter, the burial of nobles and others for the advantage of the monastery, or the honour of the abbot himself, as he was often wont to do, and as his predecessors were wont to do, the abbot's expenses were to be borne by the house; and if at any time he should wish to ride or walk about outside the monastery for his own recreation, he might go with a proper retinue, but at his own expense. That if any gifts were presented to the abbot he was to have them and rejoice therein, and reward the bearers; but, if he allowed the gifts to go to the common use of the monastery, the bearers were to be rewarded from the common chest.

And the notary says that all these things were done as above written, and that, beside those mentioned at the commencement, there were also present those discreet men John Carnell, bachelor of law, and Henry Fortescue, clerk of the said diocese, these having been specially called and summoned; and piously concludes, And thus peace, faith, hope, and charity here met together, which the undivided blessed Trinity abandons in discord, but cherishes in concord. Amen.

There are many errors in the spelling, grammar, &c., but the sense is apparent, the mistakes are easily corrected, and I print the document as it stands.

In Dei Nomine. Amen.

Per presens publicum instrumentum cunctis appereat (*sic*) evidenter quod Anno ab Incarnacione Dñi secundum cursum et computacionem ecclesie Anglicane millesimo cccc^{mo} vicesimo primo, Indicciones quinta decima, Pontificatus sanctissimi in Christo Patris et Domini nostri Domini Martini Divina Providencia Pape quinti Anno quinto mensis Januarii die xx^{mo} vj° in domo capitulari Monasterii de Buckfast Ordinis Cisterciensis, Exoniensis
{ 26 Jan. 1421.

Diocesis, in mei Notarii Publici et Testium subscriptorum presencia honorabilibus et religiosis viris Domnis Willielmo Beagle Abbate ut asserit Monasterii de Buckefast predicti et Willielmo Abbate Monasterii beate Marie de Hayles Wigorniensis [Diocesis], Fratre Michaele de Moretoneo Magistro de Langbinyngton Lincolniensis Diocesis ut asseritur, ac Fratre Thoma Roger Priore dicti monasterii de Buckfast predicti (*sic.*) [cum] toto Conventio ejusdem Monasterii de Buckfast personaliter constitutis;

Dictus Honorabilis et religiosus Vir Domnus Willielmus Abbas Monasterii de Hayles assertus (?) mihi notario infrascripto Cedulam in papiro scriptam tradi fecit, supplicans quod eandem cedulam legerem in aperto; quam post ejus inspeccionem legi; cujus cedule tenor talis est:—

Nuper exorta materia perturbacionis et discordie inter honorabilem et religiosum virum Domnum Abbatem Monasterii de Buckfast Ordinis Cisterciensis Exoniensis Diocesis et suum Conventum ibidem de et super regimine et gubernacione Spiritualium et Temporalium dicti Monasterii infra et extra, ceterisque causis, punctis et articulis aliis, que omnia et singula in presenti longum esset en arrare; Deo tamen annuente qui est pacis Auctor, discrecione, labore, et industria reverendi in Christo Patris et Domini Domni Willielmi Dei gracia Abbatis Monasterii beate Maria de Haylez Wygorniensis Diocesis, et religiosi viri fratris Mychaelis de Moretones Magistro de Langbinyngton Lincolniensis Diocesis, Ordinis antedicti, ad visitandum Monasterium de Buckfast in capite et in membris legitime deputatorum, dicta materia sedata est et quievit per visitatores predictos in hunc modum:—

In primis quod dictus honorabilis et religiosus vir Domnus Willielmus Abbas antedictus secundum antiquum, honestum et solitum usum dicti Monasterii de Buckfast hospites et advenas suos cum ad idem monasterium declinaverint juxta eorum statum bene recipiat, hillaremque vultum eis ostendat, suis eciam et dicti Monasterii famulis quibuscumque in licitis et honestis jubeat, precipiat et commoneat quod eisdem intendant in aula, mensa et camera prout sui status honestas debite exigit et requirit.

Item quia dictus Domnus Willielmus abbas prelibatus jam in matura etate constitutus corporisque invaliditudine multipliciter detentus diversis infirmitatibus sepius occupatus [est] et confractus, quod omnia que in sua persona errent juxta sui Ordinis statuta adimplenda personaliter nequeat propter premissa providere nec adimplere, adeo quod dictum monasterium dampnum patitur in presenti et plus timendum ei in futuro; quare consideratum est et decretum quod dictus Domnus Willielmus Abbas prelibatus nullo modo se intromittat in gubernacione et regimine spiritualium aut temporalium quorumcumque nisi cum fuerit per Priorem et Conventum suum debite ad hoc requisitus, et tunc eorum voluntati adquiescat in hiis que tangant dicti monasterii utilitatem et sui status et ordinis exigenciam omnimodo.

Item concordatum et decretum est quod dictus honorabilis vir et Domnus Willielmus Abbas prelibatus non acquirat per se aut suos aliqua privilegia exempciones et similia a Curia Romana que possunt vergi in derogacionem dicti Ordinis Cisterciensis et statutorum ejusdem; &, si qua hujusmodi privilegia habeat, aut habere eum de cetero contingat, quod eisdem non utatur quovis modo.

Item consideratis considerandis concordatum et decretum est per visitatores predictos commune consensu pariter et assensu dictorum Abbatis et Conventus Monasterii de Buckfast predicti quod dictus Willielmus Abbas . . . dum Abbas fuerit percipiet annuatim ad quatuor anni terminos per equales porciones a dictis Priore et Conventu pro vestura et aliis necessariis dicti Abbatis x libr.

Item concordatum et decretum est, si contingat dictum Domnum Willielmum Abbatem extra Monasterium invitari aut vocari pro dicti Monasterii utilitate, ipsiusve Abbatis honestate, videlicet ad installacionem Episcopi Exoniensis loci Diocesani, sepultura et obitio Magnatuum et Prelatorum ac aliorum generosorum, amicorum et vicinorum, prout sepe solebat et predecessores sui Abbates solebant, hec omnia semper fient expensis dicti Monasterii cum contingant.

Item si aliquando dictus domnus Abbas extra dictum Monasterium pro sui ipsius disporto et voluntate equitare aut spaciare voluerit, tunc decente familia, sed expensis propriis, ista fient.

Item concordatum est et decretum quod si qua munera, donaria, bonaque alia quecumque dicto Domno Abbati offerantur et donentur, eadem habeat et inde gaudeat, dum tamen contemplacione persone ejusdem hoc fiet; tunc ex propriis remuneret deportantes prout placet. Et si eadem in communem usum et dicti Monasterii utilitate convertat, de communi thesauro remunerentur.

Et dum nec omnia premissa fideliter observanda hinc et inde tam dicti Abbas quam frater Thomas Roger Prior dicti Monasterii tactis Dei Evangeliis per eosdem corporaliter prestiterunt.

Acta sunt hec omnia prout suprascribuntur et recitantur sub anno Domini, Indiccione, Pontificatu, die, mense, et loco predictis; presentibus tunc ibidem discretis viris Johanne Carnell in Legibus Bacallario, et Henrico Fortescu Clerico dicte Exoniensis Diocesis, testibus ad premissa vocatis specialiter et rogatis.

Et sic pax, fidis, spes, et charitas hic in unum obviarunt, quas inter discordes concedat, inter concordes foveat, Trinitas indivisa. Amen. (MS. Reg. 12, E. xiv., fol. 62-64 recte.)

142. The aged and infirm abbot enjoyed his home and pension for several years. Let us hope he often walked abroad with his becoming retinue "pro sui ipsius disporto spatiari." His successor, Thomas Rogger, was not blessed until the 13th April, 1432, more than eleven years after the settlement of the discords detailed by the notary.

143. Of Thomas Rogger and the succeding abbots we know little more than their names. Rogger was succeeded by John Ffychet, 16th October, 1440. He was concerned in legal proceedings with reference to the Erne river, as appears from the following extracts in Norman French from the year-book 1441 :—

Trespas. En Trēs Lo pl' counta v̄s l'Abbe de Bulkfast de san gort debrus' en Ermingt̄. ¶ Yelverton. Est un douce eau courrant en t̄ dit Ermingt̄ tanq; al' haut mer, qui est appell' Erine, ou le dit Abbe ⁊ touts ses p̄dec ⁊c. ont uñ ouv̄ture de vj pieds de largeur en chaqū gort en le dit Erine, ⁊ illec tāq; a haut mer de temps, ⁊c. ou le cours d̄ cē eau plus pfondem̄t court ⁊ disous q̄ le dit gort dont il ad luy complaiñ est [B] en la dit Ermingt̄, ⁊ q̄ c̄ fuit estoppe, ⁊ nous ceo debrusames accord a nr̄e ouverture avādit. Juḡ si acc̄. ¶ Markham. A ceo disons nous, q̄ le Sñr de Hunt̄ long temps devant le trespas fuit seisi de m̄ le gort en son demaiñ come de fee, ⁊ nous lessa pur t̂me de x ans, le t̂me commenc̄, ⁊c. Quel t̂me dure unc̄, ⁊ vous debrusastes m̄ le gort hors de cest lieu dont vous ave; ple par ij pches pcheiñ at̄ t̂re, sur q̄ nous avōs conceu nostr̄ acc̄. Juḡ. Et priōs q̄ vous soie; atteints. ¶ Yelverton. Lōg temps devāt cest leus le Sñr de Hunt̄ a no⁹ lessa m̄ le gort pur t̂me de ñr vie, p forc̄ de q̄l nous fumes seisis ⁊ debrusames come v̄n a nous list. ¶ Markham. De v̄re tort demeñ sans tiet cause. ¶ Newton. Ceo n'est ple : car si jeo port̄ br̄e de Trns v̄s vous ⁊ vous dic̄s que le lieu ou, ⁊c. fuit v̄re franct̄ (Juḡ ⁊c.) n'e rñs pur moy, adire, De v̄re tort demcñ sans tiel cause. Ergo nec hic. Et puis. ¶ Markham. Way va la ple, ⁊ trav̄s le leas a t̂me de vie.— (Year-Book De Termino Trinitatis, Anno xx. Henrv VI.)

144. It was also about this time perhaps that Richard Dove, monk and scholar of Buckfast, drew up the statutes of the house, with the oaths to be taken by the novices, monks, scholars, and others. They are very interesting, and I am glad to be able to present them in the appendix to this paper.

145. The following, perhaps about the same date, relates to land in Brent :—

Bukfast.
La Ya in
Brent.

Hoc convencio facta inter f'rem Minorensem Abb̄m Buckfastre &c. ex una p̄te et Ric̄um de Cotelaford ex alt'a viz. p̄dict abbas &c. dedere &c. unū ferling t̄re in la Ya in manc̄io de Brenta q̄d Rob̄tus de la Ya quond̄ tenuit &c. Habend̄ de dicto Ric̄o Cotelaford et Hered̄ &c. In cujus rei test̄ sigilla sua alternatim apposuer̄. Hijs Test̄. Joh̄e de Boyvile. Witto de Kilbury, Stepho Stoyll, tunc Scenescho p̄dictorū Religiosorū Benedicto le Boñ Witto de Harbenford, Witto de la Ford [sans date*] p. 540.—(Brit. Mus. Add. MSS. 28,649, p. 413.) [Prince's excerpts from Pole's MS.]

From the Assize Roll, temp. Henry VI., we learn that Gode claimed as his freehold a tenement in Buckfastleigh, of which the abbot of Buckfast and William Budde and his wife, and another Budde and his wife, had dis-seized him. The verdict was against the abbot.

146. John Matthu was confirmed 3 Oct. 1449, and he it was probably who obtained from the King,—Edward IV., surely not Henry VI., as stated in Fox's Kingsbridge,—a grant of a weekly market, and a fair for three days in the year at Kingsbridge, and a fair for the same number of days once a year at Buckfastleigh. The Kingsbridge market and fair still continue to be held. A copy of the grant is given in the book just mentioned.†

147. It has been said that John Bothe, afterwards Bishop of Exeter, was Abbot of Buckfast; but, on examining the events of his life before his consecration as bishop, it would seem that this could not have been.

148. John Kinge is found as abbot 25 Feb. 1483, and John Rede 24 Nov. 1498.

149. In the interesting little book entitled " The Parish of Ashburton in the Fifteenth and Sixteenth Centuries," being extracts from the churchwardens' accounts from 1479 to 1580, in the year 1499-1500 a receipt of 4s. is credited from a gift of the Lord Abbot of Buckfast, Saint Clere Pomeroy, Galfrid

* So in MS.
† Kingsbridge and its Surroundings, by S. P. Fox, pp. 34—248.

Harepath, and others. I thought at first that this was an unmentioned abbot of Buckfast, but on consideration I do not think the entry bears this out. If in the original entry there is a comma after "the Lord Abbot of Buckfast," it would I think show that the abbot and Saint Clere Pomeroy were different persons. Prince says that Edward Pomeroy and Margaret Beavil his wife had issue Henry, Scinclere, and John.* Sir William Pole says that Edward Pomeroy died 24 Henry VI. 1445.† Both Prince and Pole trace the descent of the elder son Henry, and do not refer to the second and third; but in the Heralds' Visitation of 1620 we find in the pedigree of Ford ‡ that St. Cleere Pomeroy was the son of John Pomeroy, and that he married, and had issue, in which case he could not have been the abbot of Buckfast. I believe this to be the same person as that mentioned in the Ashburton accounts. Beyond this there is no reference elsewhere, so far, to a Pomeroy being abbot of Buckfast; but, if it should prove to be the case, it will be very interesting to find that a descendant of its early benefactors was connected with the Abbey in its latter days.‖

150. In the accounts just referred to is another entry, under date 1512, ijs. for ringing the knell of the late abbot of Buckfast. This must have been for either Saint Clere Pomeroy (if he was the abbot) or John Rede, for on Palm Sunday, 20 April, 1512, Alfred Gille succeeded the deceased abbot. Gille, after ruling the house for thirteen years, was succeeded by John Rede, whom Dr. Oliver thought might have been a nephew of Abbot John Rede before mentioned. He had a care for the welfare of Kingsbridge and Churchstow, and readjusted the revenues of the churches. He was confirmed abbot 13th April, 1525, and lived about twelve years after. He may be considered the last abbot, for his successor was foisted upon the monks, and was simply put in to carry out the designs of the King.

151. Gabriel Donne or Downe was a student in Trinity Hall, Cambridge, and afterwards a monk of Stratford, a Cistercian house at West Ham, Middlesex. A suit, followed by an appeal to Rome, between the abbot and convent and the vicar William Shragger arose, and on the 7th Feb. 1517, a "composition real" between the abbot and the vicar was executed, and "the provident and religious man Gabriel

* Prince's Worthies, p. 645, ed. 1812.
† Pole's Collections, p. 20.   ‡ Har. Soc. 1872, p. 108.
‖ I have since examined the original entry, and I do not think that it is any evidence as to Saint Clere Pomeroy having been an abbot of Buckfast.

Donne, monk of the Blessed Mary of Stratford, of the Order of Cistercians" was proctor for the brethren.

152. His abilities and zeal soon brought him into more public notice, and he was employed by Cranmer, More, and others to assist in the apprehension of Tyndale at Antwerp. He accompanied Henry Phillips, "a tall, comely, good-looking young man" travelling as a gentleman, as his counsellor, disguised as a servant. There can be little doubt that he was the author of the plan which resulted in the capture, imprisonment, and death of Tyndale. Donne resided for six months after Tyndale's arrest with Phillips or Buckenham at Louvain, assisting in preparing the case against Tyndale. He returned to England in June, 1535, and was shortly after thrust into the abbey of Buckfast, doubtless as a reward for his services to the King, the Archbishop, Bishops, and Cromwell. In June, 1536, he attended the meeting of Convocation at St. Paul's, and he signs the articles then promulgated, as "GABRIEL, *Abbas de Buckfastria.*"

153. Within two years of his election he alienated much of the monastic property, and on the 25th February, 1538, he betrayed his trust, and surrendered the house with its belongings into the hands of the King, and fifteen months after was rewarded with a large pension; the Prior of Plympton alone, among all the heads of religious houses in this county, receiving so much. This pension of £120, equal to £1,800 of our money, was enjoyed by him until his death in 1558. On the 16th March, 1541, he was made Prebendary of St. Paul's, and three years later Cromwell gave him the rectory of Stepney "sine cura." Upon Bonner's deprivation in Sept. 1549, Cranmer, according to Strype,* "constituted Gabriel Donne residentiary of St. Paul's, to be his official and keeper of the spirituality, and to exercise all manner of episcopal jurisdiction in the said city and diocese."

154. Donne died 5th December, 1558. By his will, after directing payment of his debts and certain legacies, he bequeathed the residue of his estate to Trinity Hall, Cambridge. With this residue a scholarship was founded, which continues to be enjoyed to the present day by the student called "Mr. Gabriel Donne's scholar." In the chapel of Trinity Hall, among the shields in the roof, are still to be seen the arms of the ex-abbot: "*Azure, a wolf rampant, a chief argent.*"†

* Memorials of Cranmer, vol. i, p. 274, ed. 1812.
† I am indebted for many of the facts here given relating to Donne's Life to the sketch given by Christopher Anderson in his Annals of the English

155. He was honourably buried before the high altar in Old St. Paul's, four days after his death, and the inscription on his tomb has been fortunately preserved by Dugdale.*

> Mole sub hoc Gabrael Donnus detruditur, hujus
> Qui præses Templi, Presbyter atque fuit.
> Mortua terreno clauduntur membra sepulchri
> Vivens cœlicolo spiritus orbe manet,
> Ossibus urna locum dat, pulvere terra recumbit,
> Sydera sunt animæ cœlica tecta suæ.
> Illius (adde Deus) menti tua gaudia clemens
> Corpus in Elizii pace quiescat. Amen.

156. Donne was doubtless a time-server, and trimmed his sails according to the varying breezes of the time. His share in the persecution of Tyndale cannot be excused, but he sinned with Sir Thomas More, Archbishop Cranmer, and others no less distinguished. The great blot in his memory must ever be his consenting to be forced upon the monks of Buckfast as their abbot, taking the solemn oaths he was compelled to by the rules of his order, well knowing that he was sent to the monastery for a purpose, and that in a short time he would be called upon to fulfil the undertaking he had doubtless given, betray the solemn trust committed to him, become a perjured man, and an accomplice in an act of sacrilege and robbery.

157. At the time of the surrender, the following brethren were in the house:—
> The Abbot, Gabriel Donne.
> The Prior, Arnold Gye.
> John Cowle.
> John Watts.
> Richard Taylor.
> William Shapcott.
> Matthew Pryston.
> Richard Splat.
> Thomas Gylle.
> William Avery.
> John Doyge.

158. With the exception of the Prior, Arnold Gye, all these received pensions from £6 13s. 4d. paid to John Doyge, down to Thomas Gylle who had but £5. Why was the

Bible. The author is strong in his denunciation of the ex-abbot, but all alleged against him is the part taken against Tyndale.
* History of St. Paul's, ed. 1658, p. 61.

prior left out? Was he less compliant than the others, or had he passed away before the pension list was completed and so spared the sight of the spoliation of his house.

159. For spoliation soon came. The Abbey, the church, and the monastic buildings, with their sites and precincts, and the cemetery, grange, and farm buildings, were granted by the King to that avaricious knight, Sir Thomas Dennis, who not only succeeded in deceiving the monks, pretending to be their friend, and obtaining offices of trust, and of course emolument, from them, but who also by his subserviency and cringing made himself to be well thought of at Court. He was appointed steward for the management of the lands of several religious houses, and the reversion of the same office was granted his son. He also pretended to give valuable advice to the monks in the critical position in which they were placed, in return for which he succeeded in obtaining annuities from many of the abbeys and priories, and so well did he play his game that he succeeded after their dissolution in obtaining confirmation of such annuities from the Augmentation Court. Dr. Oliver well says, "if the mammon of iniquity could confer happiness, this very rich man must have been supremely happy."

160. I have found a curious letter written by him which seems to imply that he had been charged with appropriating lead from the abbey buildings. It is endorsed "Sir Thomas Dennyes as touchinge vj. fodores of lead of the late P'ory of Buckefast." To show that the lead was worth taking a little trouble about, I may mention that a fodder weighed upwards of two thousand pounds.

Sr Thomas Dennyes as touchinge vj Fodores of lead of the late P'ory of Buckefast.

Ryght wurshipfull aft my hartye comend doo pseve by Mr Totyll ye be my verye good maist accordyng to trouthe for vj. fodder of leed supposed by Grove Mr Arundell avaunt that I shulde have the custodi of. Wherfor trouthe I never sawe no suche leed nor psell therof and yf I had I am sure the mater is not so lyght but he wolde have had for his dischardge a byll of my hand of the recept or some other sufficyent wytnesh to testyfye the same. I never was at Buckfast but one tyme synnes I dyd purchasse yt therfore yf yt maye please yor maistership & the rest of my maysters in comyssion wth you to derect a comyssion in to the countreye to enquyre for the trouthe herof yf then shall appere that I or any one of my Servauntȩ to my knoledge or consent ever had any parte of the seid leed I wyll promes you by this my wrytting to geve you for everye fodder of leed a c^{li} & in this wyes I trust you shall come to the knoledge of the trouthe & knowe hym to be as he is & I a trewe man good M\(^r\) Barnes for youre Jentylnes in this behalfe shoued I shall thynk no lesse but my selff alwayes bounden to gratefye you or any Frynd of yours duryng my lyef w\(^{th}\) such plesures as shall lye in my huyll powre as knowetbe the hollye Trynite to whome I comyt you.

Yours assured
Thom's Denys.

To the right Worshipfult master Willyam Barñs Esquyer geve this.

(Land Revenue Records, Bund. 1392, File 31, No. 1.)

161. The lead from the roof is also mentioned, with the five bells in the tower of the church, in an inventory dated 29th November, 1555, headed "A brieff Declaraton of all the Bell belonginge to late suppressed & dissolved Monasteries and Pryores in the foresaide counties made by Mathiewe Colthurst esquier late Auditor & Robt. Grove some tyme s'vant to S\(^r\) Thomas Arundell Knight, late Receyvo\(^r\) there, at the comaundyment of Willm Barnes, Thomas Myldemay & John Wiseman Esquiers by their letters unto us directed."

V. Buckfaste xxxiiij\(^{li}\). v\(^s\).

A Brieff Declaracōn of all the leadd belonginge to the late Monasteries and P\(^i\)ories [as before].

Buckfast vj foders ccc lib.
 remayneng w\(^{th}\) the farm s of the said
 houses as it apereth by report of Edmonde
 Wynter Esquyer.

(Land Revenue Records, Bund. 1392, File 33, N. 1.)

162. In 1553, besides the abbot, there were six monks still alive and in receipt of pensions, viz., Matthew Preston, John Watts, Richard Taylor, William Avery, and Richard Splate, 5l. 6s. 8d. each, and Thomas Sylle, 5l.[*]

163. There is little interest in tracing the subsequent history of the Abbey lands. From Sir Thomas Dennis, with the manor of Buckfast, they descended to his son, Sir Robert, whose daughter Margaret is said to have married Sir Arthur Mainwaring.[†] In 1629, according to Chapple, quoted by Dugdale and Lysons, they were in the possession of Sir Richard Baker, the historian. The property passing to the

[*] Brown Willis, Hist. Abbeys, vol. ii. p. 60.
[†] See Pole's Collections.

family of D'Oleys, it was by them dismembered and sold off in parcels. The actual site of the Abbey was purchased by Mr. Berry, by whom it was sold to Mr. William Searle Benthall, and it is now the property of Dr. James Gale, of Dovescourt, Newton Abbot.

164. Before 1806, when the remaining portions of the buildings were almost entirely destroyed, the ruins were very extensive, and, doubtless, the plan could have been made out without difficulty. Westcote and Risdon speak of the "skeleton of a huge body whereby may be conceived what bigness once it bore, whose ruins may move the beholders both to wonder and pity."* Buck's view is dated 1734, but nothing certain can be learnt from it. It appears that the church was as usual chancel, transepts, and long nave, the chapter-house on the south, and the conventual buildings running down towards the river, the normal plan of the Cistercians being followed. (See Buckland Abbey, par 12.)

165. In the Gentleman's Magazine for 1796, Mr. James Laskey gives an account of the ruins, which, although very unsatisfactory to an archæologist, is worth rescuing from the pages of the old periodical. Of course we are not bound to agree with all Mr. Laskey's speculations, some portions of his story being, to say the least, curious.

After saying that the ruins were of great extent and worthy of a more particular description than he could give, the author proceeds:—

"There now remain of this magnificent ruin two arches which appear to have been the entrance, and some ruins on a large scale which we took for the lodge. The arches are situated one behind the other and stand across the road leading from Buckfastleigh to Ashburton; the iron staples for gates to hang on still remain and are of great bigness, which led us to think they were of massy structure. The ruins of what we took to be the lodge stand on the eastern side, its length about twenty paces, breadth eight paces (not being supplied for a minute measurement we were obliged to content ourselves with it thus roughly, taking care to diminish rather than exaggerate). On the same side are several apartments, one of which is inhabited, another is converted into a poundhouse, in which stands a moorstone trough of great bulk, for the purpose of breaking apples for the pound. The following measurement I received from a learned gentleman who has paid great attention to these ruins. The diameter of this

* Risdon, p. 152.

stone is 9 feet 4 inches, depth 3 feet 6 inches, one-half of which is sunk in the ground; the supposed weight before it was hollowed he computes must amount to above 100 tons. It is of the granite kind and affords matter of surprise by what means it was brought there, stones of that quality not being to be found within the distance of many miles; round the abbey being one continued limerock, which is worked at many places to a depth, height, and extent surprising, and forming a vast cavern at once terrific and beautiful, which proves an inexhaustible fund of gain to the owner. The remainder of these ruins are situated in an orchard on the western side of the road, at the bottom of which runs with silent murmur the River Dart, seemingly regretting the downfall of the abbey. The first thing that presents itself, tradition says, was the abbot's cellar, which is entered by a small Gothic gateway and is about twenty-eight paces long and twelve wide arched overhead. * * * *
At one end remain a few steps which led to the ruin above, which our guide told us was the abbot's kitchen; it is now converted into a kitchen garden. At the south end is the skeleton of a set of apartments, which appear to have been the cells of the monks, which was approached by winding steps, fifty-one of which now remain. It is of particular form, having, as well as we could guess, seven sides. The immense bushes of ivy, dropping in rich festoons, almost buried its form. On removing some of these we could plainly observe the holes in which the joists and sleepers rested for support on the flooring, from which we judged the rooms to be about 6 feet in height in the clear, one above the other. These we were told solely belonged to the abbot. Joining this was their court of judicature and judgment seat, and behind a dungeon for those that by their offences were thought worthy of the same. On the north-east side appear the walls and foundation of this once spacious and splendid seat of superstition; the abbey church and the remains of its tower all lying in such massy fragments, that it is scarcely to be conceived by what power so vast a fabrick could be disjointed. The walls appear to be of the thickness of 9 or 10 feet and entirely composed of small stones in layers and a compost of lime and sand, which we supposed to have been thrown on these layers hot, after the method antiently used in such large buildings, which incorporating together formed a mass as solid as the native rock. The ruins of this church appear to be about 250 feet in length, and the ruins of the tower towards the

south seem like huge and vast rocks piled on one another in extensive confusion—

> by Time's fell hand defac'd,
> The rich proud cost of outworn bury'd age.—*Shakspeare.*"

166. The author then goes on to say that, as stone for building is plentiful in the neighbourhood, the ruins will in all probability continue unmolested for ages; a prophecy unfortunately not fulfilled. (A Ramble on Dartmoor, by J. L. Gentleman's Magazine, 1796, vol. lxvi. p. 194.)

What our author here calls the cellar and the seven-sided building apparently still remain, the latter being what is now called the Abbot's Tower. It is unquestionably a domestic building of some kind, but nothing more certain I think can be said. It is square, of three stories, with a cellar under. In it are fireplaces and garderobes, with a well, and a staircase with landings to every floor; the entrance appears to have been from the south on the first floor.

167. The great barn of the grange remains, and the arches, of apparently an entrance, but the gatehouse is gone. In the lawn on the eastern side of the house graves have been found, and here was probably the cemetery. The foundations of the present house, erected about fifty years since, are said to be upon vaulted work of Early-English character. The greater part of the materials of the old buildings were used in the erection of the adjoining mill, which occupies the site of some of the conventual buildings.

168. The arms of the Abbey are *Sable, a crozier in pale argent, the crook or, surmounted by a stag's head caboshed, of the second, horned gules.* Leland gives a sketch in his Collectanea. I know of two seals only belonging to the Abbey, the first, appended to the surrender deed, is small, and shows the Blessed Virgin Mary and Holy Child under a canopy, with the legend " S. Conventus Bucfestrie." The second is a counter-seal of the abbot—in the centre an arm grasping a crozier, the legend " Sigill. Abb. Buckfesta✠."

169. Let us now see what the various possessions of the Abbey were. To commence with those we find in Domesday, let us try to identify the manors there mentioned. The first paragraph relating to each is a translation from the Exeter Book, the second from the Exchequer Book, see paragraph 69. The first is headed "The Land of the Church of the Abbot of Bulfestre in Devonshire," the second "The Land of the Church of Bucfestre."

170. PETROCKSTOW. "The abbot has a manor* which is called PETROCESTOVA, which the abbot Aluuin held in that day when King Edward was alive and dead, and it paid geld for one virgate and a half. These can be ploughed by five teams. From thence the abbot has in demesne half a virgate and one plough,† and the villeins one virgate and two ploughs. There the abbot has six villeins and one bordar and two serfs and four oxen‡ [cows?] and twenty sheep, and three furlongs of wood in length and one furlong and a half in breadth, and six acres of meadow and eight furlongs of pasture in length, and five furlongs in breadth, and worth by the year fifteen shillings, and when he received it it was valued at just as much."

"The church of Buckfestre holds PETROCHESTOV. In the time of King Edward it paid geld for one virgate of land and a half. There is land for five ploughs. In demesne is one plough and two serfs, and six villeins, and one bordar with two ploughs. There six acres of meadow pasture eight furlongs long and five furlongs broad. Formerly and now worth fifteen shillings." Exchequer Book.

The name has changed but little during the eight hundred years that have elapsed since the great book was compiled, although it is also known as Stow St. Petrock and Heanton.

The return of the jurors recorded in the Hundred Roll, temp. Edward I. shows that the abbot had a gallows there.

Shortly before the dissolution the Valor§ shows:—

* *Mansionem.* This word properly means a habitation, capital dwelling, plot of ground, on which several houses are built.
† Mr. William Basevi Sanders is of opinion that in Domesday, whenever "*car*" stands alone, it is intended for "*caruca*" or some case of that noun, and that, whenever "*carucata*" is meant to be designated, "*car*" is always followed by "*terræ*," or is written in full. "*Terra est .... car,*" and similar entries should therefore be read as meaning that there was as much arable land as so many ploughs could till.
‡ *Animalia.*
§ This was a survey taken in consequence of Parliament having passed a measure granting to the King the first-fruits of all spiritualities and a tenth of the possessions of the Church. The instructions to the Commissioners, dated 30th January, 1536, were to ascertain the whole and just and yearly value of all possessions, lands, tenements, profits, &c., as well spiritual as temporal, pertaining to any manner of dignity, monastery, church, parsonage, vicarage, or other dignity through England, Wales, Berwick, and Calais.

Manerium do Patrikstowe :—

	£	s.	d.
Redditus assise liberorum tenencium et custumariorum	5	6	11¼
Terrarum bartone	3	1	8
Auxiliorum	0	9	6¾
Operum custumariorum	1	8	0
De finibus terrarum cum perquisitis curie et aliis proficuis ejusdem manerii per annum communibus annis	3	2	10½
	13	9	0½

And the Ministers' accounts give :—

	£	s.	d.
Petrockystowe Reditus tam liberorum quam custumariorum tenentium	7	4	6
Firma manerii	3	1	8
Perquisita curie	0	3	9
Porcio	1	6	8

and the rector paid £1 6s. 8d. to the abbey.

The manor appears to have been merged in that of Heanton Sackville in the same parish, and it has descended, as shown by Lysons, with the advowson of the church, to Lord Clinton, whose nephew, the present baron, now enjoys them.

171. AISSA. There are two Ashs mentioned in Domesday as belonging to the Abbey. One is doubtless Ash the village in the parish of South Brent, but the locality of the other is very uncertain.

" The abbot has one manor which is called AISSA, which paid geld for one virgate and a half in that day when King Edward was alive and dead. These can be ploughed by three teams. From thence the abbot has in demesne half a virgate and one plough, and the villeins one virgate and two ploughs. There the abbot has five villeins, and three bordars, and three serfs, and ten oxen, and forty sheep, and six acres of wood and six acres of meadow, and three furlongs of pasture in length and breadth, and it is worth by the year twenty shillings, and, when he received it, it was worth ten shillings."

" The abbot has one manor which is called AISSA, which the abbot Aluuin held in that day in which King Edward was alive and dead, and paid geld for a hide and a half. This ten teams can plough. Thence the abbot has in demesne a virgate and a half and one plough, and the villeins have a hide and a half, a virgate, and five ploughs. There the abbot has eight villeins, and eight bordars, and six serfs, and nine oxen, and sixty-eight sheep, and eleven goats, and three furlongs in length of wood and one in breadth, and four acres of meadow and one mile of pasture in length and a half in breadth, and worth by the year thirty shillings, and, when the abbot received it, it was worth just the same."

"The same church holds AISSE. In the time of King Edward it paid geld for one virgate of land and a half. There is land for five ploughs. In demesne is one plough and three serfs and five villoins, and three bordars with two ploughs. There six acres of meadow and six acres of wood, pasture three furlongs in length and breadth. Formerly ten shillings, now worth twenty shillings." Exchequer Book.

"The same church holds AISSE. In the time of King Edward it paid geld for one hide and a half. There is land for ten ploughs. In demesne is one plough and six serfs, and eight villoins and nine bordars with five ploughs. There four acres of meadow. Pasture one mile [leuca] long and half-a-mile broad; wood three furlongs long and one furlong broad. Formerly and now worth thirty shillings." Exchequer Book.

172. LIME or Limet, as the Exchequer Book has it, I am unable to trace.

"The abbot has one manor which is called LIMÆ, and it paid geld in that day in which King Edward was alive and dead for one hide. This seven teams can plough. Thence the abbot has one virgate and one plough in demesne, and the villoins have three virgates aud six ploughs. There the abbot has ten villeins and fourteen bordars, and four serfs and nine oxen, and four pigs and seventy-two sheep, and four acres of small wood, and three acres of meadow, and it is worth by the year fifty shillings."

"The same church holds LIMET. In the time of King Edward it paid geld for one hide. There is land for eight ploughs. In demesne is one plough and four serfs and ten villeins and fourteen bordars with six ploughs. There three acres of meadow, and four acres of small wood. It is worth fifty shillings." Exchequer Book.

173. DONA, Downe, or Done, is Down St. Mary. The Manor and Water Mill, Barton Estate, Donne and Cliffe Wood, with the advowson and rectory of Downe Church, belonged to the house at its fall. SELE, Zeal Monachorum, is near it, and they are entered in the accounts together. The latter is the manor mentioned in the Hundred Roll as having come to the abbey by the gift of King Cnut.

"THE abbot has one manor which is called DONA, which paid geld for two hides in that day in which King Edward was alive and dead. This ten teams can plough. Thence the abbot has in demesne half a hide and one plough and the villeins one hide and a half and five ploughs. There the abbot has twelve villeins, and nine bordars, and seven serfs, and six oxen, and four pigs, and sixty-six sheep, and eight furlongs of small wood, and eight acres of meadow, and twelve acres of pasture, and it is worth by the year three pounds."

"The same church holds DONE. In the time of King Edward it paid geld for two hides. There is land for ten ploughs. In demesne is one plough and seven serfs and twelve villeins and nine bordars with five ploughs. There eight acres meadows and twelve acres of pasture and seven furlongs of small wood. It is worth three pounds." Exchequer Book.

The Valor gives:—
Manerium de Sele et Donne—

	£	s.	d.
Redditus assise liberorum tenencium	0	17	3½
Custumariorum tenencium	15	19	8¼
Terrarum bartone	11	17	9
Firma molendini	1	10	0
De finibus terrarum cum perquisitis curie et aliis proficuis ejusdem manerii per annum communibus annis	6	4	5½
Inde solutum Priori Sancti Johannis Exonie et successoribus suis de quodam annuali redditu per annum	1	10	0
Et remanet clare	34	19	2¼

And the Ministers' accounts—

	£	s.	d.
Sele et Downe Redditus liberorum tenentium	0	17	3 ob.
Sele Redditus custumariorum tenentium	4	17	4 ob.
Downe Redditus custumariorum tenentium	12	12	4 ob. q.
Sele et Downe Firma certe terre vocate le barton ground	11	17	9
Perquisita Curie	0	8	9
Sele et Downe Porcio de rectorie	2	13	4

174. TRUSHAM. "The abbot has a manor which is called TRISMA, which paid geld for one hide that day in which King Edward was alive and dead. This four teams can plough.

Thence the abbot has in demesne one virgate and one plough and the villeins three virgates and three ploughs. There the abbot has four villeins, and nine bordars, and ten serfs, and six oxen, and nine pigs, and one hundred and three sheep, and twenty-two goats, and sixteen acres of wood, and three acres of meadow, and ten of pasture, and it is worth by the year thirty shillings, and when he received it it was worth twenty-five shillings."

" The same church holds TRISMA. In the time of King Edward it paid geld for one hide. There is land for three ploughs. In demesne is one plough and ten serfs and four villeins, and nine bordars with three ploughs. There three acres of meadow and ten acres of pasture and sixteen acres of wood. Formerly twenty-five shillings, now worth thirty shillings." Exchequer Book.

Trisma is Trusham, granted by the King to a Southcote, in whose family it continued for several generations, and is now the property of Sir Lawrence Palk.

The Valor gives:—

	£	s.	d.
Trisme.			
Redditus assise liberorum tenencium	0	7	2
Custumariorum tenentium	5	9	0½
Ac terrarum bartone	5	5	7
De quibus terra cum perquisitis curie et aliis proficuis ejusdem manerii per annum communibus annis	2	13	7
	13	15	4½

Ministers' Accounts.
Trisme—
Redditus liberorum tenentium . . 0 7 2
Redditus custumariorum tenentium . 10 14 10 ob.
Porcio . . . . . . 1 lib' cere.

175. AISERSTONE. "The abbot has one manor which is called HAISERSTONA, which paid geld for one ferling and a-half and three acres in that day in which King Edward was alive and dead. There the abbot has one villein who pays forty pence a year."

" The same church holds AISERSTONE. In the time of King Edward it paid geld for one ferling and a half and three acres of land. There one villein pays forty pence." Exchequer Book.

Aiserstone, it has been suggested, is Ascerton in the parish of Sidmouth, but there is no evidence that I can find, showing that the abbey ever had any land there, and we may find it much nearer the abbey, Staverton being perhaps the place, the monks having a mill there in later years.

With reference to Staverton the Valor gives :—
Staverton—
Molendinum ibidem valet per annum   £ s. d.
   ultra 6 13 4
Solutum decano et capitulo Exoniæ et
   successoribus suis per annum . .   3 6 8

Ministers' Accounts :—
Stafarton—
Redditus Molendini   . 10 0 0

176. HEATHFIELD. "The abbot has a manor which is called HETFELT, which the abbot Aluuin held in that day in which King Edward was alive and dead, and paid geld for two hides. These twelve teams are able to plough; from thence the abbot has in demesne half a hide and one plough, and the villeins have one hide and five ploughs. There the abbot has ten villeins and nine bordars and six serfs, and eleven oxen, and five pigs, and sixty sheep, and sixteen goats, and two acres of small wood, and forty acres of pasture, and it is worth by the year forty shillings, and, when the abbot received it, it was worth thirty shillings."

"The same church holds HETFELD. In the time of King Edward it paid geld for two hides. There is land for twelve ploughs. In demesne is one plough and six serfs, and ten villeins and nine bordars with five ploughs. There forty acres of pasture and two acres of small wood." Exchequer Book.

Hetfelt or Hetfeld or Hethfylde is the manor of Heathfield, in the parish of Aveton Giffard. Here, it is stated in the Hundred Roll, the abbot had a gallows, and consequently power of life and death.

The Valor gives :—
Manerium de Hethfyld—   £ s. d.
Redditus assise tam liberorum tenen-
   tium quam custumariorum . .   17 16 7½
Terrarum bartone 12 9 9
Auxiliorum 1 6 8
Operum custumariorum tenencium .   1 10 1½
De finibus terre cum perquisitis curiæ
   et aliis proficuis ejusdem manerii
   per annum communibus annis .   2 1 9
                                             35 4 11

Ministers' Accounts.

Hethfyldc—	£	s.	d.	
Redditus liberorum tenentium	4	18	11	
Venditio operum cum auxilio tenentium	2	17	7	ob.
Redditus custumariorum tenentium	7	12	8	
Redditus terr' berton'	18	18	10	
Perquisita curie	0	1	1	

177. BULFESTRÁ. "The abbot has one manor which is called BULFESTRA, and is the head of the abbacy, and that never paid geld. There the abbot has one smith [or carpenter] and ten serfs, who have two ploughs, and there the abbot has three pigs and one mile in length of wood and a half in breadth."

" BUCFESTRE is the head of the abbacy. It never paid geld. There is one blacksmith and ten serfs, with two ploughs. Wood one mile long and half a mile broad." (Exchequer Book.)

Bulfestre and Bucfestre, of course, stand for the *caput abbatiæ*. At Buckfastleigh there appear to have been four manors, those of Buckfast Abbey, Buckfast, Brooke Mainbow, and Kilbenland. The Earl of Macclesfield and Dr. Gale hold these now, or what portions of them remain.

The Valor gives,

Manerium de Buckfastleigh cum Kelbury.

	£	s.	d.
Redditus assise tam terrarum dominicalium cum pastura bosci circa manciouem dicti monasterii	8	0	0
Ac piscaria de Dert	1	0	0
Quam liberorum tenencium		4	6
Ac custumariorum tenencium	50	0	11
Firma molendini	4	0	0
Incrementum redditus	2	7	4
Finis terre	4	1	0¼
Ac perquisita curie per annum communibus annis	1	18	7½
	71	12	5

Manerium de Kylbury.

	£	s.	d.
Redditus assise tam liberorum tenencium quam custumariorum cum molendino ibidem valet per annum.	18	15	9½

Maynebowe.

	£	s.	d.
Redditus assise tam liberorum tenencium quam custumariorum tenencium	2	2	9
De finibus terre cum perquisitis curie et aliis proficuis ejusdem manerii per annum communibus annis	1	14	3¼
	3	17	0¼

Ministers' Accounts.

	£	s.	d.	
Buckfastleigh. Scitus cum terris pratis pascuis et pasturis	11	3	6	
Redditus liberorum tenentium	0	4	6	
Redditus custumariorum tenentium	30	1	7	
Firma duorum molendinorum aquat' granat'	4	0	1	
Kenynton, alias Lowertowne. Redditus custumariorum tenentium	20	8	11	ob.
Buckfastleigh. Perquisita curie	6	6	8	
Kylbury. Redditus liberorum tenentium	0	0	1	ob.
Redditus custumariorum tenentium	20	12	0	
Maynbow. Redditus liberorum tenentium	1	4	0	
Redditus custumariorum tenentium	0	18	4	
Perquisitæ curie	0	2	4	
Buckfastleigh. Porcio	0	16	8	
,, ,, Firma Rectorie	11	13	4	

178. NOTONA. "The abbot has one manor which is called NOTONA, which the Abbot Alwin held in that day in which King Edward was alive and dead, and it paid geld for two hides. These ten teams are able to plough. From thence he has half a hide and one plough in demesne and the villeins one hide and a half and five ploughs. There the abbot has nine villeins and twelve bordars and six serfs and four oxen and three pigs and seventy sheep, and two furlongs of wood in length and one in breadth, and two acres of meadow and

twenty acres of pasture. This is worth forty shillings, and when the abbot received it thirty shillings."
"The same church holds NOTONE. In the time of King Edward it paid geld for two hides. There is land for ten ploughs. In demesne is one plough and six serfs and nine villeins and twelve bordars with five ploughs. There two acres of meadow and twenty acres of pasture. Wood two furlongs long and one broad. Formerly thirty shillings, now worth forty shillings." (Exchequer Book.)

To this place we can assign no modern name.

179. CHEREFORDA *may* be Churstowe, although this is only a guess.

"The abbot has one manor which is called Chereforda, which the Abbot Alwin held in that day in which King Edward was alive and dead, and paid geld for one hide. This eight teams are able to plough. From thence the abbot has one virgate and one plough in demesne and the villeins three virgates and three ploughs. There the abbot has seven villeins and six bordars and four serfs and six oxen and forty-four sheep and two acres of meadow and twenty acres of pasture. This is worth thirty shillings, and when the abbot received it twenty shillings."

"The same church holds CHEREFORD. In the time of King Edward it paid geld for one hide. There is land for eight ploughs. In demesne is one plough and four serfs and seven villeins and six bordars with three ploughs. There two acres of meadow and twenty acres of pasture. Formerly twenty shillings, now thirty shillings." (Exchequer Book.)

The Valor gives,

Manerium de Churchstowe—

	£	s.	d.
Redditus assise liberorum tenencium .	2	14	8¼
18 libre cere et dimidium			
Custumariorum tenencium . .	17	7	8
Terrarum dominicalium . . .	21	0	0
De finibus terre cum perquisitis curie et aliis proficuis ejusdem manerii per annum communibus annis .	3	13	5½

£44 15 9¾

18 libre cere et dim.

Kyngesbrigg—
	£	s.	d.
Redditus assise liberorum tenencium et convencionariorum	8	8	0½
Firma molendinorum	3	6	8
Exitus mercatorum et nundinarum	5	0	0
Ac perquisita curie per annum communibus annis	0	18	0
Inde solutum Philippo Champernon militi et heredibus suis pro redditu gurgitis molendini fixati super terram suam apud Dodbrooke per annum	0	2	0

Et remanet clare . £17 10 8½

Ministers' Accounts.

Churstowe—
	£	s.	d.
Redditus tam liberorum quam custumariorum tenentium	3	3	2 q.

Kyngesbrigge—
	£	s.	d.
Redditus custumariorum tenentium	9	1	8
Exitus mercat' sive nundinarum	5	6	8
Redditus liberorum tenentium	4	4	8 ob.
Perquisita curie	0	18	6
Churchstowe cum capella de Kingsbridge—Firma rectorie	32	14	6

180. BRENT. "The abbot has one manor which is called BRENTA, which the abbot Alwin held in that day in which King Edward was alive and dead, and paid geld for two hides. These ten teams can plough. From thence the abbot has half a hide and one plough in demesne, and the villeins one hide and a half and five ploughs. There the abbot has ten villeins, and eight bordars, and five serfs, and fourteen oxen, and fifty-five sheep, and five acres of wood, and four acres of meadow, and thirty acres of pasture. This is worth forty shillings, and when the abbot received it thirty shillings."

"The abbot has one manor which is called BRENTA, which the abbot held in that day in which King Edward was alive and dead, and paid geld for two hides. This six teams are able to plough. Thence the abbot has half a hide and one plough in demesne, and the villeins one hide and a half and three ploughs. There the abbot has eight villeins and six bordars, and four serfs and eleven oxen, and seventy sheep, and thirty goats, and one mile of wood in length and one furlong in width, and two acres [of meadow]* and one mile of pasture in length and a half in breadth. This is worth thirty shillings, and when the abbot received it twenty shillings."

"The same church holds BRENTA. In the time of King Edward it paid geld for two hides. There is land for ten ploughs. In demesne is one plough and five serfs, and ten villeins and eight bordars with five ploughs. There four acres of meadow and four acres of wood, and thirty acres of pasture. Formerly thirty shillings, now worth forty shillings."

"The same church holds BRENT. In the time of King Edward it paid geld for two hides. There is land for six ploughs. In demesne is half a plough and four serfs, and eight villeins and six bordars with three ploughs. There two acres of meadow, pasture one mile long and half a mile broad, wood one mile long and one furlong broad. Formerly twenty shillings, now thirty shillings." (Exchequer Book.)

The two Brentas stand for manors, both probably in the parish of South Brent. The Brent property appears in the Valor and Ministers' accounts, as under:—

The Valor gives,

Manerium de Brent.	£	s.	d.
Redditus assise liberorum tenentium	8	6	7½
Et custumariorum tenencium	87	17	3
Firma molendini	6	16	8
Piscaria	0	3	4
Incrementum redditus	9	17	6½
De finibus terrarum cum perquisitis curie et aliis proficuis ejusdem manerii per annum communibus annis	11	5	2¼
	121	6	7¾

Ministers' Accounts.

	£	s.	d.
Brent. Redditus liberorum tenentium manerii	8	17	3
Redditus custumariorum et conventionariorum tenentium	102	15	7 q.
Brent. Porcio de vicarie	0	4	0
Brent. Firma rectorie	18	2	10

181. I have now been through the whole of the land mentioned in Domesday, and shown as nearly as possible that it continued to be held down to the time of the Dissolution.

* Omitted, but see Exchequer Book.

Besides the above the Abbey held some other land scattered through the county, mentioned thus :—
In hundreto Mortone . . . . Abb de Bulfestra i virgā. Fol. 65b., p. 59.
In hundreto chridiatone . . . De his ht' Osbuūs epš iiii. hid & dim. & abbas de bulfestra dim' hida. Fol. 66b, p. 60.
In hundredo Taintone .. . . . et abbas bulfestrensis fertium [ferlium ?] & dim'. Fol. 69b, p. 64.
In hundredo dippeford . . . . et abbas bulfestrensis ii. hid. Fol. 69b, p. 65.

182. Of course the property had greatly increased in value since Domesday, but that was owing to the general progress of the country, and the care bestowed upon it by its owners, but it cannot fail to be noticed that the additions made during the time between the Great Survey and the Dissolution were few and unimportant. They were, following still the Valor and Ministers' Accounts, as follows :—

183. PALSTON, in South Brent, probably belonged to one of the Domesday manors, thus mentioned in the Valor:—
                                                £ s. d.
Redditu bertone ibidem per annum   . 3 0 0
And in the Ministers' Accounts—
Redditus terrarum dominicalium vocat'
Palston 3 0 0

184. ENGLEBURNE, Ingleborne, or Engelbourne, is in the parish of Harberton. It was leased by Gabriel Donne to Sir Phillip Champernowne for a term of sixty years, and subject to this was sold by the Crown. About the end of the last century it was divided into parcels and sold.

Valor.
Manerium de Engleburne.
                                                £ s. d.
Redditus assise liberorum tenencium . 0 9 0
                                             1 libra cere.
Custumariorum tenencium in Totnes,
  Aisheberyngton, Churston, quam
  Engleburne predicta   .   .   . 10 7 2
                                          et 1 libra cere.
Ac terrarum bartone   .   .   .   5 13 4
De finibus terrarum cum perquisitis
  curie et aliis proficuis ejusdem
  manerii communibus annis   .   . 2 5 0¼
                                          ─────────
                                          18 14 6¼
                                          2 libre cere.

Ministers' Accounts.
Engleburne—   £   s.   d.
Redditus liberorum tenentium   .   .   0 12   1
Redditus tam custumariorum quam
  conventionariorum tenentium .   .   11   0   6
Firma manerii 5 13   4

185. BROMSTON or Brownston is a manor in the parish of Modbury and was given to the abbey by John de Morville. On the Dissolution Sir Thomas Dennis secured this for himself.

Valor.
Brounston—
Redditus assise custumariorum tenen-
  cium ibidem per annum .   .   .   5   1   0½
                                            1 par. cirotecarum.

Ministers' Accounts.
Bromston—
Redditus assise   .   .   .   5   0 10 ob.

186. BOTTOXBURGH, Bottokysburgh, or Battisborough, is a manor in the parish of Holbeton.

Valor.
Bottokysburgh—
Redditus assise liberorum tenencium .   1 15   5½
Custumariorum tenencium   .   .   6   6   8
Terrarum bartone   12   5   4
Firma molendini   2   0   0
Ac perquisita curie per annum com-
  munibus annis   0   5   3½
                                           ―――――――――
                                            22 12   9

Ministers' Accounts.
Bottoxburgh—
Redditus liberorum tenentium   .   .   1 15   5 ob.
Redditus conventionariorum tenentium   7   9   0
Firma capitalis mesuagii   .   .   .   13   3   0
Perquisita curie   0   4   8

187. CHYSCOMBE was a piece or parcel of land in the parish of Dene Prior, of the yearly value of 6s. 8d. both in the Valor and the Ministers' Accounts.

188. At SPYCHEWYKE, in the manor of the same name, in the parish of Widdecombe, the abbey had two tenements returned at an annual rent of 28s. both in the Ministers' Accounts and in the Valor.

189. NORTH BOVEY. Here was a tenement included in the Valor and Ministers' Accounts as producing an annual rent of 10s.

190. Hoo or Hooe, in the parish of Plymstock, described in the Valor as being below the parish of Plympton. Here was a tenement entered in both accounts as being worth 8s. per annum.

191. PLYMPTON. Here the Abbey had a garden, the rent being returned in the Ministers' Accounts and Valor at 5s. yearly.

192. EXETER. Like most of the other abbeys, Buckfast had a house in the city for the residence of the abbot, the successive owners of which are traced by Dr. Oliver. In the Valor and Ministers' Accounts it is entered as producing only 6d. per annum for firewood. The reason of this probably was, that it had been leased for a money payment, this small amount being reserved. It was not until 1543 that the King disposed of it.

193. BICATON, a village in the parish of Broadhempston, according to Oliver, belonged to the house, but I have not met with any mention of it in any original document, nor does the name or parish occur in either the Valor or Ministers' Accounts.

194. We also find enumerated in the Valor the usual payments made out of the annual revenue, amounting to £15 16s. There was a corrody of £3 per annum to James Knottysford.

195. The spiritualities, which are entered separately, amount with the pensions paid to £68 14s. 3d. and one pound of wax from the Rectory of Petrockstow.

196. Taking then the figures as they stand in the Valor, we find that the total annual income of the Abbey in 1534 was—

1534.
26 Hen. VII.
cap. 3.

				£	s.	d.
Rents, &c.				430	19	7¾
Spiritualities				68	14	3
				499	13	10¾
out of which payments—						
Temporalities	.	15 16	0			
Spiritualities	.	17 6	8			
				33	2	8
				£466	11	2¾

Thus leaving the total nett income £466 11s. 2¾d., besides twenty pounds of wax and one pair of gloves, an income larger than any other Cistercian house in Devon. And yet, unlike some monastic establishments, there appears to have been no greed of wealth, no undue accumulation of riches; the monks did their best with their land, and often had, as we have seen, to struggle to maintain their rights; but in the centuries which elapsed between the Conquest and the Dissolution it cannot be said that they had been covetous; and the sneer of Richard Cœur de Lion, when he told Fulke that of his three daughters, Covetousness, Pride, and Lust, he would bestow the first upon the white monks, could not apply to the monks of Buckfast.

197. Besides being the chief farmers of the day, the Cistercians were great promoters of the industrial arts. It has recently been discovered that the Cistercians were the predecessors of the ironmasters of the nineteenth century, the monks of Kirkstead and Louth Park Abbey having promoted iron-mining and smelting, and carried on the work on an extensive scale.

Rather than covetous, the Cistercians should be called thrifty and industrious, developing the resources of the neighbourhood in which they settled, and endeavouring to make two blades of grass grow where only one grew before. It would be a pleasant task, and the results valuable, to trace out the various occupations in which these monks engaged, and what effects their labours have had upon the commercial and agricultural interests of the country.

198. Buckfastleigh owes what prosperity it has to the monks of Buckfast, for the Cistercians were the great wool traders of the times in which they lived, and the owners of the large mills, some of which are built up with the materials of the Abbey and its belongings, are but carrying out in the same locality, in other ways, the work of former years.

You may break, you may shatter the vase if you will,
But the scent of the roses will cling round it still;

and so, when we use the "Abbot's Way" across the breezy moor, we think of those busy men who often trod it, and carried their merchandise along it; and when we follow the "Monk's Path" by the Dart, flowing on as it did long years ago,

Giving a gentle kiss to every sedge,
It overtaketh in its pilgrimage;

the lives of those who prayed and laboured, laboured and

prayed, hard by, must occupy our thoughts, and "Abbot's Way" and "Monk's Path," and the moor and the river, tell us more, and do more to keep alive the memory, of the old dwellers in the Abbey of Bulfestre, than the few scanty remains of the buildings which they raised.

APPENDIX (A).

List of the Abbots of Buckfast.

Name.	Approx. date.	Authorities.
Alwine	1066	Domesday Book.
Eustachius	1143	Archives Dean and Chapter, Exeter
William	1196	Foundation Deed, Torr Abbey.
Nicholas	1207?	Grant to John Lambrith.
Michael	1225	Pedes Finium Henry III.
William	1246	Coll. Sir William Pole, B.M.
Howell	1247	Oliver.
Durandus	1258	Oliver.
Henry	1268	Coll. Sir William Pole, B.M.
Simon	1272	Episcopal Registers, Exeter.
Robert	1280	Do. do.
Peter	1290	Agreements with Hubernford and others, &c.
Robert	1316	Episcopal Registers.
Stephen	1330	Do. do.
John de Churstowe	1332	Do. do.
William Giffard	1333	Do. do.
Philip	1340	Do. do.
Robert Simons	1358	Do. do.
William Paderston	1395	Do. do.
William Slade	1400	Do. do.
William Beaghe	1415	Do. do.
Thomas Rogger	1432	Do. do.
John Ffychet	1440	Do. do.
John Matthu	1449	Do. do.
John Kynge	1483	Will of Ambrose Franke.
John Rede	1498	Episcopal Registers.
St. Clere Pomeroy?		See par. 149.
Alfred Gille	1512	Episcopal Registers.
John Rede	1525	Do. do.
Gabriel Donne	1537	Do. do.

APPENDIX (B).

The following documents are printed (from transcripts made for me from the originals in the British Museum) as they stand, with the contractions and errors. I have thought it best to adopt this course with all the documents throughout this paper, the greater part of which are printed for the first time.

SLOANE MS. No. 513. (fo. 210B.)

Anno Dñi M^{mo} ꝛc̄. In crastino p'ificacōis Bē Marie v'g̃ cōpleta visi^{ae} in mo"stio de B. p pre; Abbatē statuta sūt ea q̃ secût' f'mit obśvanda. In p'mis statuit' Anno Dñi ꝛc̄. Nos Fr̃ R. dc̄us Abbas—visitantes filam nr̄am Abbaciā de B. statuim^q ꝛ p̃cipim^q ea q̃ seqût' inviolabilit obśvāda In p^{is} statud dec^{e}vim^q ꝛc̄. Et in fine sigillū visitator appo"t' Qñ aliq̨ officiū tc̄pale iniūgi^{ir} ¶ Mo"cho alic^i vt o̵vso p Abbm suū h^o juramentū sb sc'ptū tenea' p̃staɼ corā Abbe suo ꝛ senioribɜ de c̄oventu p cōstitucōes Dñi Bñdci pape xij^{mi}.

¶ Juramentū.

Ego fr̃ R mo"ch^q vt o̵vsus Moñ de B. ordis Cist̄ juro p i^{ta} sc̄a Dī ev"nge" q̨ ab i^{to} die in antea in offo m^i p vos Abbęm meū cōmisso ꝛ i oibɜ ꝛ sin^l m^i in offo p̃dc̄o cōmiss fidelit me h̃ebo ꝛ q̨ de p'ciis reddāibɜ f"ctibɜ seu pvētibɜ quibɜcūɜ inde p̃veientibɜ ꝛ expñsis quocic̄s ꝛ qñ p Abbęɜ meū requisit^q fūo fidęlē ǫpotū reddā pt Dʒ m^i ded^{o}it ꝛ potō ꝛ reliq̄" quecūɜ supfʼūit Mo"stio vt bursario h^q Moñ mei integ"lit assignabo s^e me Dʒ adjuvet ꝛ ista sc̄a Dī Ev"ngelia.

¶ Juramentū novicōrɇ.

¶ Ego fr̃ N c̃ticus juro p ista sc̄a Dī ev"nge^a q̨ ab isto die in antea nullū apponā repugnacōis obstāctm ūlhn pc'abo defencōis p̃sidm̃ q̃m ad jussiōm Abbis mei offa si qua m^i committēt^r in fut'o dimittā absɜ o̵"diccōne q"cūɜ sic me Dʒ adjuvet ꝛc̄.

Quiliɜ novici^q in ordīe Cist̄ petens instant ut pfessiom̃ suā faciat inf"" annū pbōis sue ꝛ si cōced' ei sic̄ licite pt ut ex" de relig̃ ꝛ t"nsit ad religiōm c^o ad ap̃licam Tūc pref ꝛ faciat ins'ptā renūciacōm in cn^o corā Abbe suo ꝛ cōventu.

Pfessio Monachorɇ.

Ego fr̃ R c̃ticus Exorcista Accolit^q sbdiacon^q † sac̄doʃ pmitto stabilitē meā ꝛ cōvsiom̃ morɇ meorɇ ꝛ obedien^{as} s^m regtaɜ sc̄i Bñdc̄i ordis Cist̄ corā Dō ꝛ omībɜ sc̄is ej^q quorɇ

reliquie hic hñt͛ in hoc loco qui voca͛ Bucfast ord̃ Cist̄
constructo in hoñe beatissime Dc̄ genitricis semp ip͡ꝗ Ṽginis
Marie in p̃sencia dñi Witti Abb̃is.

¶ Juramentū Abb̃is.

Ego f͞r N cl̄cus Abb̃s h͡ꝗ Moñ b̃e Marie de B juro p̱ ista
sc̃a D͞i evn͞͞ge͞ᵃ p̱ me tacta q̱ possessiones reddit͡ꝗ ꝉ jura
mobilia ꝉ imobilia isti͡ꝗ Moñ nõ vendā nᵉ alienabo vł impig-
norabo ne͡ꞇ de novo infeodabo ne p̱ am̃ modum donabo n¹
q͞͞tenus statutū Pape B͞nd͞ci ꝉ jura ordis mei p̱mittūt sᵉ me
D͡ꞇ adjuvet ꝉ ista sc̃a D͞i Ev͞͞nge͞ᵃ p̱ me tacta ꝉ ṽacił
osculata.

Juramentū scolaris mittendi ad studiū.

Ego f͞r N cl̄cus scolaris huj͡ꝗ Moñ be Mᵉ de B ordis Cist̄
juro p̱ ista sc̃a D͞i evn͞͞ge͞ᵃ q̱ ab istu die in antea ordis
mei p¹vilegia libtates ꝉ appbatas͛ ꝯsuetudic̃s atq͡ꞇ statuta a¹d
clam vł palā p̱ me ł p̱ aliũ attēmptaṝ impet͞͞re seu ꝉ in a͟ꝯ
illicite sive p͟ꞇve cꝗ͞͞ire nõ p̃sumā uñ p̃dc̄us ordo meus in p̱te
vł in toto dampnū a¹scādalū inc͞͞reṝ valeat vł g͞͞vamen sᵉ me
D͡ꞇ ꝉc.

Juramentū scolaris p̱movēdi ad g͞͞dū scolasticum.

Ego f͞r N Monachus ꝉ scolaris Moñ bc̄ Mᵉ de Bucfas̄t ordis
Cist̄ juro p̱ ista sc̃a D͞i ev͞͞nge͞ᵃ q͡ꞇ cū ad bacl̄aṝ vł Magist͞͞tū
theologice facultatᵖ pveñ͞o cꝗ͞͞ instituta ordis mei p¹vilegia ꝉ
libtates a¹d in fut͛is nõ attēptabo p̱ me ł p̱ aliũ seu alios nᵉ
quocū͡ꞇ doloso coloṝ quesito pc͛abo seu p̱ me pc͛ari paciar
ip̱etrando q͞͞ instituta ꝉ libtates ordis mei añd͞ci Nec eidm̃
p̃sumā vł ꝉ pc͛abo p̱ me vł p̱ aliũ clam vł palā infⁱnge seu
qᵒmodoli͡ꞇ alias inpugr͞͞ sᵉ me D͡ꞇ ꝉc.

Juramentū Monachi vocati ad cōsiliū Abbatis.

Ego f͞r N. Mo͞͞chᵖ ꝉ pfessus Moñ bc̄ Mᵉ de B. ordis Cist̄
juro p̱ iᵗᵃ sc̃a D͞i ev͞͞nge͞͞ q̱ secretū ꝉ consiliū q̱cū͡ꞇ m¹ per
vos Abb̃m meū vł aliũ seu alios noīe vr̄o jā revelandū fidelił
tenebo at͡ꞇ ꝯvabo ne id ullatenⁱ in post̃u alicⁱ vł a¹d p͟ꞇ con-
scīa͡ꞇ vr̄a͡ꞇ p̱ me nᵉ p̱ aliā seu p̱ alios qᵒscū͡ꞇ revelabo ne͡ꞇ
denudabo nᵉ ꝉ revelaṝ seu denudaṝ faciam vł pcurabo sic me
d͡ꞇ ꝉc.

Juramc̄t Monachi m¹tc̄di ad curiā Ro͞͞nā p̱ nego¹ˢ domꝗ.

Ego f͞r N. Mo͞͞ch͡ꝗ ꝉ pfess͡ꝗ h͡ꝗ Moñ b̃e Mᵉ de B. juro p̱ ista
sc̃a D͞i ev͞͞nge͞͞ p̱ me corpat tacta q̱ nego͞ᵃ dñi mei Abb̃is ꝉ
dc̄e Mo͞͞sⁱtⁱi mei ꝯmissa ꝉ cōm¹tenda fidełⁱ in cuṝ ro͞͞na pseq͞͞r
ꝉ p̱ posse meo dił͞t͞n͞r p̱movebo cū exacta diligencia ac pᶜcunia͡ꞇ

m¹ delibandā in usus ꝛ utiliᵗᵉˢ dĉorꝑ negociorꝑ m¹ cōmissorꝑ ꝛ coṁittēdoꝫ ꝛ nō in alios vsus frivilos expendā ꝙꝗꝫ ūllam īp et“cōm in dcā cuꞃ p̄l alibi p me p̄l p aliū seu alios faciā p̄l ꝼi peu“bo ꝗ tendᵖe potꞇit ad incᵉmentū honorꝑ seu status dei dni mei abbis p̄l mei aᵗ eoliꝫ de cōventu sive Moñ me piudiciū p̄l ruinā qᵒvismᵒ ac ꝛ inꞇ“ tᵗduū adventꝗ mei pⁱmo ad dcaꝫ cuꞃ g̃n̄ali peu“tori orᵭis mei si eiꝗ copiā heꞃ potuo me fidelit̃ pntabo sᵉ me ds ꝛc.

Juramēt Mo“ch ꞇ eꝯꝟsi dirᵉti ad cuꞃ ro“na p absolueōc.

Ego fr N. Mo“chꝗ ꝛ pfessus hᵖ Mo“stⁱⁱ de B. iuro p ista sĉa di ev“nǥᵗ ꝗ casᵖ quē stimulante ꝯsĉia meā dno meo abbi exposui ꝛ p qᵒ ad ēndm sedē aplicā ꞇiam ab eo petivi p̄ᵖ ost ꝛ vacit̃ m¹ accidit ūllo simulacōis p̄l fraudis coloꞃ pmixto ꝛ ꝗ p tēpe quo ex“ dem Moñ meū ex causa p̃dca ꝼūo itiñatu“s mansurus p̄l qᵒmᵒcūꝫ moraturus nullū ōio actū p̄l instᵃ mentū seu aᶦd aⁿd ꝗeūꝫ ñoie consent“ eꝗ“ pⁱvilegia orᵭis mei añdei p̄l statuta aᵗ cosuetudios appbatas eiusdm p me p̄lꝓ alios seu aliū peu“bo aᵗ alias arte p̄l ingenio impetrabo ꝗ in piudiciū aᵉᵖ psone eꝯeūꝫ statᵖ digniᵗᵉ p̄l condiĉois existat p̄l g“vamen ac ꝛ inꞇ“ tᵗduū pᵖ advētū meū pⁱno ad cuꞃ ro“nā g̃n̄ali peu“tori orᵭis mei si copiā ipⁱᵖ heꞃ poꞇo me fidelit̃ presentabo sᵉ me ds ꝛc.

Obligaĉo recipiendi in Noviciū.

Ego N. de cꞇicus Exorcista accloitᵖ sbdiaconᵖ diaconᵖ p̄l saĉdos dio instinctu motus cupiens vitam Mo“chalem ducᷓe in isto Moñ be Mᵉ de B. orᵭis Cistᷓ Exoñ dioĉ obligo me do ꝛ be Mᵉ sp v̄gi di geniᵗᵉi ac ōibꝫ scis ꝛ pat̃ abba ꝗ die m¹ limitato tonsurā ꝛ hitū novicioꝛꝫ assumā ac integrū annū pbaĉonis mee p̄l ꝗntū in hᵒᵃ reḡlam sci bndei fuit indultū fidelit̃ pimplebo sᵐ forᵃm orᵭis añdĉi.

¶ Peticio novicij in Capitulo.

Dñe peto instanꞇ̃ ꝛ hm¹ᵖ supplico ꝗtenᵖ valeam a vobis recipi ad faciend̃ pfessīom meā in isto Moñ de B. ad ꝟviend do ꝛ scis eius hic inꝑ vos in hitu Monachali secdm reḡlam sci bndei orᵭis Cistᷓ ad p̃minū vite mee sᵐ legem di ꝛ p̄ra documenta. ¶ Tūc exponat illi abbas auriciā orᵭis vt est modus.

¶ Renūciaĉo.

Ego fraꞇ̃ Riĉ eꞇeꞇᵖ Novicius in isto Moñ bte Marie de Bukfast orᵭis Cistᷓ dio instictu motus cupiens ordinem monasticū in isto p̃deo Moñ sᵐ reḡlaꝫ sci bndicti solempnit̃ pfiꞇⁱi in sbsidū novicijs religiosis de iure indultū nōvi n̄ᵉ metu induct⁹ s̄ȝ p̄o sponte siplit⁹ ꝯt absolute residuo d̄cti anni p̄bac̄onis mee in hijs sc̄ᶦptꝑ renūc̄o ꝯt peto instantꝑ me recipi ad p̄fessīom p̄dcam faciendam ṣᵐ for̃ᵐ ordinis antedci.

Itm̃ cū refrigescente devoc̄one m̃ltoȝ pauce psoᵉ p̄th dolor ad cꝯỹsiōem vc̄iant hijs diebȝ vñ in nōullis mūdi p̱tibȝ monasc̄ia n̄ri ordis magnū paciūt̃̃ defectū psonaȝ pptꝑ q̃d cult⁹ d̃iu⁹ minuit̃̃ ꝯt monasteria ip̄a in tēpalibȝ magnā sustineāt lesionē vt autē de receptis novicijs cici⁹ adiuvet̃̃ caᵐ geˡᵉ diffiʳᵃ alias editā de novijs ante annū p̄bac̄ois finitū ad p̄fessionē solempnē admittens ip̄is qȝ b̃ndic̄edis vsqȝ ad revo-cac̄oem pdurandū progat ꝯt renovat sic tamc̄q̃ ip̄i novici' añq̃ᵐ b̃ndicāt̃̃ sciant psaltiū ꝯt ea que de ñccitate sūt scic̃da ꝯt q̇rtūdecimū sue etatis cōplevint ꝯt residuo tp̄is anni sue p̄bac̄ois de feo renūcient exp̄sse vt pȝ supᵃ. Ista diffinic̄o compilata fuat anno d̃ni Mith̃mo ccc lxxiij apud Cist̃ ī c⁰ geˡⁱ.

212 b. Revendo ī xᵒ p̄ri ac d̃no d̃no E. di gr̃a Exoñ Ep̄o sui h̃miles ꝯt devoti filij Ab̃bs ꝯt Convent⁹ Monast̃ij Bukfestr̃ ordis Cistᵉciensis Exoñ dioc̃ revencias tanto p̄ri debitas cū honor̃ Revende patr̃nitati ṽre. J. b. accolitū virum liberū ꝯt legitᵐ boneqȝ cōvsac̃ōis ꝯt honeste ṽre dioc̃ p̄sentamˢ h̃militꝑ sup-plicātes ꝯt devote q̄tinꝗ eūdc̃. J. ad om̃s sacros ordies p sac̃̃rū manuū ṽraȝ iposic̄ōem caritꝑ ituitu pmoṽe dig̃ei. On⁹ aᶜ p̃moc̃ōis sive p̃visōis eiusd̃ ī nos ꝯt successores n̄ros to*ʳt̃r suscipimˢ vos autē successoŕsqȝ ṽros ī hac p̱te idēpnes cōsvar̃ pmittimˢ p p̄ntes. In c⁹ rei testioȝ sigillū n̄rȝ c̃ōe c̃ app̄.

APPENDIX (C).

SLOANE MSS. No. 513, fo. 213.

In visitacōne faciēda p⁰ d₃ Abbas visi^{tat} p̃muniř visitand sc^lbendo s^i vł ej^q locū tenēti de te^e advēt^q sui cā visi^{is} celebñde P^u g̃^i die visi^{is} añq^{u–} intret ca^m d₃ p̃muniř Abbm ł ej^q P^lorem dom^q ⁊ p⁰ intř eccm^{u–} ad vigi^{as} vł ad p^lmam ut filii sui s^i obediať mage devote. Intñs g̃ ca^m post lcom regle plectā dicto ut moř c̄ bndi^{te} sbjūgat Carissī fřes ⁊ filii lateř vos nō d₃ cā instanł advēt^q nr̃i q^{l}li₃n pať Abbas p^l scite s statuta ordis tene^r annuati p se ł p aliū sing^la Mos^{u–}tia s^i im̃e^{te} sbjecta visitař ⁊ ea q̄ ivenlit corigēda zelo di ⁊ ordis tā in spualib₃ q^{u–} in corpalib₃ emēdař Ad h⁰ g^i vēi ut actū visi^{is} pficiā i vobis dīa g^{u–}tia dirigēte ⁊ q₃ c^{u–}tā form^{u–} i hac pte hem^q mutādā iō s^{u–}gat cātor ⁊ legat corā vobis Deiñ pte^{u–} carta visi^{is} ⁊ lega^r tūc plectẹ diffinib₃ legēdis dicat visitator. Ecce kmi vos audistā bonā inforc^{u–}ōm nob a scis p̃rib₃ nr̃is t^{u–}ditā q^{u–}bř nos ⁊ vos hem₁^q pced^pe i p̃nti visitacōe nr̃a ⁊ iō do^e Abba debetẹ fřes vřos rognř p̃cipe ⁊ moneř ut ea q̄ corigēda no^vint puplice ł p^lvati nob suggerant ⁊ pponant s₉ form^{u–} corā nob lectam Postq^{u–} v⁰ Abbas fec^pit molcōm suā Dicat visitator ⁊ nos autori^{te} p̃rna q^{u–} fūgim^r i hac pte vob ōib₃ ⁊ sin^l p̃cipim^q i hac pte i v^ltute §ce obedi^e q^{u–}tin^q veīatẹ ad nos puplice ł p^lvati p meli^q indicavite faciēd ⁊ oñdatẹ ea q̄ corigēda sūt i mos^{u–}tio i spualib₃ ⁊ tēpalib₃ tā i capite q^{u–} iu mēb^ls ptestam^r q₃ vobis p pte nr̃a q₃ q^lcq^i nobis caritatio suggestū fu^pit ⁊ ex bono spu pati sum^q id effica^{te} emēdař p̃^l D₃ mīstv^{u–}erit gt^{u–}iā ⁊ ip̃i^q ⁊ ordis honorē aīarẹ vr̃arẹ salutē paceq₃ ⁊ utilite₃ oñiū i cōř Tūc dicat visitator volum^q p^q ca^m visitař officia iō vos officiales sitẹ in officiis vr̃is ⁊ vos P^lor pvideate de Frīb₃ q^i vadāt nobiscū ⁊ p^q novā hebitẹ pliamētū Insup durāte visitacōe res^pvam^q in man^q nřas pulsacōm ad p^lmā ⁊ ad ca^m ⁊ phibem^q ne a^lo Mo^{u–}ch^q de Monastio se absentet sñ licen^{u–} nr̃a spali ⁊ q₁ opus bonū incipe d₃ cū orone ut finē meliorē heat in effcu iō ut pñs act^q nr̃e visi^{is} meli^q pspe^{u–} dico^q i p^ln⁰ veni cř spc pr̃ nř ave et collca Accōnes nr̃as ⁊c.

De comissar̄

Qñ comissari⁹ visitat dicat loqᵘᵐʳ de ordie nr̃o deɱ̃ sbjūgat
ķi vos scitę cā₃ advēt⁹ nr̃i Venimus sv̄ vocati sum⁹ ad moᵘ⁻
st̃iū istud p comissioɱ̃ pr̄is vr̄i dñi v₃ Abb̃is tt̃is loci s₃ ī pinᵒ
volu⁹ q̨ audiatę forᵘᵐ cōmissiois nr̃o qᵘ ptca dicat comissar̄
Ecce socii vos audist̃ę forᵘm ist̃i⁹ cōmissiois admittitę istā
cōmissō₃ ꞇ nos s ej⁹ forᵘm q¹b₃ annuc̄tibus dicat cōmissari⁹
sʳgat cātor ꞇ legat forᵘᵐ visiⁱˢ ꞇc̄ ut sᵘ De relaxacōe pene
vī mitiganᵒ p̃nie Amice nos itellexim⁹ ob qᵘm cā₃ pōit⁹ es ī
p̃nia ꞇ sic̃ dc̄m c̄ not̃ ɱ̃ito hᵒ pat̃is ad istanciā tn̄ Abbis ţui ꞇ
socōrę tuorę remittim⁹ ꞇ relaxam⁹ pcīa₃ istā iᵃ p de cet̃o te
emc̄des ī q̨ᵐ pot̃is erga ordic̄₃ at₃ dɱ̃ Qᵃ die dc̄a collacōe si
qᵘ fŭit faciat p̃sidēs postea pelamacōes pt mat̃iā inveñlit in
suo pliamc̄to ꞇ alibi sup pⁱore suppⁱore cantor̄ succētor̄ celle-
raris sboelllernr̄ de sp̃ualib₃ ꞇ tēpalib₃ ꞇ sup articlos ǫtc̄tę in
sc̃)pto visiⁱˢ Pⁱorc̄ sic alloquens. Dñe Pⁱor tu es pelamat⁹
p co q̨ nō fac ę debitū officii tui c̓ca ordię₃ obs̃vād Frc̄s nō
sedet in clautro festivis dieb₃ ꞇ aliis tēpe lc̄ois nec tu ad boᵐ
exᵐ aliorę hᵒ facis ut deberes. Silenciū in 4 locis pⁱncipalib₃
nō obs̃vatᵘ nec ꞇ in aliis locis ꞇ tēpib₃ debitę ꞇ p̃cipue ad
mc̄sā. Frc̄s nō veniūt ad s̃viciū dñm ꞇ horas canoicas in eccīa
qt̄is sic̄ deberet s₃ aliq̨ⁱ s₃ absentāt sepi⁹ intendētes vagacōi ꞇ
alii potacāb₃ in ordinatę post cōpletorɱ̃ ꞇ añ remanc̄t ꞇ de
vigiliis ꞇ de cōpletor̄ nec ea psolvūt in iſ̃'mitoris tepe debito
ut tenc̄tʳ Nō veniūt ad qfom ōi septiᵘ nᵉ celebrāt missas suas
cōiţ sic̄ decet. Formā ꞇ b̃i Bernardi pr̄is nr̃i ī cantu ꞇ Pᵈⁱᵃ
nō obs̃vatę devote morose ac vivaciţ cantādo s₃ nimis tepide
festinatę ꞇ indevote cōplet̃ę s̃viciū dnm q̨ᵃ p̃eoptū

S⁹vite dño ī t̃iorᵖ Pᵖᵖtea dñc Pⁱor deberᵖs ex offo tuo
excitar̄ cantorc̄ in ecetīa ꞇ alies ǫfres tuos ut dn̄ū officiū cu
tior ꞇ tremor̄ inibi psolvant remissos sv̄ negligētes ī caᵒ
pelamar̄ coriq̨ᵖe ꞇ emc̄dar̄ s₃ ista nō facę q̨ⁱⁿ vi⁹ dissitās in
pietm ario tue ꞇ det¹mentū nō modicū religioⁱˢ. Illa que
dixim⁹ pⁱori t̃ⁱ ꞇ suppⁱori iponim⁹ q₃ nō facedebitū tuū
qᵘntū ad obs̃vācias regtares ī ppⁱa pᵃ aut aliena qᵘr q̨ⁱ
delibar̄ volum⁹ q̨ vobis p vr̄a necligēcia sit facicd̄ catę sessū
us₃ in crastinū judiciū exspᶜtantes. T'cia die dīco a p̃sidēte
bñdⁱᵗᵉ expoᵘq₃ regta sbjūgat loqᵘᵐʳ de ordic̄ nr̃o ꞇ petita
vēia a Pⁱore ꞇ aliis pⁱdie pelamatę dicat p̃sedēs Dñc Pⁱor
ɱ̃lta fŭut t̃ⁱ īp̃oita hestⁱʰna die hic ī caᵒ uñ magnā peñia₃
meruisti ex ordis rigor̄ S₃ mīa moti volum⁹ ad p̃us punic̄ǫ₃
ōio differr̄ sb̃ spc emc̄dac̄ois usq₃ ad pxīa₃ visiᵉˢ ī qᵘ si
nō invenⁱim⁹ debitā emc̄dacōm ī te ꞇ in aliis nⁱ vobis
ppōim⁹ oñder̄ gr̃o decet̃ᵒ ĩ favor̄ s₃ cōstet vobis dc cet̃ᵒ s₃

Sic, bis.

statuta ordis nr̃i oç rigorē justicie q" vos volum⁹ obs̃vare ꝛ
iō facinte oĩa ꝛ sinᵐ bn̄ emc̄dari ꝛ ente sessum Tūc dicat t̃ri
frēs ꝛ filii ǫsidᵖate attēci⁹ ꝛ videte q"lit̃ pn̄teç visieʳ nr̃aç·
pfcein⁹ ĩ vob ōi rigor̃ ordis pc̄it⁹ p̃misso pponimʹⁱ n p nc̄
on̄dcr̃ vobis soᵐ gr̃aç ꝛ favoē movēdo ꝛ vitando? q tiu⁹ dn̄m
officium devocōe debita psolvate or̃om atç leccōi tepibç debite
insistate Abbi vr̃o ꝛ aliis sr̃ioribç vr̃is obedieneiā ꝛ revencciā
exhibeate caritatē tr̃nitatis ꝛ bonū pacē ivicē obs̃vādo debetis
insup vagacōç oĩodā evitar̃ defcus vestros atqç negligēeias
emc̄dar̃ ut sᵉ gr̃aç vobis tc̄aç in pn̄ti visitacōe iveiam⁹ ĩ pxiǫ
advētu nr̃o vos in vacuū nt̃tate⁹ recepisse Sup iste vᵒ efficat̃
obs̃vād Pⁱori ꝛ suppriori cōmittimᵖ vices nr̃as ut faciāt istā
monicōm nr̃um ab oĩbç sbs̃vari. Nichil ad faciēd c̄ ad p̃us
ki nⁱ cū orōne ut mor̃ c̄ visitaᵉˢ nr̃aç l̃iarᵖ. Recomēdamᵖ g̃
vobis ꝛ oron̄ibç vr̃is statū ꝛ unitatē ecēio un⁹it capud ipiⁱ
intˡuccoū? dn̄m siç Sūmū pont̃ cū toto clero sⁱ fidetr
adherc̃to ut sūt cardonales Archiop̃i Ep̃i Abbes Pⁱorᵖs ocˊtiç
rectorᵖs ac curā aĩare ht̃ntes p̃cipue g̃ recomēdo orōibç vr̃is
ordĩoç nr̃m Cisˈcii cū oĩbç plñt ꝛ sbdit⁹ ĩ cod ꝛ spalit̃ domū
vr̃aç Mr̃nā Ex-aˢ ptc recomēdo orōibç vr̃is pspitatē ꝛ pacē tociⁱʹ
Xⁱanissi ꝛ spālit̃ Reḡ ꝛ pp̃ti Anglicani illustʹissimū p̃ncipē
Dn̄m ñrm regē Dn̄āqç reginā sēsqç incolas Dn̄os ꝛ coc̄s hⁱ⁹
ẽr̃ ꝛ p̃cipue ōs Fūdatorᵖs patᵒnos ꝛ bn̄factores nr̃i ordis ĩ cōi
çᵒ recomēdo orōibç vr̃is ōs fideles vivos ꝛ defūctos ꝛ spalit̃
aĩas dormicciū qui ĩ p̃rgatorio diñā m̃iaç p̃stolan⁽⁾ ut det it̃ ds
requiē ꝛ gt̃iaç sēpit̃nā.
    Igitʳ aĩe istore ꝛ aĩe patrū nr̃ore matrū fratū sorore ōniūqç
pentū ꝛ bn̄factore nᵉnō ꝛ omn̄ fideliū defūctore p di m̃iaç ĩ
pace reqˡescāt Vos ex pte Pⁱore qⁱ este sacerdot̃ celebrabitis
ꝛ qˡliç vr̃m celebrabit unā missā p̃ defūcte ꝛ qˡliç vr̃m qⁱ ostis
ex pte Abbis unā missā de b̄a vgine Maria Recomēdam⁹ vos
dn̄o ki mtu rog"cianẽ vobis de mora nr̃a ꝛ illā pacē q"m ds
reliquit suis disciptis tʰnsicns ex hᵒ mūdo ad p̃reç vobis
ṗoptam̃ʹⁱ ꝛ pax di q̃ exsupat ocēç ssᵐ exultet ĩ cordibç vr̃is
custodiēs corda vr̃a ꝛ inteligēeinas vr̃as. nr̃i si placeat ꝛ con-
vent̃ʹⁱ nr̃i i vr̃is orōnibç cotidie memorāte Et ad dm̃ site filii ꝛ
Frēs ꝛ bndicēo Dĩ oĩpotēte p̃riʎ ꝛ f. ꝛ s. s. descēdat ꝛ
maneat sup vos in ct̃num amen.
    Q. Ricardus Dove Monachus ꝛ scolaris de Bukfast—R. D.
M. de B.

THE
CISTERCIAN HOUSES OF DEVON.

IV.
NEWENHAM.

THE

CISTERCIAN HOUSES OF DEVON.

NEWENHAM.

199. This Abbey was situated in the parish of Axminster, at a short distance from the town. Founded by William de Mohun in 1245, the site of the Abbey was blessed, and the cemetery consecrated in the course of the following year.

200. It is not my intention to write the history of this house. This has been already done by the late Mr. James Davidson, in a manner which leaves little further to be said, and to his Memoir I would refer my readers.* I intend only to print some unpublished documents relating to the Abbey and to certain proceedings of its inmates hitherto unknown.

201. The second Abbot was Henry de Persolte, and in the first year of his abbacy a purchase of part of Shapwick was made of Henry de Burton and Mabilla his wife for a money consideration, the convent yielding in addition annually, on the Feast of the Nativity of St. John Baptist, a pair of white gloves. I give the original of the agreement entered into at Exeter on the Morrow of the Ascension, 1249. The payment appears to have been thirty marks, not thirty-five, as mentioned by Davidson, p. 158.

Hec est finaƚ concordia fca In Cuȓ dni Regᵽ apud Exoñ ln C⁰⁻stino Ascensionis Dñi Anno regni Regᵽ Henȓ fiƚ Regᵽ Joh̄ Triccsimo ƚcio Corā Rogo de Thurkelby Gilƀto de Prestoñ Maḡro Siñ de Wautoñ ꞇ Joḩe de Cobbeḩ Justicē Itiñ̄anē ꞇ aliis dni Regᵽ fideƚ tūc ibi ᵽsentibȝ Inƚ Henȓ Abƀem de Nowenḩ queȓꞇ Henȓ de Burtoñ ꞇ Mabiƚ vx ei⁹ impeđ de vna Carucē ƚre ꞇ dimiđ cū ptiñ in Shepwykᵽ. Unde plac̄ Waȓ carte suñ fuiƚ inᵽ eos in ead Cuȓ Sciltꝙđ ᵽđci Henȓ ꞇ Mabiƚ rec̄ ᵽđcam ƚra cū ptiñ esse ius ipius Abƀis ꞇ Ecctie sue de Neweham vt illā q̅ᵐ Id Abƀs ꞇ eccta sua pđca ƕnt de dono

* The History of Newenham Abbey, in the County of Devon, by James Davidson. London and Exeter. 1843.

U

p̃dcorᵹ Henr̃ ꝗ Mabit. Habenꝑ ꝗ tenendꝑ eid Abb̃i ꝗ succ̃ suis ꝗ ecctie sue p̃dc̃o de p̃dc̃is Henr̃ ꝗ Mabit ꝗ h̃ed ipius Mabit impp̃ Reddendo inde pann̄ vnū par̃ albarᵹ Cyrothocarᵹ ad Natitate sc̃i Joh̃ Baptᵒ p omī ṣuic̃o ꝗ exacc̃one. Et p̃dc̃i Henr̃ ꝗ Mabit ꝗ h̃ed ipius Mabit War̃ p̃dc̃o Abb̃i ꝗ succ̃ suis ꝗ ecctie suo p̃dc̃e p̃dc̃am ꞇram cū ꝑtiñ p p̃dc̃m ṣuic̃ cont⁻ om̃es h̃oies impp̃. Et p hc̃ rec̃ war̃ fine ꝗ concordia Idem Abb̃s dedit p̃dc̃is Henr̃ ꝗ Mabit Triginta Mᵘʳcas arḡnti.

Foot of Fines, Devon. Henry III. No. 446.

202. The next is the abridgment of John Prince (the author of "The Worthies of Devon," who was born in the house at Newenham Abbey,) of the account of the ceremonies attending the laying the foundation stone of the church. Prince heads his abstracts,—

[*Cartæ sequentes ob nimia prolixitate* abreviunter p J. P.]

Aᵒ gratie 1254 Idûs Septem̃. positus est primus Lapis super Fundamentū Ec̃te Bᵗᵉ Marie de Nyweham a venᵉˡˡ viro Dño Reginaldo de Moun Fundatore ejusd̃ abbathie; qui etiā tres Petras posuit, cruce signatas; et quartam petram posuit Dñus Witt̃mus de Moun frater dicti Reginaldi; Quintā petrā posuit Dñus Wymondus de Ralegh miles; et in secundo Anno postea Dñus de Smaleridge. Posite sunt he quinque petre in honorē sᵗᵉ Trinitaꞇ et bᵗᵉ Marie Virginis et ōium Sanctorū, pᵒsenꞇ tunc Dño Henrico tunc Abbate et omni Conventu.—(Add. MSS. 28,649, p. 370.)

203. The date given in the following copy of the deed of Reginald de Mohun, directing that his body should be buried before the high altar in the Abbey Church of Newenham, is different from that in the copy referred to by Davidson, and it appears to vary in other particulars.—See Davidson, p. 35.

Oĩbus sᵗᵉ Matris Ec̃te filijs &c. Regiñ de Moun Miles Dñus de Dunsterro Saluꞇ in Dño Sempiter̃. Affectione qua nos Novᶜᵗⁱˢ versus Monasteriū de Nyweham Exoñ Diocos quia nostra existit fundaꞇ Ab̃tem et Monachos Ord̃. Cisꞇ. ibidc̃ Deo et Gloriose virḡ Marie famulantibus ex devotione gerimus p̃sentibus,—— declaramus, volentes Corpus nostrū, cu ab cod Anima fuerit separata, in Ec̃ta de Nywehā ante majus altare honorifice sepeliend̃ legamus, et insuper expresse concedentes q̃d ubicūq, et quocunq, decesserim preterquā in Terra sancta p Heredes [vel] Alios Amicos Execuꞇ nostros Corpus ñrum apud Nyweham Sepeliend̃ deferatur. alioqui liceat memorato Ab̃ti et Monachis qui p tempore in dicto Monasterio existunt corpus ñrum p se vel p certos nuntios ad hoc specialiter Deputatos requirere et apud Nywehā deferre, vt p aliquos Amicorū ñrorum alibi (q̃d absit) humatū esset. In cujus rei testimoñ Sigillū meum apposuimus. Hijs Test̃. Dño Witto de Moun, Wimondo de Ralegh, Gervasio de Horton tunc vicecoñ Devoñ, Joñe Arondell, Warino de Ralegh Militibus; Witto de Bray, Reginaldo de Bath, Gilb̃. de Castello, Rado de Monte Sorell, Riĉo de Membyry, Ada Hunt et alijs. Dat̃ apud Dunstor iiij Kal. Jul. A° D. 1255.—Ibid. p. 423.

204. The record of the death of the founder follows:—

A°. D^l. 1257. 13 Kal. Feb. die Dominica in festo storū Fabiani et Sebastiani Reginaldus de Moun Dñus de Dunstorre et Fundator Abbathie de Nyweham viā universe Carnis ingressus est apud Torr in Coñ Devoñ.—Ibid. p. 371.

205. The kindness of Mr. J. M. Davidson, the son of the historian of Newenham, enables me to print a complete copy of the monkish rhymes in praise of Bishop Broncscombe with the original Latin extended.

        Plus de viro referam
        Qualiter et Nyweham
        Fovet et decorat
            Prout vobis dicere
            Possum necnon pandere
        Plurimum honorat.

        Ibi multum laboravit
        Et thesauros erogavit
        Eorum laboribus
            Quod nunc patet et patebit
            Gaudet homo que gaudebit
        Futuris temporibus.

        Primo sex altaria
        Per sua donaria
        Ibidem levavit
            Quæ de Dei gratiâ
            Manu suâ propriâ
        Post et dedicavit.

        Ex his autem senis aris
        Pars habet aquilonarie
        Ternas iu basilicâ.
            Quorum sancto Gabrieli
            Cunctis angelisque cæli
        Dedicatur unica.

Thomæ magistri secunda
Cujus luxit vita munda
Cunctisque martyribus
    Qui vi crucis triumphalis
    Caput hortis infernalis
Trivarunt sub pedibus.

Sanctæ quoque Katerinæ
Et virginibusque sine
Virili concubitu
    Ara tertia sancitur
    Illis eis et largitur
Laus devoto spiritu.

Aliæ quidem tres aræ
Latæ nunc ad angulare
Locis stant dividuis
    Quarum prima dedicatur
    Johanni qui plus amatur
In Dei discipulis.

Lucæ, sanctoque Matthæo,
Et ei quem signat leo,
Cunctis et apostolis,
    Quos gens Christianæ legis
    Jussis pœnâ summi Regis
Habet pro didasculis.

Annæ secundaque piæ,
Matri scilicet Mariæ,
Sanctisque conjugibus
    Qui per nuptialem vitam
    Aulam cœli concupitam
Habent pro laboribus.

In honore Nicholai
Preca leni qui vult trahi
Ad opem merentium
    Omniumque confessorum
    Qui fragrarunt in amorem
Stat altare tertium.

Multa post hæc fecit ibi,
O tu lector, quæ non tibi
Modo recitantur;
    Dicant hi de Nyweham
    Qui per Dei gratiam
Inde jam lætantur.

Igitur vos Sancti Dei
Subvenite, precor, ei
Implorantes veniam
    Qui nos tantus sit honore
    Et pro Christo sic labore
In domo de Nyweham.

Hinc vos qui de Nyweham
Estis ut memoriam
Præsulis habendo
    Deprecor ne taceat
    Vox laudis sed valeat
Gratias agendo.

Orantes cum credulis
Pro salute præsulis
Vos qui via honorat
    Germinat ut lilium
    Ante Dei filium
Pro quo sic laborat.

Pro Waltero confessore
Mentis visu cordis ore
Rogatis, carissimi.
    Ut in die mortis diræ
    Hunc dignetur custodire
Filius altissimi. Amen.

206. The following is the agreement with William de Staunton, permitting the monks to take stone from his quarry of Staunton, which was situated, it is stated, between the quarry of the monks of Ford and the grantor's arable land.

Oībus x^u fid p̃scñ Scripṫ visuṙ vel Auditūṙ Wiṫts fiṫ Wiṫti de Staūton miṫ saluṫ. Nov^{etis} me dedisse et concesṡ Deo et b^{te} Marie et fabrice Ecte in honorē eorund apud Nyweham incepte et Monachis ejusd Loci unā Acram de Quarrarea mea de Staunton jacentē inter Quarrariā Monachorū de Forda et P̃ram meā arabilem, et se extendenṫ ab oriente Longitudine 16 pticarū, et in Latitud versus Austrū 8 pticarū et adeo profunde sicut melius videretur expedire. Concessi etiā p me dictis Monachis et ministris q̃d hab̃ Liberū et idoneū ingresṡ et egresṡ p terram meam cū Carro et Carreta ad petrū Cariand &c. Pro hac autē donatione et concessione dedere mihi Abbas et Convenṫ de Nyweham septē marcas sterling̃ premanibus &c. In cujus rei testim̃ p^{esenti} Scripto sigillū meū apposui. Testibus Dño Henṙ de Aulton, Dño Andrea Rectore Ecte de Staunton Robto de Staunton fre ejus Rog⁹o de La Breche, Dño Hug tunc Priore de Newham et alijs. Dat mense Apr A°. D¹. 1279.—(Add. MSS. 28,649, p. 370.)

207. The next document is of some interest. It is the record of a dispute between the Abbot of St. Michael's Mount,—not the Cornish, but the French Abbey, that of St. Michael "*in periculo Maris*,"—and the Abbot of Newenham, as to rendering "*secta*" in respect of land in the manor of Yarcombe in the hundred of Axminster. The verdict of the jury was in favour of the French abbot. William de Saham, one of the justices itinerant, was a judge of the Court of King's Bench. William de Giselham, whose name often appears in the legal records, was the King's advocate, the names of Attorney and Solicitor-General not having been adopted until the reign of Edward IV. In 1229 Giselham was appointed one of the Judges of the Common Pleas.*

Ptita de Juratis ꝛ Assisis Coram Salam de Roffi ꝛ Sociis suis Justiciaȓ Itiƀantibꝫ Apud Exoñ In Com Devoñ In Octab Sči Martini Anno Regni Reg Edwardi fit Reg Henȓ Nono Incipiente Decimo. Boylund.

¶ Abbas sči Michis in picto mar sum fuit ad respond Abbi de Neweham de ptito qd fač sectam ad hundȓm suum de Axmenystre qᵃm ad illud face debet ꝛč Et unde dicit qd quidam Galfrs p̃deč suus fuit sēs de p̃dča secta p manⁱ cuj⁹dam Thurstani Abtis de Monte sči Michis in picto mar p̃deč p̃dči Abbis de Manlio de Yartekumbe ut de tribus sept in tres sept ut de feodo ꝛ Jure tpe pacis tp̃e Dñi H Reg pat̃s Dñi Reg nūc capiendo inde expleč ad valenč ꝛč Et qd tale sit Jus ꝛč off⁹t Et Abbas p Atorñ suū veñ Et defenď Jus suū ꝛ seisiᵃm p̃dči Galfri p̃deč ꝛč Et totū ꝛč. Et poñ se in magnam assiᵃm Dñi Reg. Et pet reč fieri utᵐ ip̃e maj⁹ Jus ħt tenendi p̃dčm manliū suū de Yartekumbe absq̃ hoc q̃d aliq̃m sᵃtam ei faciat p eodm ad hundredū p̃dči Abbis de Axemenystre sič tenet An idm Abbas de Newehᵃni ħndi p̃dčam sectam de t̃)bus septs in tres septis ꝛč. Et off⁹t Dño Regi dimid marc p ħnda mcoē de t̃pe Et Recipit' ꝛč. Et Witts de Radlegħ. Rads de Done. Rič̃s Coffyn ꝛ Ričs de Hydoñ qᵃtuor milites veñ ꝛ oligūt istos scitt Ričm de Hydoñ. Wiltm de Radlegħ. Radm de Done Ričm Coffyn Hugone de Radlegħ Wiltm de Albemarle. Henȓ de Radlegħ Joħem de Valle Torta de Clist Witm Punchardon. Radm fit Riči Warinum de sicca vill Joħem Punchardon Michem Trenchard Rogum

---

* Foss, Judges of England, p. 301.

fit Pagani Johm de Umfmivyt 𝄆 Wiltm le Prouz, qui dñt sup sacr̄m suū qd p̃dc̄us Abbas de Monte sc̄i Michis in picto mar̄ maj⁹ Jus ht tenendi p̃dc̄m mañliū de Yattecombe absq, p̃dc̄a secta faciend ad hundr̄m p̃dc̄i Abbis de Axemynstre de tribus septis in tres septiñ sic̄ tenet qᵃ p̃dc̄s Abbas de Neweh*m hndi p̃dc̄am sectam ad hundr̄m suū p̃dc̄m de l̃bus sept in tres sept Et I⁹o conɜ est q̄d Abbas de Monte sc̄i Michis in picto mar̄ 𝄆 succ̄ sui teneāt p̃dc̄m Mañliū de Yattecombe absq, p̃dc̄a secta faciend ad hundr̄m p̃dc̄m qⁱete de p̃dc̄o Abbe de Neweh*m 𝄆 succ̄ suis inppet Et Abbas de Neweh*m in mïa Et Wilts de Gyselh*m appoñ clañ p dño Rege.

Assize Roll Devon $\frac{\text{M}}{\overline{1}\atop{34}}$ 1 Memb: 13-d.

208. In 1301-2 at the Cornish Assize at Launceston the Abbot was called upon to show by what authority he claimed to hold the hundred and bailiwick of Stratton. This is referred to by Davidson, and I give the original entry from the Assize Roll.

Placita de Jur̄ 𝄆 assiɜ · · apud Lancenetoñ In Coñ Cornub In Octab sc̄i Michis Anno regni Regis Edwardi filij Regis Henr̄ Tricesimo.

ff Abbas de Niwenham suñ fuit ad respond dno Regi quo waranto clamat hre hundredum 𝄆 ballivam de feodo sine aliquo dando de hundredo de Strattoñ. Et Abbs per attorñ suū veñ Et dicit q̄d ip̃e 𝄆 eius p̃docessores sui a tempore quo nō exstat memoria habuerunt p̃dc̄am ballivam 𝄆 ea vsi fuerūt hucusque absq, aliqua interrupc̄oe. Et de hoc ponit se super patriam. Et Joh de Mutf* simitr In hundr̄o nichil clamat. Ideo reñ Regi. Jur̄ quo ad ballivam p̃dc̄am dicunt sup sacr̄m suū q̄d p̃dc̄us Abbas 𝄆 oñes predec̄ sui a tempe fundac̄ois Abbathie sue p̃dc̄e 𝄆 oñes alij qui Mañiūm de Nortoñ tenuerunt ante fundac̄oem p̃dc̄am huerunt ballivam p̃dc̄am 𝄆c̄ Ideo p̃dc̄us Abbas inde sine die salvo 𝄆c̄.

Assize Roll. $\frac{\text{M}}{\overline{1}\atop{21}}$ 1. m. 37.

209. The next, from the De Banco Roll, date 1317, refers

* *Joh'nes de Mutford*, in other Pleas—*qui sequitur pro Rege*.

to a claim by the Abbey against William Gel, chaplain, for the payment of £20 due from him.

Ptita apud Westm̃ coram Witts de Beresford ⁊ sociis suis Justic̄ Dñi Reḡ de Banco Termino Pasch̃ anno regni Regis E. filii Regis E. decimo.

De tribus septim̃ Pasch.

¶ Essoñ Abbtis de Nywynh*m op. se iiij. die versus Witto Gel Capellanū de ptito q̃d reddat ei viginti libr̃ quas ei debet ⁊ injuste detinet ⁊c̄ Et ip̃e nõ veñ Et p̃coptū fuit vic̄ q̃d sum̃ eū ⁊c̄ Et vic̄ nich inde fecit set mand̃ q̃d nich hot ⁊c̄ Et testatū est hic q̃d satis hot in eodē Com̃ tuo ⁊c̄ P̃o sicut p̃us p̃coptū est vic̄ q̃d sum̃ eū q̃d sit hic a die Sc̄i Michis in xv dies ⁊c̄. De Banco Roll, Easter, 10 Edw. II.

210. The next, 20 Edw. II. from the Pole Collections, refers to the gift of the Tyntens, of lands in Shapwick to the Abbey. See Davidson, p. 71.

Oĩbus X^{ti} fidel. &c. Frater Johes de Tynten Abbas de Neweham et ejus Loci convent̃ ex una p̃te et Alicia de Tynten Dña de Colury (?) et Johes Tynten mit̃ fil. ejus ex alt̃ pte de terris in Shapwick in Mañ de Axmister D. Dat̃. A. R. R. E. fil. R. E. 20, p. 56. Add. MSS. (B. M.) p. 381.

211. I give the next to preserve the names of the parties and of the witnesses. It is from the same source as the last. The Abbot is Walter de la Houe, the sixteenth abbot.

Sciant &c. q̃d Ego Henricus de la Ford persona Eccles. de Meriet* dedi &c. Johi de Carru mil. omnes ter̃ meas quas habui in La Moore in pochia de Loueputt. In cujus test. &c. Sigillũ meũ apposui Test. D^{no} Walt̃ Abbe de Newham Johe Franceis Witto Uphey Johe de Greneway Dat̃ apud Nyweham 27 E. 3.—Ibid. p. 381.

212. The next entry, from the De Banco Roll, relates to proceedings taken against Thomas Morton, a defaulting collector of the Abbey, who did not appear, and against whom judgment was given.

Waltus atte Hone Abbas de Nyweh"m p Wiltm de Elleworth att̃ suū op. se iiij. die ṽsus Thom̃ de Mortoñ de ptito q̃d reddat ei r̃onabilem compotū suū de tempe quo fuit receptor denar̃ ip̃ius Abbis ⁊ Johis de Gaytyngtoñ nup Abbis de Nyweham p̃decessoris p̃dc̄i Abbis ⁊c̄ Et ip̃e nõ veñ Et poec̄

* Probably Merriott, co. Somerset.

fuit viĉ q̃ disīr cū ɫc̃ Et viĉ modo manď qď nich hct ɫc̃ I°o preĉ est viĉ q̃d cap̃ eū ɫc̃ Et salus ɫc̃ Ita q̃d heat corpus eius hic in Octab̃ s̃ce Trinitaī p Justic̃ ɫc̃ Et vñ ɫc̃ Ad quē diē viĉ nō misit b̃re Io siĉ p'us preĉ est viĉ q̃d cap̃ eū si ɫc̃ Et saluo ɫc̃ Ita q̃d heat corpus eius hic in Octab̃ s̃ci Michis p Justic̃ ɫc̃.—De Banco Roll, Easter, 17 Edw. III. memb. 18 d.

213. A Mayor of Exeter is mentioned in the following entry relating to another debtor.

Preceptū fuit viĉ q̃d corpus Henr̃ de Lacy de com̃ suo si laicus esseī capet et in p'sona Regp̃ saluo custodiri faĉ donec Abb̃i de Nyweh'm de q'ndecim libr̃ plene satisfaĉ quas p̃dc̃us Henr̃ p'mo die ffebruar̃ anno regni dñi Regp̃ nūc Angł q'ntodecimo corā Henr̃ de Hugheton̄ nup maiore ciuitaī Exoñ ɫ Rob̃to de Lucy tūc ctico ad recogñ debitorȥ apud Exoñ accipienď deputaī recogñ se debere p̃dc̃o Abb̃i et quas ei soluisse debuit ad fm s̃ci Michis Archangeli tūc pẍ sequeñ et eas ei nōdū ɫc̃ Et qualiī ɫc̃ scire faĉ hic ad hūc diē sciī a die Pasche in xv dies ɫc̃ Et viĉ modo manď q̃d cepit corpus p̃dc̃i Henr̃ ɫ illud saluo ɫ securr̃ custod̃ faĉ sc̃dm tenorẽ b̃ris ɫc̃ I°o p̃dc̃us Abbas heat inde b̃re p statuī ɫc Et qualiī ɫc̃ viĉ scire faĉ hic in Octab̃ s̃ci Michis ɫc̃ Et vñ ɫc̃.—Ibid. memb. 49.

214. Walter Bourdenile had neglected to furnish a proper account, and proceedings were taken against him.

Walīus Abbas de Nyweham p Wiłtm de Elleworth atī suū op. se iiij. die ṽsus Waltm Bourdenyle de p̃tito q̃d redď ei rōnabilē compotū suū de tempe quo fuit receptor denar̃ Johis nup Abb̃is de Nyweham p̃decessoris ipius Walēi nūc Abb̃is de Nyweh'm ɫc̃ Et ip̃e nō veñ Et p̃reĉ fuit viĉ q̃d cap̃ eū ɫc̃ Et viĉ modo manď q̃d nō est inuent ɫc̃ I°o siĉ p'us preĉ est viĉ q̃d cap̃ eū si ɫc̃ Et saluo ɫc̃ Ita qď heat corpus eius hic a die s̃ce T'nitatis in xv dies p Justic̃ ɫc̃ Et viĉ sit ɫc̃.—Ibid. memb. 161 d.

215. Thomas Morton turns up again the following year [see 212], and Robert Cayphas was called upon to answer for the like neglects as Morton.

Walīus atte Hone Abbas de Nyweham p Wiłtm de Elleworth atī suū op. se iiij die ṽsus Thom̃ de Morton de p̃tito qď redď ei rōnabīlem compotū suū de tempe quo fuit receptor denar̃ ip̃ius Abb̃is ɫ Johis de Gaytyngton nup Abb̃is de Nyweham p̃decessorȷ p̃dc̃i Abb̃is ɫc̃. Et ip̃e nō veñ p̃c fuit viĉ q̃d cap̃ eum si ɫc̃. Et viĉ modo manď q̃d nō est inuent ɫc̃ I°o sicut prius p̄c̄ est vic̄ q̄d cap̄ eū si ꝉc̄. Et saluo ꝉc̄ Ita q̄d ħeat corpus eius hic in Octab̄ s̄ci Michis ꝉc̄.—Ibid. Easter, 18 Edw. III. memb. 46.

Walтus Abbas de Nywcham p Wilтm de Elleworth atт suū op. se iiij. die v̊sus Robтm Cayphas de ptito q̄d reddat ei r̄onabilē compotū suū de tempe quo fuit receptor denar̄ ip̄ius Abb̄is ꝉc̄ Et ip̄e nō veñ Et prec̄ fuit vic̄ q̄d capet eū ꝉc̄ Et vic̄ modo mand̄ q̄d nō est inuentus ꝉc̄ I°o sic̄ pluз prec̄ est vic̄ q̄d cap̄ eū si ꝉc̄ Et saluo ꝉc̄ Ita q̄d ħeat corpus eius hic a die s̄ci Michis in xv dies ꝉc̄ Et vic̄ sic ꝉc̄.—Ibid. memb. 134.

216. William Abraham, in 1343, was charged with stealing hay and rushes, and committing other depredations, and did not appear to defend himself.

Abbas de Nyweham p Wilтm de Elleworth atт suū op. se iiij. die v̊sus Wilтm Abraham de ptito q͏̃"re vi ꝉ armis clausit ip̄ius Abbis apud Axemynstre fregit ꝉ fenū ꝉ ruscos ad valenc̄ quadraḡ libr̄ ibidem inuenta cepit ꝉ asptauit ꝉ alia enormia ei intulit ad g⸗ue dampnū ip̄ius Abb̄is ꝉ cont⸗ pacē ꝉc̄ Et ip̄e nō veñ Et sic̄ prius prec̄ fuit vic̄ q̄d cap̄ eū ꝉc̄ Et vic̄ modo mand̄ q̄d nō est inuent⁹ ꝉc̄ I°o sic̄ plur̄ prec̄ est vic̄ q̄d cap̄ eū si ꝉc̄ Et saluo ꝉc̄ Ita q̄d ħeat corpus eius hic in Octabis s̄ci Michis ꝉc̄ Et vic̄ sic ꝉc̄.—Ibid. memb. 46 d.

217. The next is a complaint against the Convent. John at Sloo asserts that the Abbot and John Sangere had deprived him of forty sheep, of the value of one hundred shillings.

Ad huc de Octab̄ s̄ci Hillar̄.

⁋ Joħes atte Sloo op se iiij¹⁰ die v̊sus Walтm Abbтm de Nyweham ꝉ Joħem Sangere de ptito quare vi ꝉ armis quadraginta oves ip̄ius Joħis atte Sloo precij Centū solidorᶻ apud Rouerigge inventas ceperunt ꝉ abduxerunt ꝉ alia enormia ei intulerūt ad grave dampnū ip̄ius Joħis atte Sloo ꝉ cont⸗ pacem Reḡ ꝉc̄ Et ip̄i non veñ Et prec̄ fuit vic̄ q̄d distr̄ eos ꝉc̄ Et vic̄ modo mand̄ q̄d p̄dc̄us Abbas distr̄ p cat̄ ad valenc̄ duodeñ denar̄ Et m̄ p Joħem Scot et Henr̄ Dare I°o ip̄i in m̄ia Et sicut prius prec̄ est vic̄ q̄d distr̄ oū p om̄es ꝑras ꝉc̄ Et q̄d de exit̄ ꝉc̄ Et q̄d ħeat corpus eius hic a die Pasche in xv dies p Justic̄ ꝉc̄ Et de p̄dc̄o Joħe Sangere mand̄ vic̄ q̄d nichil ħet ꝉc̄ I°o prec̄ est vic̄ q̄d capiat eū si ꝉc̄ Et salvo ꝉc̄ Ita q̄d ħeat corpus eius hic ad ꝑfatū ꝉmiñ ꝉc̄ Et vñ ꝉc̄.—De Banco Roll, Hilary, 26 Edw. III. m. 21.

218. In the next the grievance is somewhat similar, but the Abbot is plaintiff, not defendant.

¶ Abbas de Nyweham p Johem de Cruk att̄ suū op. se iiij⁹ die v̄sus Rog̃m de Cabus de Lym de p̃tito quare vi ꝛ armis ducentos multones ip̄ius Abb̄tis preēij viginti libr̄a apud Swapwyk inventos cepit ꝛ abduxit ꝛ alia enormia ei intulit ad grave dampnū ip̄ius Abb̄tis ꝛ cont̄ pacem Reḡ ꝛc̄ Et īp̄e non ven̄ Et sicut plur̄ preē fuit vic̄ q̄d capet eꝛ si ꝛc̄ Et salvo ꝛc̄ Ita q̄d h̄eret corpus eius hic ad hunc diem scit̄ in octabis sc̄i hillar̄ ꝛc̄ Et vic̄ modo mand̄ q̄d non est inventus ꝛc̄ nec aliquid h̄et ꝛc̄ I⁹o preē est vic̄ q̄d exigi faē eū de Com̄ in Com̄ quousq̄ sedm legem ꝛ cons̄ ꝛc̄ vtlaget* si non compūlit Et si ꝛc̄ tūc eū cap̄ ꝛ salvo ꝛc̄ Ita q̄d h̄eat corpus eius hic in Octabis sc̄i Mich̄is ꝛc̄ Et vnde ꝛc̄.—Ibid. m. 41.

219. Here William Gilemyn is a defaulter in his accounts, and does not appear to justify himself.

¶ Joh̄es Abbas de Nyweham p Joh̄em de Chudd att̄ suū op. se iiij. die versus Witt̄m Gilemyn de p̃tito q̄d reddat ei r̄onabil̄e compotū suū de tempo quo fuit receptor denar̄ Rob̄ti de Pebbesbury quodā Abbatis de Niweham p̄decessoris p⁹dc̄i Joh̄is Abb̄tis ꝛc̄ Et ip̄se nō venit et fuit attach̄ p Witt̄m de Trenant ꝛ Ric̄m de Trenant īo ip̄i in m̄ia Et p̄cep̄t est vic̄ q̄d distr̄ eum p om̄es ter̄ ꝛc̄ Et q̄d de exit̄ ꝛc̄ Et q̄d h̄eat corpus eius hic In Octabis sc̄i hillar̄ ꝛc̄—Ibid. m. 33.

220. William de Stamford, the executor of the will of Simon of Farham, sues the Abbot on behalf of himself and his co-executors for £12 stated to be due from the former to the estate.

¶ Witt̄s de Staunford exec̄ test̄i Simonis de ffarnam p Thom̄ P*t att̄ suū op. se iiij¹⁰ die v̄sus Abb̄em de Nywenham de p̃tito q̄d reddat ei ꝛ Joh̄i Descures Rad̄o de Bereford ꝛ Witt̄o Dunmuire coexec̄ p̄dc̄i Witt̄i de Staunford duodecim libr̄ quas ei iniuste detinet ꝛc̄ Et ip̄e non ven̄ Et huit diem nūc hic posstq*m compuit in Cur̄ hic ꝛ cepit inde diem p̃ce pciū ꝛc̄ Io preē est vic̄ q̄d distr̄ eum p ōes fr̄ ꝛc̄ Et q̄d h̄eat corp⁹ ei⁹ hic in octabis Pur̄ b̄e Marie ꝛc̄. Et quia p̄dc̄i Joh̄es Rad̄us ꝛ Witt̄s Dunmuire ad p̃xm diem compuerūt hic ꝛ modo non secuntur ꝛc̄ Iō p̄dcus Witt̄s de Staunford sequat* sine ꝛc̄—Ibid. m. 337.

221. The next refers to another defaulting collector of some of the revenues of the Abbey.

¶ Abbas de Neuwenham p Johem de Chuddelegh att͠ suū op. se iiijᵗᵒ die v̄sus Walt̄um de Burdevill de p̄lito q̄d redd̄ ei r̄onabilem compotū suū de tempe quo fuit receptor denarior̄ ip̄ius Abb̄tis t̄c̄ Et ip̄e non ven̄ Et sicut plur̄ distr̄ p cat̄ ad valenc̄ duor̄ sulido₃ Et Mañ p Walt̄m de Bodget t̄· Johem de Kerle Iō ip̄i in m̄ia Et sicut plur̄ p̄ceptū est sic̄ q̄d distr̄ p om̄es p̄r t̄c̄ Et q̄d de exit t̄c̄ Et q̄d h̄eat corpus eius hic a die Pasche in xv dies t̄c̄ · Et vicⁿ sit t̄c̄—Idem. m. 263 d.

222. In 1366-7 Richard Branescombe, the Abbot, commenced proceedings against several persons for entering his land at Newenham and cutting down and carrying away trees of the value of £20, and against William Constance for cutting down growing trees at Clocombe [*Valor* Clokham] and digging stone at Foxhole.

¶ Abbas de Nywenham p Johem Prestecote att͠ suū op. se iiijᵗᵒ die v̄sus Rob̄m Strange Johem ffowel Johem Alhot Walt̄m West Wit̄tm Bertelot Wit̄tm Conyn̄g senior̄ Marḡiam Hayward Marḡiam Belle Johem South Roḡm Diegher Wit̄tm Hembury Juñ Wit̄tm Hembury senior̄ Johem Dulymere Wit̄tm Purs ad̄ Pratenesse Johem Toterigge t̄ Walt̄m Toterigge de p̄lito quare ip̄i simul cū Wit̄to Constance vi t̄ armis clausū ip̄ius Abb̄is apud Nywenham Park freḡunt t̄ arbores suas ad valenc̄ viginti libra₃ ibidem nup crescent̄ succiderunt t̄ asportaverunt t̄ alia enormia ei intulerunt ad gᵃve dampnū ip̄ius Abb̄is t̄ contra pacem Reḡ t̄c̄ Et ip̄i non ven̄ Et sicut plur̄ prec̄ fuit vic̄ q̄d capet eos si t̄c̄ Et salvo t̄c̄ Ita q̄d h̄eret corpa eo₃ hic ad hunc diem scit̄t a die sc̄i hillar̄ in xv dies t̄c̄ Et vic̄ modo mand̄ q̄d non sunt invent̄ t̄c̄ Io prec̄ est vic̄ q̄d eos de Com̄ in Com̄ quosq̄ t̄c̄ om̄es p̄ter p̄dc̄e Marḡia t̄ Marḡia vt̄lagentᵃˢ t̄ p̄dc̄e Marḡia t̄ Marḡia waiventᵃˢ si non t̄c̄ Et si t̄c̄ tunc eos capiat Et salvo t̄c̄ Ita q̄d h̄eat corpa eo₃ hic a die sc̄i Michis in xv dies Et vñ t̄c̄— Ibid. 41 Edw. III. Hilary. m. 198.

¶ Abbas de Newenham p Johem Prestecote att͠ suū op: se iiijᵗᵒ die v̄sus Wit̄tm Constance de p̄lito quare vi t̄ armis clausū ip̄ius Abb̄is apud Clocombe freḡ t̄ arbores suas ibidem nup crescentes succidit t̄ in quarrera sua apud ffoxhull fodit t̄ petras inde prectas ac arbores p̄dc̄as ad valenciā decem libra₃ cepit t̄ asportavit t̄ alia enormia t̄c̄ Et ip̄e non ven̄ Et p̄c̄ fuit vic̄ q̄d distr̄ eū t̄c̄ Et vic̄ modo mand̄ q̄d nichil h̄et t̄c̄ Io p̄c̄ est vic̄ q̄d capiat eū si t̄c̄ Et salvo t̄c̄ Ita q̄d h̄eat corpus eius hic a die Pasche in vnū Mensem p Justic̄ t̄c̄.— Ibid. m. 232 d.

NEWENHAM ABBEY.

223. In 1394, the Abbot, John Leggas, sued William, the Vicar of Axminster, for intruding upon his free warren at Axminster without licence, and taking fish, hares, rabbits, pheasants, and partridges.

¶ Abbas de Newenham p atī suū op. se iiij^{to} die v̄sus Wiłtm vicaī ccctie de Axmynstre Wiłtm fīt Joħis Toker de Cleyhill ꝗ Joħem Blakeforđ de p̄tito quare vi ꝗ armis libam warennā ip̄ius Abbis apud Axmynstre intraver̄ ꝗ in ea sine licencia ꝗ voluntate sua fugaver̄ ꝗ in sepali piscaria sua ibiđ piscati fuer̄ ꝗ piscē inde ad valenciā viginti libraȝ ac lepores cunic̄los phasianos ꝗ p̱drices de warenna pdc̄a cepunt ꝗ aspor· taver̄ ꝗ alia enormia ꝗc̄ ꝗ cont^a pacem Regis ꝗc̄ Et ip̄i non veñ Et prec̄ fuit vic̄ q̄d attach eos Et vic̄ modo mand q̄d nichil ħent Iō prec̄ est vic̄ q̄d capiat eos si ꝗc̄ Ita q̄d ħeat corpòra eoȝ hic a die Pasche in xv dies ꝗc̄ ad quem diem vic̄ non mis b̄re Iō sicut prius capiant^{us} q̄d sint hic in Octab̄ sc̄i Micħis.—De Banco Roll 18 Ric. II. Hilary m. 46d.

224. The following are records of similar proceedings to those already mentioned:—

¶ Abbas de Newenham p Joħem Dennynḡ atī suū op. es iiij^{to} die v̄sus Roḡum Carter cticum de p̄tito quare· vi ꝗ armis clausū ip̄ius Abbis apud Newenham fregit et arbores suas ibm nup crescentes ad valenc̄ decem libraȝ succidit ꝗ aspor- tavit ꝗ blada ꝗ herbam sua ibidem nup crescencia ad valenc̄ Centū solidoȝ cū quibusdā av̄ijs depastus fuit conculcavit ꝗ consumpsit ꝗ alia enormia ꝗc̄ ad grave dampnū ꝗc̄ et cont^a pacem Regis ꝗc̄ Et ip̄e non veñ Et prec̄ fuit vic̄ q̄d capet eū Et vic̄ modo mand q̄d non est inventus ꝗc̄ Iō sicut prius prec̄ est vic̄ q̄d capiat eū si ꝗc̄ Et salvo ꝗc̄ Ita q̄d ħeat corpus eius hic a die Pasche in tres septimanas ꝗc̄.—Ibid. M. 202d.

¶ Wiłłs Lange de Axmynstre p Thomam Brokhampton atī suū op. se iiij^{to} die v̄sus Abb̄m de Newenham de p̄tito q̄d reddat ei decem libras Et v̄sus Joħem Ryde de Colyforđ de p̄tito q̄d reddat ei centūm solidos quos ei debent ꝗ iniuste detinent ꝗc̄ Et ip̄i non veñ Et sum̄ ꝗc̄ Juđm attach q̄d sint hic a die Pasche in tres septimanas ꝗc̄.—Ibid. m. 217d.

225. The next appears to be a record of the fresh proceed- ings in the protracted litigation between Thomas Carew, on the death of Robert Grymeston in 1401, and the Convent, with respect to the right of presentation to the Church of Luppit. See Davidson, p. 75 *et seq.*

¶ Thomas Carreu Chivaler p attorñ suū op sc iiij^to die vsus Johem Abbem de Nyweham ꞇ Vincencium atte Hille Capellm de plito q̃d pmittant ipm presentare idoneam psonam ad ecctiam de Lovepitte que vacat ꞇ ad suam spectat donacõem ꞇc̃ Et ipi non veñ Et huerunt inde diem p ossoñ suos hic vsq̨ ad hunc diem ꞇc̃ Iõ prec̃ est vic̃ q̃d distr̃ eos p omēs l̃ras ꞇc̃ Et quod heat corpa eoꝝ hic in Octab sc̃i Michis ꞇc̃.— De Banco Roll 1 Henry IV. Trinity. m. 71d.

226. The following year we have some further entries. In the second Thomas Carew is still pursuing his action against the Convent. His proceedings were ultimately unsuccessful.

¶ Jacobus Chuddelegh Miles p attorn suū op. sc iiij^to die vsus Ric̃m Abbem de Dunkeswell ꞇ Johem Abbem de Nyweham de plito q̃d vl̃q̨ eoꝝ reddat ei viginti libras quas ei debet ꞇ iniuste detinet ꞇc̃ Et ipe non veñ Et prec̃ fuit vic̃ q̃d Attach eos ꞇc̃ Et vic̃ modo mand̃ quod vl̃q̨ eoꝝ Attach est p Johem Holme ꞇ Thomam fforster Iõ ipi in m̃ia ꞇc̃ Et prec̃ est vic̃ q̃d distr̃ eos p omnes l̃ras ꞇc̃ Et q̃d de exit ꞇc̃ Et q̃d heat corpa eoꝝ hic A de sc̃i Michis in xv dies ꞇc̃— De Banco Roll, 2 Henry IV. Trinity. m. 176d.

¶ Jur^a inꝑ Thomam Carreu Chivaler quer̃ ꞇ Johem Abbem de Nyweham de plito quare ipi impedit ponit" in respem hic visq̨ a die sc̃i Michis in xv dies Nisi Justic̃ d̃ni Regis ad assĩas in Com̃ p̃dco capiend̃ assigñ p formam statuti ꞇc̃ die veñis px̃ post fm sc̃i Jacobi Apli apud Exoñ prius veñint p defcu Jur̃ quia nult veñ Iõ vic̃ heat corpa ꞇc̃.—Ibid. m. 319d.

227. An account of a daring deed is preserved in the next extract from the De Banco Roll. Thomas Usher and others appear to have taken the Abbot, Leonard Houndalre, prisoner and carried him from Newenham to Bykele, and also detained his goods and chattels to the value of £40. The defendants did not put in an appearance.

¶ Abbas de Nywenham p attorñ suū op. sc iiij^to die vsus Thom̃ Ussher Ric̃m Tryst ꞇ Radm̃ Paym de Colmptoñ de plito quare ipi siml cū Johe Prentys de Honytoñ Reginaldo Baker de Bradenynche ꞇ Johe Vautard de Clyst vi ꞇ armis ipm Abbem apud Nywenham ceperunt ꞇ ipm abinde usq̨ Bykele duxerunt ꞇ ipm imprisonaverunt ꞇ malo tractaverunt ꞇ ipm sic in prisona ibm̃ quousq̨ idem Abbas finem p decem libras p delibac̃õne sua henda cū pfat Thoma Ric̃ Rado Johe Reginaldo ꞇ Johe fecisset detinuerunt ꞇ bona ꞇ catalla suā ad valenc̃ quadraginta libraᵣ apud p̄dc̃am villam de Nywenham inventa ceperunt ꝛ asp̄ortaverunt Et alia enormiū ꞇc̃ ad g"ᵛe dampnū ꞇc̃ Et contᵃ pacem Regꝑ ꞇc̃ Et ip̄i non veñ Et sicut pluꝛ prec̃ fuit vic̃ qđ capet eos ꞇc̃ Et vic̃ modo manđ qđ non sunt inventi ꞇc̃ Iđ sicut pluꝛ capiantʳ Ita qđ sint hic a die sc̄i Michis in xv dies p justic̃ ꞇc̃.—De Banco Roll, 5 Henry IV. Trinity. m. 307.

228. The following relate to other legal proceedings, and sufficiently describe themselves. The third shows that the Abbot was a receiver for the Prince of Wales, probably of the revenues of the Duchy of Cornwall.

¶ Abbas de Nywenham p attorñ suū op. se iiijᵗᵒ die v̄sus Ric̃m Trīst de p̄lito quare cum de ꞉c̄oi consilio regni Reḡ Angꞇ pvisum siꞇ q̃d non liceat alicui vastum vendic̄c̄em seu destruc̄c̄oem facõ de ꞇris domibᴣ boscis seu gardinis sibi dimissis ad ꞇmiñ vite vel annoᵣ idem Ric̄us de domibᴣ boscis ꞇ gardinis in Tuddeheys que Ric̄us Excestre nuꝑ Abbas de Nywenham pdecessor p̄dci nunc Abbis p̄fato Ric̃o dimisit ad ꞇmiñ annoᵣ fecit vastum vendic̄oem ꞇ destruc̄c̄oem ad oxhedac̄ᵉᵉm ecclio ip̄ius Abbtis be Marie de Nywenham ꞇ contᵘˢ formā pvisionis p̄dc̃e Et ip̄e non veñ Et attach est p Johem Mey ꞇ Ric̃m Masoñ I'o ip̄i in m̄ia Et prec̃ est vic̃ q̃d distꝛ eū p om̄es ꞇras ꞇc̃ Et q̃d de exit̄ ꞇc̃ Et q̃d heat corpus eius hic a die sc̄i Michis in vnū Mensem ꞇc̃.—De Banco Roll, 8 Hen. IV. Trinity. m. 79.

¶ Johes Palmer de Brydport p attorñ suū op. se iiijᵗᵒ die v̄sus Leonardū Abbem de Newenham de p̄lito quod reddat ei quadraginta solidos Et v̄sus Aliciam que fuit vx̄ Johis Cole de Southmoltoñ de p̄lito q̃d reddat ei decem marcas Et v̄sus Stephm Burdescombe de p̄lito q̃d reddat ei quadraginta solidos quos ei debent ꞇ iniuste detinent Et ip̄i non veñ Et prec̃ fuit vic̃ q̃d suñ eos ꞇc̃ Et vic̃ manđ q̃d p̄deus Abbas suñ est Judm attach q̃d sit hic in Octabis sc̄i Michis Et de p̄dcis Alicia ꞇ Stepho manđ vic̃ q̃d nichil hent ꞇc̃ I'o capiantᵘˢ q̃d sunt hic ad p̄faꞇ ꞇmiñ p Justic̃ ꞇc̃ ad quem vic̃ non mis̄ bꝛe I'o pdc̄us Abbas sicut prius et p̄dci Alicia ꞇ Stephus sicut prius [to Hil. then to Easter.]—Ibid. m. 433d.

¶ Honꝛ Princeps Wall p attorñ suū op. se iiijᵗᵒ die v̄sus Abbem de Newenham de p̄lito q̃d reddat ei ꝛonabilem compotū suū de tempore quo fuit receptor denaꝛ ip̄ius Principis Et ip̄e non veñ Et suñ ꞇc̃ Judm attach q̃d sit hic a die sc̄i Michis in tres sepꞇias ꞇc̃.—Ibid. m. 527d.

¶ Jur" in? Johem Calmadya in ppria psona sua quer et Leonardū Abbem de Neweham do ptito t"nsgr ponit" in respēm coram Dño Rege vsq, in C"stino sēi Johis Bapte vbicūq, tc p defcu Jur Quia nullus tc I'o vic heat corpa tc Idem dies dat est ptib; pdcis tc.

¶ Jur" in? Ricm Calmadya in ppria psona sua quer' et Leonardū Abbem de Neweham Michm the Abbotes servant of Neweham t Thomam the Abbotes servant of Neweham de ptito t"nsgr pōit" in respēm coram Dño Rege vsq, in C"stino sēi Johis Bapte vbicūq, tc p detēu Jur Quia nullus tc I'o vic heat corp tc Idem dies datus est ptib; pdcis tc.—Coram Rego Roll. Easter, 11 Henry IV. m. 8d.

¶ Abbas de Newenham qui tam p dno Rege q"m p se ipo sequit" p att suū op. se iiij^to die vsus Johem Colewille de ptito contemptus t t"nsgr cont" forma statuti eo svientib; nup editi et ipe non ven et pceptum fuit vic qd capet eū et vic rotorn qd ipo non est invent tc I'o pceptū est vic qd Exigi fat eū de Com in Com quousq, tc vtlaget" si non tc et si tc tunc eum capiat Et salvo tc Ita qd heat corpus eius corā dno Rege in Crastino Pur be Marie vbicūq, tc Et vnde a die Pascho in xv dies.—Ibid. m. 8d.

229. The first of the last three documents I am able to quote shows that the Abbey had property upon the water as well as on the land, the Abbot of Abbotsbury, in the county of Dorset, and others, being charged with having taken a ship the property of the Monks of Newenham. Nicholas Wysebeche, the Abbot, appeared at Exeter in person to support the complaint.

¶ Nichus Abbas de Nyweham in ppria psona sua op. se iiij^to die vsus Robtm Abbem de Abbotysbury in Com Dors Radm Cokwyll de Abbotysbury in pdco Com Dors yoman Johem Walshe de Dorchester in eodem Com Dors yoman Ricm Hille de Waymouth in pdco Com Dors yoman Wittm Sandwyche de Seton in pdco Com Devon yoman de ptito quare vi t armis quandam navem ipius Nichi Abbis precij quadraginta libra; apud Seton invent ceperunt t abduxerunt t alia enormia tc Ad g"ve dampnū tc Et cont" pace Reg tc Et ipi non ven Et prec fuit vic qd attach eos tc Et vic modo mand qd quilibet eo; attach est p Ricm ffoys t Johem Gyon I'o ipi in mia I'o prec est vic qd distr eos p omes tras tc Et qd de exit tc Et qd heat corpora eo; hic a die sce Trinitatis in xv dies tc [Further postponed to

Mich., Hil., Easter, and Mich. following.]—De Banco Roll.
6 Henry V. Easter, m. 248.

¶ Nichus Abbas de Nyweham p Johem Trelay att̃ suū op. se iiij¹⁰ die v̄sus Withm ffrankeleyn de Setoñ in Com̃ p̄dc̃o Bocher de p̃lito quare vi ↄ̃ armis bona ↄ̃ catalla ip̄ius Abb̃tis ad valenciam centū solidoȝ apud Bere inventa cepit ↄ̃ asportavit Et alia enormia ↄc̃ ad g"ve dampnū ↄc̃ Et cont" pacem ↄc̃ Et ip̃e non veñ Et sicut plur̃ prec̃ fuit vic̃ q̃d capet eum si ↄc̃ Et salvo ↄc̃ Ita q̃d h̃eret corpus eius hic ad hunc diem scitt a die Pasche in xv dies Et vic̃ modo mand q̃d non est inventus ↄc̃ I'o prec̃ est vic̃ q̃d exigi fac̃ eum de Com̃ in Com̃ quousq̨ ↄc̃ vtlaget"si non ↄc̃ Et si ↄc̃ tunc eum capiat Et salvo ↄc̃ Ita q̃d h̃eat corpus eius hic in crastino aiaȝ Et vnde.—Ibid. m. 269 d.

¶ Walt̃us Coo̊k cticus in pp̃ia psona sua op se iiij¹⁰ die v̄sus Nich̃m Abb̃em de Nywenham in com̃ p̃dc̃o de p̃lito q̃d reddat ei centum solidos Et v̄sus Adam Geraunt de Axemynstr̃ in eodem com̃ Husbondman ↄ̃ Johannam vx̄em eius de p̃lito q̃d reddant ei centū solidos quos ei debent ↄ̃ iniuste detinent ↄc̃ Et ip̃i non veñ Et prec̃ fuit vic̃ q̃d attach̃ eos ↄc̃ Et vic̃· modo mand q̃d utq̨ coȝ attach̃ est p Ric̃m Brouñ ↄ̃ Johem Coll I'o ip̃i in m̃ia ↄc̃ Et prec̃ est vic̃ q̃d distr̃ eos p om̃es t̃ras ↄc̃ Et q̃d de exit̃ ↄc̃ Et q̃d h̃eat corpora coȝ hic in Octabis sc̃e Trinitatis ↄc.—Ibid. m. 271.

¶ Joh̃es Cole in pp̃ia psona sua op se iiij¹⁰ die v̄sus Nich̃m Abb̃em de Nywenham in com̃ p̃dc̃o de p̃lito q̃d reddat ei octo libras ↄ̃ duodecim solidos Et v̄sus Leonardū Abb̃em de Clyff in com̃ Som̃s de p̃lito q̃d reddat ei octo libras ↄ̃ decem solidos Et v̄sus Joh̃em Parys de Dertemouth̃ in com̃ Devoñ mercatorem de p̃lito q̃d reddat ei octo marcas Et v̄sus Ric̃m Worthy de Dertemouth̃ in eodem com̃ Devoñ Bocher de p̃lito q̃d reddat ei quadraginta ↄ̃ sex solidos ↄ̃ octo denar̃ Et v̄sus Joh̃em Brouñ de Wyke in p̃dc̃o com̃ Som̃s husbondman [q̃d] reddat ei quadraginta solidos quos ei debent ↄ̃ iniuste detinent ↄc̃ Et prec̃ fuit vic̃ q̃d distr̃ p̃dc̃os Abb̃em de Nywenham ↄ̃ Abb̃em de Clyff ↄ̃ Joh̃em Parys Et eciam sicut prius q̃d capet p̃dc̃os Ric̃m ↄ̃ Johem Brouñ ↄc̃ Et vic̃ modo mand q̃d vtq̨ p̃dc̃oȝ Abb̃tum distr̃ est p catalla ad valenc̃ quadraginta denar̃ Et vtq̨ coȝ m̃ p Ric̃m Poyer Joh̃em Waye Joh̃em Treysewe ↄ̃ Henricū Waye I'o ip̃i in m̃ia Et sicut prius prec̃ est vic̃ q̃d distr̃ eos p om̃es t̃ras ↄc̃ Et q̃d de exit̃ ↄc̃ Et q̃d h̃eat corpora coȝ hic a die sc̃e

Trinitatis in xv dies Et de p̃dc̄o Joħe Parys manđ vic̄ q̃d nichil ħet ꝉc̄ Et de p̃dcis Ric̄o ꝉ Joħe Broun manđ vic̄ q̃d non sunt invenꝉ ꝉc̄ l'o p̃dc̄us Joħes Parys capiat[us] et eciam sicut plur p̃dc̄i Ric̄us Broun̄ capiant" Ita q̃d sint hic ad pfatū t̄miñ ꝉc̄ Ad quē dic̄ vic̄ non misit bre ꝉc̄ l'o sicut plur̃ p̃dc̄i Abt̄es distr̃ ꝉc̄ [for Mich term, then in Hilary term all the defendants to be here].—Ibid. m. 329 d.

230. The arms of the Abbey were apparently those of the founder De Mohun. The common seal was the Blessed Virgin seated, with the Holy Child, under a canopy, with shields on each side,—one bearing the engrailed cross of Mohun, the other the Maunche. The legend is ꝉ. COĦ=VENTVS MONASCERH DE NVIMEĦAN. Three of the Abbot's seals are mentioned and described by Davidson, p. 87.

231. For a description of the remains of the buildings I must refer my readers to the History of Mr. Davidson, to which work my paper is only supplemental. The monastic buildings were on the south side of the church, and probably the whole ground-plan could be traced by excavation. Of the magnificent church, nearly three hundred feet in length, within the walls of which the bodies of many distinguished persons were laid, not a vestige remains above the ground, and the other scanty remains are gradually disappearing. The east end of the building, with the Early English triplet light, of which Mr. Davidson gives an engraving, has now fallen. The little stream, the invariable accompaniment of a Cistercian abbey, sometimes overflows its banks, and washes out from the adjoining soil human bones, indicating the site of the monks' cemetery. No crime of its inmates, no conspiracy against the common weal, brought the stately house of Newenham thus low. The pension list attests that the abbot and his monks were honest and of good conversation, and they and their property but shared the common fate of thousands as guiltless as themselves.

232. The evidence for the history of this house is full and interesting. The cartulary and some of the original books of the Abbey are in existence. They are referred to by Mr. Davidson and fully described, and Dr. Oliver prints in the appendix to his notice in the *Monasticon Devoniensis* some interesting documents.

APPENDIX.

LIST OF THE ABBOTS OF NEWENHAM.

Names.	Dates.	Authorities.
John Godard	1246-1248	
Henry de Persolte, or Spersholte	1248-1250	
John de Ponte Roberti . .	1250-1252	
Geoffry de Blanchville . .	1252-1262	
Hugh de Cokeswell . .	1262-1265	
John de Northampton . .	1265-1272	
William de Cornubia . .	1272-1288	To 1347 the chartulary
Richard de Chichester . .	1288-1293	of the Abbey com-
Richard de Pedirton . .	1293-1297	piled in the abbacy of
William de Fria . . .	1297-1303	Walter de la Houe.
Richard de Pedirton, again .	1303-1304	
Ralph de Shapwick . . .	1304-1314	
Robert de Pupplisbury . .	1314-1321	
John de Cokiswille . . .	1321-1324	
John de Geytyngton . .	1324 1338	
Walter de la Houe . . .	1338-1361	Davidson,
Richard Branescombe . .	1361-1391	Oliver's Monasticon,
John Legga's	1391-1402	the Bishops' Regis-
Leonard Houndalre . . .	1402-1413	ters, &c., &c., are the
Nicholas Wysebeche . .	1413-1431	authorities for the
Trystram Crucherne . .	1431-1456	names and times of
William Hunteford . .	1456- ?	election of the suc-
John ? . .	? 1512	ceeding Abbots.
John Ellys	1512-1525	
John Ilmynster, alias Cabell .	1525-1530	,,
Richard Gyll	1530-1539	,,

THE
CISTERCIAN HOUSES OF DEVON

V.

DUNKESWELL.

THE CISTERCIAN HOUSES OF DEVON.

DUNKESWELL.

233. Dunkeswell Abbey, one of the three Cistercian houses, the others being Newenham and Ford, situated within a comparatively short distance of one another in the east of the county, has but a meagre history. Founded in 1201, by the piety of William Lord Briwere or Bruere, it flourished for nearly three hundred and fifty years.

234. In 1199 William Briwere purchased the manor of Dunkeswell of Henry de la Pomeroy, which purchase was confirmed by King John at York, 28th March, in the first year of his reign. There seems however some little confusion here, for the property formerly belonged to William Fitzwilliam, who was compelled by his necessities* to borrow money of a Jew and mortgage Dunkeswell manor. It is said that William Briwere redeemed the land from the Jew, but the evidence offered by the confirmation charter of King John above mentioned contradicts this.

235. Early in the new century the new Abbey was founded, —*Dunkewelle fundata est*, say the Annals of Waverley,† and by a deed dated at Southampton on 13th April, in the seventh year of his reign, King John confirmed the lands the donation of William Briwere, as well as those the gifts of others.

236. The gifts of William Briwere were all his lands in Doneke-well and Wolford and the advowsons of the churches there; the abbot and convent of Ford gave their right in Biwood; Richard de Hydon all his land in Burcheghe; Richard de Treminett all his land in Bautescnapp; William de Pynn all his land in Bautescnapp; John de Thoriton a ferling of land in Stenetewde; Ivo Fitz-Allen the manor of Sobbecumbe; Richard de Mannesley a tenement in La Cumba [Marlecombe]; Thomas de Duna all his land in

* Lysons' Devon, p. 170.
† Ann. Waverleia, Ann. Monast. vol. ii. p. 253.

Uggaton, and a tenement in Codeford; Philip de Gatesden a ferling of land in Uggaton (this was a purchase); Robert Fitzanne all his right in the tenement of Lynor and Bywood; and Ursellus Fitzwilliam his right in the same tenements.

237. In the 11th year of the succeeding monarch, Henry III., we have a further confirmation of the possessions of the Abbey, from which we find that the founder and others had bestowed further gifts upon the house. Besides the lands of Dunkeswell and Wolford, Briwere had given it all his lands in the manor of Ufculme, with the mill there, and the monks of Ford had bestowed upon their newly settled brethren, besides Biwood, all their lands in Bolcham, Freschic, Bocland, Lodreford, and Hickersdon; Robert, the nephew of Robert le Goiz, his right in Lynor, and Avicia de Dun her land at Hoked.

238. It is easy to understand the gifts of the Cistercians of Ford, for Dunkeswell was her daughter, the new Abbey having been colonised by monks from the house of the foundation of Adelicia de Brioniis.

239. The powerful founder selected Dunkeswell as the place of his interment, passing by the other religious foundations which owed their existence to his bounty, and there in the year 1227, in the choir of the Abbey church, his body was laid. It is supposed that his lady was also buried there, for a short time since two stone coffins, covered with plain slabs of Purbeck, were found, each containing a skeleton, one of a man, the other of a woman. In all probability these were the bones of Lord Briwere and his wife, thus disturbed after a period of nearly six hundred and fifty years. All the bones were placed in one of the coffins and reinterred; the other coffin still remains above the ground, and may be seen under the south-east wall of the present churchyard of Dunkeswell Abbey.

240. We have but few documents illustrative of the history of Dunkeswell. The course of its existence appears to have been uneventful. We do not even know who the first abbot was, and the names of his immediate successors are wanting, but I am able to furnish the name of an abbot earlier than any yet recorded. This is Richard, who in 1228 bought of Richard de Crues three hundred and sixty-eight acres of land in Coleton.

Hec est finał concordia fca in Curia Dñi Reḡ apd Exoñ die sċi Jacoḃ Apłi Anno Regñ Reḡ Henr̃ fit Reḡ Joħis

Duodecim. Corā Thoṁ de Muleton Roḃto de Lexinton Rad Musard Joħe de Baioc̄ ꝫ Jordañ Oliỽ Justic̄ Itiñantib; ꝫ aliis dñi Reḡ fidelib; ꝉc̄ ibi p̄sentib;. Inͭ Rīc de Crues petentē ꝫ Ricard Aḃḃem de Donekewitt Tenentē de Tricent̄ ꝫ sexaginta ꝫ octo acris p͛re cū ptiñ in Coletoñ. Uñ placīt fuit inͭeos i p͛fata Curia. Scit qd̄ p̄dēs Rīc remisit ꝫ q'et clamavit de se ꝫ ħedib; suis Ip̄i Abbati ꝫ successorib; suis ꝫ Eccͭic sue de Donekewitt in ppetuū. Totū Jus ꝫ clamiū quod habuit in tota p̄dc̄a t̄ra cū ptiñ. Et p hᵃ⁻ remissioē q'eta clamācia fino ꝫ cōcordia Idē Abbas dedit p̄dc̄ō Rīc q'nq̨m arc̄ argñti. —Feet of Fines, Henry III. Devon, No. 83.

241. The next Abbot of whom we have any mention is Ralph, *Vir quidem morum gravitate ac sapientiæ fulgore non mediocriter adornatus.* He it was probably who obtained, in 1242, Sept. 21st, from the nephew of the founder, William Briwere Bishop of Exeter, an appropriation of the emoluments of the parish church of Dunkeswell, and a few days afterwards, 30th Sept., the Bishop gave to the Abbey the advowson and revenues of another church dedicated to St. David, and called Doddington, which cannot now be traced. In 1251 Ralph, who had been a monk of Tintern, was appointed Abbot of Waverley, in Surrey, and left the banks of the Culme for those of the Wey. He succeeded on the death of Abbot Walter Giffard, the 10th Abbot, in 1252. The Annals of Waverley say:—" Litera dominicalibus B. dies Paschæ xvi. Kal. Maii. Eodem anno dominus Radulphus monachus Sancte Mariæ de Waverleia, qui quondam abbatizaverat in domo de Tinterna, electus est in abbatem de Donekwell: vir quidem morum gravitate ac sapientiæ fulgore non mediocriter adornatus."—Ann. Wav. p. 336.

242. Ralph was succeeded by Thomas, whose name occurs as early as 1253. In 1259, Dec. 5th, Bishop Bronescombe dedicated a new parish church at Dunkeswell. In the following February he issued a decree with reference to the church of Doddeton, the font and bells of which had been removed, and the building altogether disused for divine service. The Abbot and convent were cited to appear, and admitting the facts, submitted themselves to the Bishop's directions, which were that the church should be re-opened and daily service said therein. During the rule of this Abbot he greatly increased the possessions of the convent by exchanges and dealings with the Prior of St. John of Jerusalem.

243. Between Thomas and John the next Abbot, according to Oliver, is a long lapse of time, and there is little doubt but that the names of some intermediate Abbots are wanting. I am able to furnish some information as to what took place in connection with the house during this period, but unfortunately the names of the Abbots mentioned are not given. The first is from the Hundred Roll, the jury finding that the Abbey held the manor of Broadhembury, in the Roll called " de Hambiri."

           Hoc est veredcm Hundr̃ de Harrig̃.
Henr̃ de Kyngesford. Joh̃es Norman. Robt̃s de Cliffewilmo. Rič̃s de la Forde. Walt̃s de Ba. Witt̃s le Engleys. Witt̃s de Godeford. Petrus de Fonte. Pħs de Siccavilla. Rog̃s de la More. Drogo de Foforde, ꝉ Robt̃s le Engleys duodecim Jur̃ de Harrig̃g̃ d̃nt sup sacr̃m suum quod   *   *   *
   *   *   *   *   *
Ītm d̃nt q̃d Abbas de Donkeswille tenet mañium de Hambiri q̃, quondam ptinebat ad baroniam de Toritone In t̃pe Witti de Toritone Qui Witt̃s dedit d̃em mañium cū suis ptinenč Witto Briwere ꝉ idem Witt̃us Briwere dedit d̃em mañium deo Abbati de Donkeswille in lib̃am ꝉ ppetuam elemosiam.

¶ Et Idem Abbas ht furc"'s ass" panis ꝉ c̃visie ptinenč ad ad p̃d̃em mañiū suū de Hambir̃ ex antiq⁰ ꝉ ex ec̃firmačone d̃ni reg̃ Joh̃is ꝉ d̃ni reg̃. H. p̃ris reg̃ qui nunc est. Et d̃na Amicia comitissa devonie ht furcas   *   *   *   *
—Exchequer, Treasure of Receipt. Hundred Rolls; Devon, No. 18.

244. From the Coroner's Roll I am able to refer to what appear to be important proceedings taken by the Abbot against certain persons who had wrongfully entered upon the manor of Hakepenne, and ejected the monks and conversi belonging to the abbey who happened to be there.

¶ Joh̃s de Cogan Thom̃ filius ejus Pħus de Cogan ꝉ Robt̃s de Stolkeye Joh̃s Comyn Rič̃us de la Hutt Eusth̃s le Heyward Robt̃s le Seler de Ofcomt Rog̃s de la Forde Witt̃us le Turner Rič̃s de la more Joh̃s Boneweye Watt̃s Hogh̃ Witt's le Haueker * Joh̃s Evered̃d̃ Rič̃us le Bakere. Witt̃s Scribi ꝉ Robt̃s Scotte attach̃ fuerūt ad respond̃ Abbt̃i de Donekeswell de plito quar̃ ip̃i simt cū Robt̃o le Hunte Gilbt̃o Hereward ꝉ aliis malefactorib; ignotis mañiū ip̃ius Abbt̃is apud Hakepenne vi et armis ingressi domos suas ibid̃m freg̃unt ꝉ furcas ejusd̃m

---

    * Hawker elsewhere.

Abbtis in solo suo pp'o ibidm̄ juxta libtates Abbatib; ejusdm̄ loci p pgenitor̄ regis concessas ut dicit' levatus noctant' pst"vūt asptavūt ꝗ cōbusserūt ꝗ monacos convsos abbath p̄dc̄e ibidm̄ inventos inde ejec̄runt in īpius Abbtis dāpnū gravissimū ꝗ cont" pacē ꝗc̄ Et unde idm Abbas quer' qd p̄dc̄i Johs ꝗ alii simul cū p̄dc̄is Robto le Hunte Gilbto Hereward ꝗ aliis malefactorib; ignotis in vigilia sc̄o; innocenciū Anno r̄ Dn̄i Regis nunc vicesimo septimo Mañliū p̄dc̄m īpius Abbtis de Hakepenne vi ꝗ armis ingressi domos suas ibidm fregunt ꝗ furcas ejusdm̄ Abbaī' jux" libtates p̄dc̄as ꝗc̄ ibidm levatas noctant' pst"vūt ꝗ illas asptavūt usq mañliū p̄dc̄i Johis de Cogan de Ofcomb * ꝗ ibi illas cōbusserī ꝗ monacos ꝗ convsos Abbathie p̄dc̄e in p̄dc̄o mañio de Hakepenne inventos inde ejec̄unt ꝗ svientes īpius Abbis videli Phm le Messer ꝗ Johm de Heyles vbavūt vlnavūt p quod idm Abbas amisit co; svicium p unū quartiū anni ꝗ āplius ꝗ ī sexaginta boves ꝗ viginti vaccas īpius Abbtis in p̄dc̄o mañio suo invenī ceprūt ꝗ eos fugavūt usq p̄dc̄m mañiū p̄dc̄i Joh Cogan de Ofcomb ꝗ ibi eos inpcavūt rac̄one cuj⁹ impcam̄ti tresdeciū boves de p̄dc̄is pierūt ꝗ dui boves ꝗ vacce residui deteriorati fūut ad valenc̄ viginti libr̄ in īpius Abbtis dampnū gravissimū ꝗ cont" pacē ꝗc̄ Unde dic̄ qd def̄ioratus est ꝗ Dāpnū hī ad valenc̄ Centū libr̄ ꝗ inde pducit sectā ꝗc.

Et Johs de Cogan ꝗ alii veñ Et Thom̄ fit Joh Cogan ꝗ om̄s alii except̄ īpo Johne ꝗ p̄dc̄is Eustach le Heyward Witto le Hauekere Walp̄o Hugh ꝗ Robto le Scote dn̄t qd īpi nullā p̄dc̄a; trangr̄ p̄dc̄o Abbti intulerūt cont" pacem ꝗc̄ put eis imponit ꝗ de hoc poñ se sup pat̄am Et Abbas simitr̄ Io fit inde Jurᵃ.

Et Johs Cogan Eustach Witto le Hauekere Walts Hugh ꝗ Robts Scote dn̄t qd īpi nullā t"nsgr̄ p̄dc̄o Abbti intulit contra pacem ꝗc̄ dn̄t enim qd p̄dc̄us Cogan het in p̄dc̄o mañio suo de Ufculm libtate hndi in fangenethef utfangenethef ꝗ furcas ꝗ oīa que ad huj⁹ libtatē ptinent ꝗ quia p̄dc̄us Abbas in mañio suo p̄dc̄o de Hakepenne qd est infra pcinctū p̄dc̄i mañii īpius Johis de Ofcomb levasse voluit furcas de novo in lesionē ꝗ pjudiciū libtatis īpius Johis idem Johis pcepit p̄dc̄is Eustach ꝗ aliis qd ipī p̄dc̄m Abbtem huj⁹ furcas ibidm̄ lovaī non pmitt̄ent qui quid Eustach ꝗ alii ipm̄ Abbtem de p̄dc̄is furc̄ ibidm̄ leyand impediverūt sicut eis bn licuit Et qd aliam tn̄sg ei nō fec̄unt cont" pacē ꝗc̄ poñ se sup pat̄am Et Abb dic̄ qd īpi furcas† levavit in pjudm̄ libtaī dc̄i Johis ꝗc̄ dic̄

* Ulfculm elsewhere.   † Query, *non* omitted.

enim qd dns J. Rex av⁹ dni R̃ nunc cōcessit ꝫ carta sua cōfirm̃ Abbathie de Donkwett ꝫ Monach ibidē deo ˢvient in pur̄ ꝫ ꝑpet Elemoſ qd ꝑdēa Abbatĥa Abbas ꝫ Monachi ibidē deo ˢvient ĥeant ꝫ teneant om̃es terr̄ ꝫ ten que huerūt ex dono Witti le Brewere ĩ mañlio ꝉc̄ et ꝗcumꝗ, alia que infuturū adq̢'sierint eū Socco ꝫ Sacca Tol ꝫ Theam ꝫ Infangenethief Utfangenethief Et dns H. Rex pr̄ dni Reǵ nūc eosdē libtat ꝑdēe Abbathie ꝉc̄ ꝑ cartam suam ⁹cessit ꝫ cōfirmavit ꝫ ꝑfert ꝑdēas cart̃ que ĥ testant͛ Et dic̄ qd a tempe confeccōis cartarꝯ illaᴣ oes ꝑdecessores sui Abbates ꝫ ipē huerūt in mañlio suo ꝑdc̄o de Hakepenne furcas suas quousꝗ ꝑdc̄us Joĥes Cogan furc̄ itt pstнere fecit tpē ipˢius Abbatis nunc [on the dorso is the following] ꝫ ꝑ quod ĥita inde int̢ ipōs Joĥem ꝫ Abbtem contr͛ˡversia pdēs Joĥs Cogan ꝑ sc̢ptum suum pd cōcessit ꝑ se ꝫ her̄ ꝫ assig͛ˡtis suis ipi Abbti ꝫ cōventui suo q̃d ipi ꝫ eorꝯ successores ĥeant ꝫ teneant om̃es libtates ꝫ libas consˢ in cōfirmacōibᴣ dñorᴣ Joĥis ꝫ Honr̄ Regū contentas in Puram ꝫ ꝑpetuā Elemosinam Imppm̃ Et ꝑfert ꝑdc̄m scipt̄u ipˢius Joĥis quod hoc idem testat͛ ꝫ dic̄ qd ipē statim post confoccōm ꝑdc̄i sc̢pti furcas suaᴣ reparo fecit in ꝑdc̄o mañlio suo de Hakepenne que ibi stetut ꝑ ij annos ꝫ ampli⁹ ḡusꝗ ꝑdc̄i Joĥs Cogan ꝫ alii furcas illas ꝑst͛ˡverūt sicud sup͛ˡdc̄m est Et hoc petit qd inquir̄ ꝉc̄.

Et Joĥes bn cogn̄ ꝑdc̄m sc̢ptū ꝫ quicquid in eo continetꝯ Set dic̄ qd tempe cōfeccōnis illi⁹ sc̢pti ꝑdc̄us Abbas nullas furcas ĥuit in ꝑdc̄o mañlio suo de Hakepenne nec unꝗ͛ˡ postea quousꝗ jam de novo q̃d idem Abbas furcas ibidē levasse voluit ꝫ ꝑdc̄i Eustach Witts le Hawkere Walr̄us Huǵ ꝫ Robtus Scote ꝑ ꝑceptū ipˢius Joĥis ipm Abbatē inde impediv⁹ūt sic sup͛ˡdc̄m est. Et q̃d nullam aliam t͛ˡnsg̢ssionem ei fecerūt qt͛ˡ pace ꝉc̄ ponūt se sup paŕam ꝑ Abbas sir̄ Ido fiat inde Jur͛ˡ—— Jur̄ dñt sup sacr̄m suū q̃d ꝑdc̄i Thom̃ fit Joĥis de Cogan, Ric̄us de la Hutt, Eustach le Heyward, Roǵus de la Ford, Witts le Turnur, Ric̄us de la More, Joĥes Boneweye, Walr̄us Hughe, Witts te Haweker, Joĥes Evard, Ric̄us le Bakere, Witts Scby ꝫ Robtus Scote ꝑ ꝑceptū ꝫ assensū ꝑdcoᴣ Joĥis de C ꝫ R de Scote furcas pdc̄i Abbatis in ꝑdc̄o Mañlio suo de Hakepenne in ꝑdc̄a vigiƚ innocenciū noctant̢ ꝑst͛ˡverūt ꝫ furcas illas ad mañliū ꝑdc̄i Joĥis de Cogan de Ufculm caria͞vūt ꝫ ibi eas cōbusserūt, quas quidem furcas idem Abbas sēdm libtates a Reǵ Angƚ Abbathie de Dunkeswett ꝫ Monach ꝉc̄ concessas ĥuiꝉ in ꝑdc̄o mañis suo levatas, fere ꝑ duos annos ante q̃ pstate fūūt ꝫ furcis illis sic pstratis ꝑdc̄us Joĥes de Cogan levare fecit furcas suas in solo ipˢius

Abbāt, inf'" p̄dēm manſiū ipīus Abbatis de Hakepenne. Et q̄
p̄dc̄us Abbas ps̄ene fecit furcas ipi⁹ Johis in solo ipīus Abbatis
levatas pdc̄i Thom̄ fił Johis Rīcus de ła Huił, Ewstachius,
Johes de Bonewey, Walt̄us Hug̃, Witts le Hawekere, Johes
Ev̄ard, Rīcus le Bakere, ꝛ Witts Scribi in c̄"stino die sequenī
p̄dēm manſiū p̄dc̄i Abbatis de Hakepenne int"verūt ꝛ hostiū
aule quod clausum invenīant ibidem freg̃ūt ꝛ ēvienī ipīus
Abbatis in eodem manſio inventos v̄beravūt videlʒ Phm̄ łe
Messꝛ Johem de Heyles. Et postea cepunt if'" ēudē manſiū
boves ꝛ vacc̄ ipīus Abbatis circif̄ quadrag̃ quos fugavūt usq̄,
pcū p̄dc̄i Johis de Cogan de Ufculm ꝛ ibi eos impeavūt rac̄one
cuj' impcamenī tres de eisdem pieūt ad dampnū ipīus
Abbatis quadrag̃ li. Et Juf̄ quesīt si p̄dc̄i Thom̄ ꝛ alii freg̃ūt
p̄dc̄u hostiū ꝛc̄ p̄ p̄ceptū p̄dc̄oꝛ Johis de Cogan ꝛ Robti de
Stokhey. Dicūt q̄d p̄dc̄i Thom̄ ꝛ alii p̄ p̄ceptū ꝛ assensū
ipīus Johis de Cogan ibidem venſūt sʒ idem Johes nō pcepit
eis aliquod hostiū frangē uń post factum illud illos receptavit
ꝛ adhuc plures de illis receptat in s̄vic̄o suo ꝛc̄.

$\left.\begin{array}{l}\text{M}\\ 1 \\ \text{Coroner's Roll, Devon. 34}\end{array}\right\}$ 3 27 Edward I.

245. John was blessed, as appears by Bishop Stapeldon's Register, 17th Oct. 1311, at Yarcombe, after the dedication of the high altar there. He was not Abbot long, as we find that his successor William was blessed in Exeter Cathedral on Palm Sunday, 1318. I quote two entries from the De Banco Roll.

¶ Abbas de Donekeswelle p̄ Adam de Bauntoñ atī suū op. se iiij^to die v̄sus Witłm Vyncent de ptito q̄d reddat ei ronabilem compotū suū de tempore quo fuit receptoꝛ denař ipīus Abb̄tis ꝛc̄ Et ipē non ven̄ Et sicut pluf̄ prec̄ fuit vic̄ q̄d capet eū ꝛc̄ Et vic̄ modo mand q̄d bře adeo tarde venit ꝛc̄ I'o sicut pluf̄ prec̄ est vic̄ q̄d cap̄ eū si ꝛc̄ Et salvo ꝛc̄ Ita q̄d heat corpus eius hic a die sc̄i Hillař in xv dies ꝛc̄ Et vic̄ sit.—De Banco Roll, 19 Edw. II. Mich. (m. 210).

¶ Wiłłus Abbas de Donkeswelle p̄ Adam de Bauntoñ atī suū op. se iiij^to die v̄sus Witłm Pyioun ꝛ Robtm Don de ptito quare ip̄i simul cum Henf̄ de Campo Arnulphi ꝛ Walfo Gydie cepunt avīa ipīus Abb̄is et ea iniuste detinuerunt cont"vadiū ꝛ pleg̃ ꝛc̄ Et ip̄i non ven̄ Et p̄dc̄us Witts attach fuit p̄ Walfm Gydie ꝛ Robtm Don Et p̄dc̄s Rob̄ts p̄ Witłm Pyioun ꝛ Walfm Gydie Io ip̄i in m̄ia Et prec̄ est vic̄ q̄d distf̄ eos p̄ ōes tf̄ ꝛc̄ Et q̄d heat corpa corꝛ hic a die Pasche in q'nq̄ septīas ꝛc̄.—Ibid. (m. 414 d) 19 Edw. II. Mich.

246. Little more than three years afterwards William's successor, William de Wanlake, was consecrated Abbot, 8th Sept. 1321, at the Bishop's palace at Clyst. For the Abbots succeeding William de Wanlake I can only quote Oliver* and the Bishop's Registers.

247. John followed William, and Simon was blessed at Chudleigh by Bishop Grandisson, 22nd Feb. 1341. The cellarer of Newenham was elected in the stead of Simon 22nd April, 1346. William Wedmore followed, 7th April, 1353, and Robert Orchard was blessed at the palace at Chudleigh by Bishop Brantyngham,.20th April, 1382. Alexander Burlescombe was Abbot in 1397, and two years afterwards Richard Lamport was elected, 17th July, 1399. In Richard's time we find several entries in the Banco Roll, principally relating to pleas of debt in which the Abbot was plaintiff.

¶ Abbas Monastij de Donkeswill p attorñ suū op se iiij^{to} die v̄sus Robtum Clauenesburgh Gilbtum Bobeknolle Ricm Bakere de Honytoñ hostiller ᛫ Ricm Dryewode de plito q̄d quilt co₃ reddat ei quadraginta marcas quas ei debet ᛫ iniuste detinet ᛫c̄ Et ip̄i non veñ Et sicut prius proc̄ fuit vic̄ q̄d capet eos ᛫c̄ Et vic̄ modo mand q̄d non sunt invent ᛫c̄ I'o sicut pluŕ capiant^{ur} q̄d sint hic in octab̄ sc̄i Michis ᛫c̄.—De Banco Roll Trin. 2 Hen IV. m. 52 d.

¶ Ricus Abbas de Dunkeswyll p attorñ suū op se iiij^{to} die v̄sus Thomam Ammary de plito quare vi ᛫ armis arbores ᛫ subboscum ip̄ius Abbis ad valenc̄ decem libra₃ apud Dunkeswyll nup crescent̄ succidit ᛫ asportavit ᛫ blada ᛫ ħbam sua ad valenc̄ centum solido₃ ib̄m nup crescent̄ cum quibusdam av^{9}ijs depastus fuit conculcavit ᛫ consumpsit ᛫ alia enormia ᛫c̄ ad g^{ue}ve dampnū ᛫c̄ ᛫ cont^{ra} pacem Regis ᛫c̄ Et ip̄e non veñ Et proc̄ fuit vic̄ q̄d attach eū ᛫c̄ Et vic̄ modo mand q̄d nichil ħet ᛫c̄ I'o proc̄ est vic̄ q̄d capiat eū si ᛫c̄ Et salvo ᛫c̄ Ita q̄d ħeat corpus eius hic A die sc̄i Michis in xv dies ᛫c̄.— De Banco Roll, Trin. 2 Hen. IV. m. 152.

¶ Ricus Abbas de Dunkeswill p attorñ suū op se iiij^{to} die v̄sus Nicħm Sturgioñ de plito q̄d reddat ei quadraginta solidos quos ei debet ᛫ iniuste detinet ᛫c̄ Et ip̄e non veñ Et sicut pluŕ prec̄ fuit vic̄ q̄d distŕ eum ᛫c̄ Et vic̄ modo mand q̄d distŕ est p catalla ad valenc̄ decem ᛫ octo denario₃ Et m̄ p̄ Joħem Hunt Wiħm Craweford Thomam Stowe ᛫ Wiħm Nooke I'o ip̄i in m̄ia ᛫c̄ Et sicut pluŕ prec̄ est vic̄ q̄d distŕ cum p om̄es

* Monasticon, p. 394.

tras ᵹc̄ Et q̄d de exiṫ ᵹc̄ Et q̄d h̄eat corpus eius hic in Octab̄ sc̄i Michis ᵹc̄.— De Banco Roll, Trin. 2 Henry IV. m. 159.

¶ Abbas de Dunkiswill p Joh̄em Cole attorñ suū op se iiij^{to} die v̊sus Walt̄m Dollebeare ētic̄ū de p̄tito q̄d reddat ei quinquaginta solidos quos ei debet ᵹ iniuste detinet ᵹc̄ Et ip̄e non voñ Et sicut pluṝ prec̄ fuit vic̄ q̄d capet cū ᵹc̄ Et vic̄ modo mand̄ q̄d non est invent^ꝰ ᵹc̄ I'o sicut pluṝ capiat" Ita q̄d sit hic a die sc̄i Michis in xv dies p Justic̄ ᵹc̄.

Idm Abbas p attorñ suū p̄dc̄m op se iiij^{to} die v̊sus Joh̄em Vssher ᵹ Isoldam vxorem eius de p̄tito q̄d reddant ei quadraginta solidos quos ei debent ᵹ iniuste detinent ᵹc̄ Et ip̄i non veñ Et sicut pluṝ prec̄ fuit vic̄ q̄d capet eos si ᵹc̄ Et salvo ᵹc̄ Ita q̄d h̄eret corpa eoꝛ ad hunc diem scitt in Octabis sc̄e Trinitatis ᵹc̄ Et vic̄ modo mand̄ q̄d non sunt inventi ᵹc̄ I'o prec̄ est vic̄ q̄d exigi fac̄ eos de Com̄ in Com̄ quousq̨ ᵹc̄ p̄dc̄us Joh̄es vtlaget" ᵹ pdc̄n Isabella wayviet" Si non ᵹc̄ Et si ᵹc̄ tunc eos capiat Et salvo ᵹc̄ Ita q̄d h̄eat corpa eoꝛ hic in crastino Puṝ b̄e Marie Et vnde ᵹc̄ Ad que dic̄ vic̄ non mis̄ b̄re I'o de novo exigant" in forma p̄dc̄a q̄d sint hic in Octab̄ sc̄i Michis Et vnde ᵹc̄.—De Banco Roll, Trin. 2 Hen. IV. m. 280 d.

¶ Jur" int Thomam Aunger queṝ ᵹ Ric̄m Abb̄em de Donkeswyll ᵹ frem Alex̄m Burgoyn Cōmonachum eiusdem Abbis Joh̄em Leygh̄ Wiħm Wolmañ ᵹ Wiħm Lomen de p̄tito transgṝ ponit" in respc̄m hic vsq̨ a die sc̄i Michis in xv dies nisi Justic̄ dni Regis ad assisas in Com̄ p̄dc̄o capiend̄ assigñ p formam statuti ᵹc̄ die lune px̄ post f̄m sc̄i Jacobi Ap̄li apud Exoñ prius veñint p detc̄u Juṝ quia nullus veñ I'o vic̄ h̄eat corpora ᵹc̄.—De Banco Roll, Trin. 8 Henry IV. (m. 24, 6 d).

¶ Abbas de Dunkeswill p att̄ suū op se iiij^{to} die v̊sus Thomā Aunger de p̄tito q̄d reddat ei decem libras quas ei debet ᵹ iniuste detinet ᵹc̄ Et ip̄e non veñ Et prec̄ fuit vic̄ q̄d distṝ cū ᵹc̄ Et vic̄ mand̄ p̄d nichil h̄et ᵹc̄ I'o capiat" q̄d sit hic a die sc̄i Mich̄is in xv dies ᵹc̄ ad quem diem vic̄ non misit b̄re I'o sicut prius capiat" q̄d sic hic a die sc̄i Hillaṝ in xv dies ᵹc̄.—De Banco Roll, Trin. 8 Henry IV. m. 252 d.

¶ Abbas de Domkeswell p Joh̄em Cole attorñ suū op se iiij^{to} die v̊sus Ric̄m Bakere de Honytoñ ᵹ Thomam Davy de Honytoñ de p̄tito q̄d v̊q̨ eoꝛ reddat ei viginti ᵹ duas marcas sex solidos ᵹ octo denaṝ quos ei debent ᵹ iniuste detinent

℞ Et ipi non veñ Et sicut pluṝ preĉ fuit viĉ q̄d capet eos si ℞ Et salvo ℞ Ita q̄d ħeret corpora eoz hic ad hunc diem scilt a dio sc̄i Trinitatis in xv dies ℞ Et viĉ modo mand̄ q̄d non sunt inventi ℞ I'o preĉ est viĉ q̄d exigi fac̄ eos de Com̄ in Com̄ quousq̄, ℞ vtlagent" si non ℞ Et si ℞ tunc eos capiat ł:t salvo ℞ Ita q̄d ħeat corpora eoz hic a die sc̄i Hillaṝ in xv dies Et vnde ℞.—De Banco Roll, Trin. 8 Henry IV. m. 298d.

248. John Bokeland, 10th June 1419, John Ottery, 26th April 1439, Simon, 13th February 1441, were Abbots, as shown by the Bishop's Registers, and by leases examined by Dr. Oliver, and from the former we find that Richard Pytmynster was Abbot in 1492, and as late as 1498. John Whitmore succeeded, and was Abbot twenty years.*

249. The last Abbot was John Ley, who was confirmed in 1529 by the suffragan Bishop of Exeter. On the 14th Feb. 1539 he surrendered his house to the King's Commissioners. There appear to have been seven monks in the Abbey at the time of the surrender, viz., John Webbe, William Boreman, John Gaye, John Segar, John Genyng, John Benelt, and Thomas Typson. The Abbot, John Ley, on the death of the Abbot of Ford, John Tybbes, in 1556, became Vicar of Peahembury. John Gay, one of the monks, was appointed on the Dissolution perpetual curate of Sheldon, formerly belonging to the Abbey.

250. The annual value of the property of the Abbey at the surrender was nearly £300. The site of the monastic buildings, the home farm and mill, and other lands, were granted with large possessions, of which the owners were ruthlessly deprived, to John Lord Russell by letters patent dated 4th July, 31 Henry VIII. He does not seem to have retained them very long, for we find soon after that parts originally given to him reverted to the Crown and fresh grants made. To trace the successive owners of the various lands belonging to the Abbey would be tedious and uninteresting.

251. The Abbey adopted the arms of its founder, William de Briwere,—two bends wavy. The fine common seal, upwards of three inches long, represents the Blessed Virgin with Saints on either side, all under canopies. Unfortunately

* Oliver, Monasticon, p. 394.

there is but one impression of this seal extant, which is very mutilated. Below the Saint on the sinister side of the central figure is a shield with the De Briwere arms. An impression from an Abbot's counter-seal is also preserved. It is vesica-shaped, about one and six-eighths of an inch long. The Abbot is represented standing, holding his crozier in his right hand.

252. There were four bells in the tower of the church at the Dissolution, valued at £32 5s. The lead went to the recipient of the Abbey lands, and the entry relating to it curtly says, " My Lord of Bedford had the lende wth the gifte of the land"

253. My Lord of Bedford took care to appropriate the lead, without reference to the preservation of the fabric, with everything else capable of being turned into money, and the grand buildings, for such they must have been, and the despoiled abbey, soon shared the fate of many a stately monastery, for centuries the home of labour, almsgiving, and prayer.

254. In dry summers the foundations of the church and of some of the important buildings may be traced by the grass above them being quickly scorched. The western tower has fallen within a comparatively recent period. Portions of the gate-house remain, and fragments of walls still standing indicate the positions of certain of the original edifices, and I think that a little time and some digging would enable one to make a ground-plan of the whole of the monastic buildings. A modern church has been recently built upon the site of the antient cemetery. The situation of the Abbey is very secluded, but very beautiful and very characteristic of a Cistercian selection.

APPENDIX.

LIST OF THE ABBOTS OF DUNKESWELL.

Names.	Dates.	Authorities.
Richard .	1228	Purchase from Richard de Crues.
Ralph	Abbot to 1251	Translated to Waverley in 1251.
Thomas .	1253	Lease.
John	1311-1318	Bishop Stapeldon's Reg.
William .	1318-1321	Episcopal Registers.
William de Wanlake	1321-	Do.
John	-1341	Oliver.
Simon	1341-1346	Episcopal Registers.
William Wedmore .	1353-1382	Do
Robert Orchard	1382-1397	Do.
Alexander Burlescombe	1397-1399	Do.
Richard Lamport	1399-1419	Do.
John Bokeland	1419-1439	Do.
John Ottery .	1439-1441	Do
Simon	1441-	Do.
Thomas Dullton	As early as 1474 down to 1486	Leases.
Richard Pytmynster	As early as 1492 to 1498	Do.
John Whitmore	As early as 1509 to 1529	Do.
John Ley	1529-1539	Episcopal Registers, &c.

THE
CISTERCIAN HOUSES OF DEVON.

VI.
FORD.

THE

CISTERCIAN HOUSES OF DEVON.

VI. Ford.

255. Up to the year 1842 the site of this Abbey, now a gentleman's mansion, was in the county of Devon. In that year the parish of Thorncombe, in which it is situated, was, by authority of Parliament, for the convenience of those having the transaction of magisterial and other business, transferred to the county of Dorset. There is therefore a necessity for including the history of Ford Abbey in this series of papers.

256. The Abbey was founded in 1141, and in point of date is the second Cistercian foundation in Devon. But the Annals of Waverley say, under date 1135, "*Forda fundata est quinto nonas Maii.*"* This, however, fixes the date of the migration of Richard and twelve monks from Waverley, the famous house before spoken of, to Brightley near Okehampton.

257. This is not the place to attempt to trace the parentage and descendants of Richard, stated in the Book of Ford Abbey to be the son of Baldwin de Brionne, and although the question has had brought upon it all the acumen and learning of Mr. Planché,† it is by no means settled. It is, however, clear that a Richard, connected with the great family of Redvers, made provision for Cistercian Monks at Brightley, and sent to Waverley for men to colonise the new house.

258. Richard the Monk and his companions had settled at Brightley only a few months when their patron died, 25th June, 1137. His death prevented his plans for the permanent establishment of the house of Brightley being carried into effect, and wanting not only friends, but the bare necessaries of life in the barren spot in which the temporary buildings

---

* *Annales de Waverleia, Ann. Monast.*, vol. ii. p. 225.
† See *Earls of Devon, Collectanea Arch.*, vol. i. p. 263. *The Conqueror and his Companions*, vol. i. p. 44. On the Lords of the Isle of Wight, *Journ. Arch. Assoc.*, vol. xi. p. 217.

were placed, and having no hopes of being able to carry out the wishes of their would-be benefactor, the thirteen monks, after having lost their leader and Abbot, who had broken down in the struggle, resolved to abandon Brightley and to return to their old home. The five years attempt was a noble but a hopeless one,—præ inopia et præ dira sterilitate victualiumque penura ibidem amplius morari non potuissent,— and with sad memories and disappointed hopes they set their faces again towards Waverley.

259. They had proceeded on their journey as far as Thorncombe when Adelicia, the sister of Richard the Viscount, met them. The chronicler quoted by Dugdale gives the very words of Adelicia when she saw the monks walking two and two with uplifted cross, as five years before they had set out from Waverley. " Absit a me, domini et patres sanctissimi, opprobrium tam damnabile et ignominiosum periculum, ut quod dominus meus et frater Ricardus pio devotionis affectu ad Dei honorem nostrumque omnium salutem tam solempniter quam salubriter inceperat, ego vero soror ejus, et heres cui decedendo omnia tradidit in manus, non velim aut valeam ad debitum perducere effectum. Ecce manerium meum in quo jam consistimus fertile satis et nemorosum ac abundans frugibus, quod vobis in excambium pro terra sterili de Brightleia cum tota mansione nostra et domicilio imperpetuum donamus. Manete hic donec alibi in ista possessione vobis competentius fit monasterium, nec vobis in hoc deesse possumus, sed satis juvabimus ad construendum." The fruitful and well-wooded manor which Adelicia offered the monks was that of Thorncombe, and the proffered gift induced them to change their plans and accept the lands for a new foundation.

260. The house called Westford, which accompanied the gift of the manor, was taken possession of, and there the wanderers lived until the completion of the larger and more convenient buildings. It was resolved that their site should be Hertbath (*Balneum cervorum*) and the erection of the church was at once commenced.

261. Scarcely had the new arrangements been completed when the monks sustained another loss. In September, 1142, Adelicia died, and was buried within the precincts of the church, although at this time little progress could have been made with it. The remains of Richard the Viscount and Richard the Abbot were removed from Brightley, and buried before the place of the high altar in the slowly rising church. The Abbey was soon known as Ford, taking this name from

a passage-way over the River Axe, near which it was situated.

262. The first Abbot was succeeded by Robert de Penynton, or Penigton, as we find it sometimes spelt, and who, as his name occurs in deeds under dates so far apart as 1137 and 1168, must have ruled the house for many years. It is very probable that the conventual buildings were completed in his time, and the remains of the two Richards removed from Brightley to Ford.

263. The third Abbot was Baldwin of Exeter. Originally a monk at Ford, he, in the course of a short time, became Abbot, and about the year 1181 was made Bishop of Worcester, and not long after Archbishop of Canterbury, and his life in consequence becomes a part of the history of our country.

264. Of the next Abbot, Robert, we know nothing. During his time, or in that of his successor, Maurice Somerset was a monk here, and, his writings obtaining him celebrity at Oxford, he was made Abbot of Wells.

265. John, the Confessor of the King of the same name, formerly Abbot of Bindon, succeeded Robert, and made Ford famous for its learning. He was a great theologian and was Abbot from 1191 to 1220.

266. Another John followed,* and was Abbot until 1236. We have from the Feet of Fines some entries in which his name is mentioned.

Hec est finalis concordia fca in Curia dñi Reg apud Westm̃. In Octab Purificacõis anno regni Reg Henr̃ fil Reg Johis vicesimo p¦mo Coram Robo de Lexinton Witto de Eborc Ada fil Witt ℞ Willo de Colowr̃th Justic ℞ aliis dñi Reg fidelibȝ tūc ibi p̃sentibȝ Inr̃ Galfridū de la Pomeray petentem p Hug de la Hutt positū loco ipius Galfr ad lucrandū ut perdendū ℞ Johem Abbem de Forde tenctem de tribȝ Carucatis ₹re cū p̃tiñ in Tale vnde placitū fuit inr̃ eos in end Cur̃ Scilicet q̃d p̃dcus Galfr remisit ℞ quietū clamauit de se ℞ heredibȝ suis p̃dco Abbi ℞ successoribȝ suis ℞ Ecctie sue de Forde totū Jus ℞ clamiū quod habuit in tota p̃dca ₹ra cū p̃tiñ imppetuū. Et p hac remissione quieta clamancia fine ℞ concordia idem Abbas dedit p̃dco Galfr quiquaginta ℞ tres m̃reas argenti.—Feet of Fines. Devon. Henry III. No. 196.

Hec est finalis concordia fca in Cur̃ dñi Reg apud Exoñ a

* But see *Annals of Waverley* under date 1234.

die sēi Joħ Bapt in quindecī dies anno regni Reḡ Henr̄ fił Reḡ Joħ vicesimo sēdo Coram Wiłto de Eborp̄ Rotto de Bello Campo Wiłto de Sēo Edmundo ꝛ Jordano Oliu̇ iustic̄ itiħantibȝ ꝛ aliis dn̄i Reḡ fidelibȝ tūc ibi p̄sentibȝ Inł Clariciā fił Radi petentem ꝛ Joħm Abb̄m de Ford̄ tenente de Dimid ferlingo t̄re cū p̱tiñ in Stok Vnde assisa mortis antecess̄ sumonita fuit inł eos in eadem Cur̄ scił qd p̱dēa Claric̄ recognouit totā p̱dēam t̄rā cum p̱tiñ esse ius ip̄ius Abb̄is ꝛ Ecctie sue de Ford̄ Habend̄ ꝛ tenend̄ eidem Abb̄i ꝛ succ̄ suis ꝛ Ecctie sue p̄dēe de p̱dēa Claric̄ ꝛ ħedibȝ suis inppetuū reddendo inde annuatim vnū den̄ ad festū sēi Micħ p omi seruic̄o ad ip̄am Claric̄ ūl ad ħedes suos ptinēte Et acquietando totā p̱dēam t̄rā cum p̱tiñ ūsᵖ Capitales dn̄os feodī illᵒ de omibȝ aliis seruic̄ ad eandem t̄rā ptinentibȝ. Et p hac recognic̄one fine ꝛ cōcordia Idē Abbas dedit p̱dēe Claric̄ duas Marc̄ argēti.—Ibid. No. 219.

Hec est finał concordia fēa in Cur̄ dn̄i Reḡ apud Exoñ a die sēi Joħ Bapt in quindecī dies Anno Regni Reḡ Henr̄ fił Reḡ Joħis vicesimo sēdo Corā Wiłto de Eborp̄ Rotto de Bello Campo Wiłto de sēo Edmundo ꝛ Jord̄ Oliu̇ iustic̄ itiħantibȝ ꝛ aliis dn̄i Reḡ fidelibȝ tūc ibi p̄sentibȝ Inł Thoṁ de Ford̄ ꝛ Petroniłł vxem eiᵖ petētes ꝛ Joħm Abb̄m de Ford̄ tenentē de t̄cia pte vinᵖ ferlingi t̄re cū p̱tiñ in Stokꝑ. Quā t̄ciā ptē p̱dēi Thoṁ ꝛ Petronilla clamabant esse r̄onabilē dotē ip̄ius Petronille q̄ eam contingebat de lib̄o tenemēto qd fuit Radi fił Ric̄ quondam viri sui in eadem villa. Et vnde placitū fuit inł eos in cad̄ Cur̄ scił qd p̱dēe Thoṁ ꝛ Petronilla remis̄runt ꝛ quieł clamauunt de se eidem Abb̄i ꝛ successoribȝ suis ꝛ Ecctie sue de Ford̄ totū ius ꝛ clamiū quod h̄unt in tota p̱dēa t̄cia pte cū p̱tiñ nōie dotis ippetuū. Et p hac remissione quieta clamanc̄ fine ꝛ concordia idem Abbas dedit p̱dēis Thome ꝛ Petronille Duas Marc̄ Argēti.—Ibid. No. 254.

Hec est finał concordia fēa in Cur̄ dn̄i Reḡ apud Exoñ in Octab̄ sēi Joħis Bapt Anno Regni Reḡ Henr̄ fił Reḡ Joħis vicesimo sēdo Corā Wiłto de Eborp̄ Rotto de Bello Campo Wiłto de sēo Edmundo ꝛ Jordano Oliu̇ iustic̄ itiħantibȝ ꝛ aliis dn̄i Reḡ fidelibȝ tūc ibi p̄sentibȝ. Inł Symonē de Pylesdoñ petentē ꝛ Joħm Abb̄m de Ford̄ tenentē de duabȝ Carucatis t̄re cū p̱tiñ in Lofford̄ ꝛ in Cundebur̄ vñ placitū fuit inł eos in eadem Cur̄ scił qd p̄dictᵖ Symō remisit ꝛ quieł clamauit de se ꝛ heredibȝ suis ip̄i Abb̄i ꝛ successoribȝ suis ꝛ Ecctie sue de Ford̄ totū ius ꝛ clamiū quod habuit in tota p̱dēa t̄ra cū p̱tiñ inppetuū. Et p hac remissione quieta clamanc̄ fine ꝛ concordia idē Abbas dedit p̄dĉo Symoni qᵘtuordecī marĉ ꝫ dimiđ argēti. Et si p̄dict̄ Symō ut ħedes sui deceťo aliqᵘs Cartas ut̃ aliqᵘ munimēta ūsᵖ p̄dĉm Abb̃m ūl succ̃ suos qᵘntū ad p̄dĉas duas Carucatas ťre cū p̃tiñ in p̄dĉis villis contᵃ hūc finĉ p̃tulerint p' nullis penitᵖ habebuntʳ.—Ibid. No. 283.

267. Roger succeeded, in whose abbacy the church was completed, for under date 1239, in the Annals of Waverley, we have "Ecclesia de Forda dedicata est a domino Willelmo Exoniensi episcopo." John de Warwick followed, then Adam, who became Abbot in 1240, and William, who died and was buried at Waverley.

Hec est finał concordia fĉa In cuř dñi Reğ ap̃ Exoñ a die sĉe Tⁱniſ in qⁱndecī dies nnñ Regñ Reğ Henř fił Reğ Joħ vicesimo octavo. Corā Joħe Abb̃e de Schyreburñ Rogo de Thurkelby Gilb̃to de P̃stoñ ꝫ Rob̃to de Bello campo Justiĉ Itiñantibꝫ ꝫ aliis dñi Reğ fidelibꝫ tūc ibi p̃sentibꝫ Inť Abb̃m de Forđ queř ꝫ Riĉ de Laya deforĉ de secta qᵘ Idē Abb̃s exiğ ab eodem Riĉo vnde Idem Abb̃s exigebat qđ faĉet ei sectā de tⁱbꝫ sept̃ in tres septim̃ ad Hundř suū de Thorneoūbe, Et vnde plaĉ fuit Inť eos in eadem cuř. Scittᵗ q̃đ p̄dĉs Riĉ recogñ ꝫ concessit p se ꝫ ħedibꝫ suis qđ ip̃i de ceťo faciant bis p annū sectam p̄dĉm Hunđř simł cū lib̃is homībꝫ suis ꝫ cū suo capitał Thedingman ꝫ duobꝫ aliis homībꝫ scitt semel sabto pximo pᵖt Hokeday ꝫ Iťum sab̃to pẋ pᵖt festū sĉi Michis. Ita ẽn q̃d p̄dĉs Thedigman cū p̄dĉis duobꝫ hoībꝫ ad p̄dĉos duos dies mōstᵘre debet oīa plaĉ de Thedinga ip̃i Riĉi ꝫ ħeđ suoꝫ ad p̄dĉm Hundř p̃tinenĉ ꝫ si aliqⁱs ip̃oꝫ qⁱ Ita seqⁱ debł ad p̄dĉos duos dies fuit in default Ia Abb̃ ꝫ succ̃ sui omia ip̃orꝫ amciamta Integre habnt ꝫ oīa alia amciamta de homībꝫ ip̃iᵖ Riĉi ꝫ ħeđ suoꝫ ad eundē Hundř contingĉĉ Inť p̄dĉm Abb̃m ꝫ succ̃ suos ꝫ p̄dĉm Riĉm ꝫ ħeđ suos fidelił dimidiabñtʳ oīa illa amciamta taxari debent p p̄dĉm Abb̃m ꝫ succ̃ ut̃ Balťos suos ꝫ p p̄dĉm Riĉm ꝫ ħedes ut̃ attʳnatos suos. Et p̃ea Idem Riĉ concessit p se ꝫ ħeđ suis qđ si aliqᵒđ plaĉ fuit in eodem Hundř p B̃re dñi Reğ ut latro fuit ibi Judicanđ ip̃i ut̃ attʳnati sui sequi debet Hundř ip̃iᵖ Abb̃is de Tⁱbꝫ sept In tres sept vsq̃ loquela illa p Juđm eiusdem Hundř plenař fuit ťmīata. Et p hac reĉ concessione fine ꝫ cōcordia. Idem Abb̃s rem̃ ꝫ qⁱeť clam̃ de se ꝫ succ̃ suis ꝫ Eccłia sua de Forde p̄dĉo Riĉo ꝫ ħeđ suis oīa arreragia ꝫ om̃s alias sectas qᵘs ab codē Riĉo exigibat ꝫ oīa dampñ que dicebat se huisse occasione subᵘccōis p̄dĉe secte usq̃ ad diem quo hec concordia fĉa fuit.—Feet of Fines. Henry III. No. 316.

Hec est finat concordia fĉa in Cuȓ Dñi Reḡ apud Exoñ a die sĉo Trinitatis In q'ndecim dies anno regni Reḡ Henȓ fit Reḡ Joħis vicessimo octavo coram Joħe Abbte de Schryreburñ Rogo de Thurkelby Gilbto de Preston ꝛ Robto de Bello Campo Justic̄ Itiñantib; ꝛ allis dñi Reḡ fidelib; tūc ibi p̄sentib; Inȶ Adam Abbem de Forde quer̄ p̄tr̄em Wiȶm Monachū suū poītum loco suo ad luc⁓ndū ut p̄dendū ꝛ Huḡ Peďel de Ermintoñ deforĉ de annuo rediditu decem libȓ Cere vnde Idem Abbs questus fuit qď decem libre eiusdem redditus ei aretro fuerūt de vno anno. Et vnde placitū fuit inȶ eos in eadem Cuȓ scitt qď p̄dĉs Huḡ recognouit ꝛ concessit eidem Abbti decem libr Cere p̄ annū; pcipiendas īpi Abbti successorib; suis de Molendino de Ermintoñ p̄ manū Balti ip̄ius Huḡ ꝛ hedum suo; de Ermintoñ ad festū sĉi Michis apud Exoñ inppetuū. Et p h⁓c recogñ concessione fine ꝛ concordia Idem Abbs remisit ꝛ quiet̄ clañ de se ꝛ succ̄ suis eidem Huḡ ꝛ heđ suis omīa arreragia p̄dĉi redď p̄dĉar decem libȓ Cere vsq ad diem quo hec concordia fĉa fuit.—Ibid. No. 328.

268. William of Crewkerne was the tenth abbot, and his time was famous for the great dispute between him and Bishop Broncscombe, the particulars of which are detailed by Oliver, and the documents given at length in the appendix to the *Monasticon*. His name occurs in the following legal proceedings:—

Hec est final concordia fĉa In cuȓ dñi Reḡ apd Exoñ In Octab sĉe Trinitatis Anno regni Reḡ Henȓ fit Reḡ Joħis Tricesimo tercio Corā Rogo de Thurkelby Gilbto de Prestoñ ꝛ Joħe de Cobbeħ Justic̄ Itiñanȶ ꝛ aliis dñi Reḡ fidet tūc ibi p̄sentibus Inȶ Rađm de Trewurtheth petñ ꝛ Adam Abbem de Laforde teñ de vno ferlingo ȶre ꝛ dimiď cū ptiñ in Opecote. Unde plaĉ fuit inȶ eos in eaď Cuȓ Scilt qd p̄dĉs Rađs reñ ꝛ quiet̄ clañ de se ꝛ heđ suis p̄dĉo Abbi ꝛ succ̄ suis ꝛ Ecctie sue de Forde totū Jus ꝛ clamiū qd huit in p̄dĉa ȶra cū ptiñ imppet̄. Et p h⁓c reñ quiota clañ fine ꝛ conĉ Idem Abbas dedit p̄dĉo Rađo duas M⁓cas argñti.—Feet of Fines. Henry III. No. 435.

Hec est finat concordia fĉa in cuȓ dñi Reḡ apud Westm̄ In Octab sĉi Hillaȓ anno regni Reḡ Henȓ fit Reḡ Joħis q'n-quagesimo sĉdo Coram M⁓rtino de Litlebiȓ Magro Rogo de Scytoñ ꝛ Joħe de Cobbeħ⁓m Justic̄ ꝛ aliis dñi Reḡ fidelib; tūc ibi p̄sentib; Inȶ Magȓm Thoñ de Wymundeh⁓m psonam Ecctie de Pahambiȓ petñ ꝛ Wiȶm Abbem de fforde tenĉtem de vno fferlingo ⁊ vna acra t̃re cum p̃tiñ in Talc. vnde Jurata vtrum p̃dc̃a terra cū p̃tiñ sit lit̃a elemosina p̃tiñes ad p̃dc̃am Ecctiam an laicū feodū ip̃ius Abt̃is sum̃ fuit int̃ eos in eadē cur̃. Scitt q̃d p̃dc̃s Abt̃s recogn̄ p̃dc̃am t̃rum cū p̃tiñ esse Jus p̃dc̃e Ecctie ⁊ p̃dc̃m ferlingū terre cū p̃tiñ ei reddidit in eadem cur̃ ⁊ remisit ⁊ quieteclam̃ de se ⁊ succ̃ suis ⁊ Ecctia sua de fforde p̃dc̃o Thom̃ ⁊ succ̃ suis psonis p̃dc̃e Ecctie ⁊ Ecctie p̃dc̃e Inppet̃. Et p hac recogn̄ reddic̃one remissiõc q'eta clam̃ fine ⁊ cōcordia. Idem Thom̃ cōcessit p̃dc̃o Abt̃i p̃dc̃am acram terre cū p̃tiñ. Hat̃n ⁊ Tenend(e eidē Abt̃i ⁊ succ̃ suis ⁊ Ecctie sue p̃dc̃e de p̃dc̃o Thom̃ ⁊ succ̃ suis psonis p̃dc̃e Ecctie ip̃pet̃. Redd̃n inde p ann̄ vnū clauū Gariophili ad Pasch p om̃i suic̃o cons ⁊ exacc̃õne. Et hec cōcordia fc̃a fuit ex assensu ⁊ volūtate Walt̃i Ep̃i Exoñ ⁊ eam concedentis. —Ibid. No. 603.

¶ Abbas de Forde sum̃ fuit ad respond̃ dño Regi de p̃lito   At Exeter.
quo Warranto clam̃ h̃re viś franc̃ pleḡ emend̃ assise panis ⁊   Octave of St.
c̃viś fracte furc̃ in Kentesbery ⁊ Thornecombe sine licenc̃ ⁊c.   Martin.
   Et Abbas p Atorn̄ suū venit Et quo visum f"nci pleḡ in   9-10 Edw I.
Kentesbyr̃ dic̃ q̃d nich̃ inde clam̃ Et quo ad emend̃ aśś panis   A.D 1281.
⁊ c̃uiś f"cte ⁊ furc̃ in eadem villa. Et quo ad emend̃ aśś panis ⁊ c̃viś f"cte furc̃ ⁊ visum f"nci pleḡ in Thorncombe dicit q̃d ipse ⁊ omnes p̃dc̃c sui a t̃pe quo nō exstat memor̃ huunt emend̃ aśś panis ⁊ c̃viś in Kentesbyr̃ ⁊ visum f"nci pleḡ ⁊ emend̃ aśś panis ⁊ c̃viś f"cte In Thorncumbe pet̃ q̃d inquirar̃.
   Et Witt̃s de Gyselh"m qui sequir̃ ⁊c Dic̃ q̃d huj⁹mō lit̃tates spalit̃ ptinent ad Coronam dn̄i Regis Et desic̃ nullū War̃ inde ostend̃ de dño Rege pet̃ Judm̃.
   Dies dat⁹ est coram dño Rege a die Pasch in unū mensem ubicūq ⁊c de aud̃ judic̃o.

Assize Roll Devon $\frac{M}{\frac{1}{34}}$ } 1 Memb : 20d.

269. Nicholas, who was blessed at Axminster 1st Jan. 1283, by Bishop Quivill, followed. William de Fria succeeded, and, having been able to be of great use to the Convent, was persuaded to resign it for Newenham, where similar services were much needed. However he remained there only about four years, when he returned to Ford, and resumed his place as a simple monk. Dying at Ford, his body was removed to the Abbey he had evidently loved so well, for interment.

270. Henry took the place of William de Fria on his resignation, and was Abbot until 1319. The grant of the fair at Thornecombe, which was continued down to the year 1770, I give from the Charter Roll.

p' Abbe et Conventu de Forda.

Dated 5 Feb. 1312-13.

Ŗ Archiepis ⁊ ⁊c. salƭm. Sciatis nos concessisse ⁊ hac carta n̄ra confirmasse diłcis noƀ in xp̄o Abbati ⁊ Conventui de Forda q̃d ip̄i ⁊ successores sui imppm̄ ħeant unū mercatū singtis septimanis p diem mercurii apud maneriū suū de Thorncūbe in Com̄ Devon, et unā feriā ibid̨m singtis annis p sex dies duraturam videłt in die martis in septimana Pasche, et p quniq̨ dies sequentes. Nisi m̃catū illud ⁊ feria illa sint ad nocumentū vicinoʒ mercatoʒ ⁊ vicinaʒ feriaʒ. Quare volum⁹ ⁊ firmiƭ p̄cipim⁹ p nobis ⁊ heredibʒ n̄r̄is q̃d pdc̃i Abbas ⁊ Conventus ⁊ successores sui imppm̄ ħeant p̃dc̃a mercatū ⁊ feriam apud Mañliū suū p̃dc̃m cum omnibʒ liƀtatibʒ ⁊ libis consuetudinibʒ ad hujusmodi mercatū ⁊ feriā ptinentibʒ. Nisi m̃catū illud ⁊ feria illa sint ad nocumentū vicinorʒ m̃catorʒ ⁊ vicinarʒ feriaʒ sicut p̃dc̃m est. Hiis testibʒ veñ'abilibʒ p̄ribʒ W. Wigorñ. W. Exoñ Epis Gilƀto de Clare Comite Glouc̃ ⁊ Hertford Adomaro de Valencia Comite Pembr̃ Hug̃ le Despens̃ Wiłło le Latimer. Nicħo de Seg"ve ⁊ aliis. Daƭ p manū n̄ram apud Windes̃ quinto die Febr̃ p fine contentū in alia carta inferius.*—Charter Roll 6 Edward II. No. 106, mem. 17, section 36.

Ŗ om̄nibʒ ad quos ⁊c salƭm. Sciatis q̃d cum p ƭras n̄ras patentes concesserim⁹ ⁊ licenc̃ dederimus p nobis ⁊ heƒ n̄ris quantū in nobis est dilc̃is noƀ in xp̄o Abƀi ⁊ Conventui de Ǝord q̃d ip̄i decem libratas ƭraʒ teñ ⁊ redditū de feodo suo p̄prio adquirere possint ħend̃ ⁊ tened sibi ⁊ succ̃ suis imppetuū Statuto de Ɵris ⁊ teñ ad manū mortuam ⁊c̃ put iɲ ƭris p̃dc̃is plenius continetʳ. Nos volentes concessionē n̄ram p̃dc̃m debito eftc̃ui mancipari concessim⁹ ⁊ lic̃ dedim⁹ p noƀ ⁊ heƒ n̄ris quantū in nobis est Wiłło de Pillaunde ⁊ Niċħs Portebref q̃d ip̄i vnū mes̃ vnū molendinū Triginta acras Ƭre tres acras p"ti ⁊ tres acr̃ more ⁊ alneti cum pƭiñ in Wheteham ⁊ Burg̃hstok̃ et Thome de Langedoñ q̃d ip̃e vnū mes̃ duodecim acr̃ Ƭre ⁊ tres acr̃ bosci cum pƭiñ iɲ Thornocōbe et Wiłło de Watelegħ q̃d ip̃e viginti ⁊ tres acr̃ Ƭre ⁊ duɲs acr̃ alneti cum pƭiñ in Watelegħ iuxta Wyncsham que de p̃dc̃is Abƀe ⁊ Conventuƭ ⁊ que valent p annū in om̄ibʒ exitibʒ iuxta verū va-

* This is No. 26 on the same Roll, being a Confirmation of a Charter of King John granting the church of Tornecumbe, &c., &c. Dated 10 Oct. in the tenth year of his reign. Confirmation dated 5 Feb. (as above).

† " tenentur " omitted.

lorem eoȝdem quatuordecim solid̄ ʒ quatuor denar̄ sicut p
inquisic̄oes p delēm cticum nr̄m Magr̄m Johem Walewayn
Escaet̄ nr̄m cit^m Trentam de mandato n̄ro fc̄as ʒ in Can-
cellar̄ n̄rā retornatas comptū est dare possint ʒ assiguare
eisdē Abb̄i ʒ Conventui hend̄ ʒ tenend̄ sibi et succ̄ suis
imppetuū in p̃te satisfacc̄ois decē libratarȝ ȝre ten̄ ʒ reddituū
p̃dc̄orȝ. Et eisdē Abb̄i ʒ Conventui q̃d ip̄i p̃dc̄a meš Molendinū ȝram p^utum boscum moram ʒ Alnetū cum ptin̄ a
pfatis Wilħo Nicho Thoma ʒ Wilħo recipe possint ʒ tenere
sibi ʒ succ̄ suis p̃dc̃is imppetuū sicut p̃dc̄m est tenore p̃senciū
similiȝ licenc̄ dedimus sp̄alem Statuto p̃dc̄o non obstante.
Nolentes q̃d p̃dc̄i Wilħs Nicħs Thomas ʒ Wilħs vel heredes
sui aut pȝati Abbas ʒ Conventus seu succ̄ sui ȝone statuti
p̃dc̄i p nos vel her̄ n̄ros inde occ̄onent^r molestent^r in aliquo
seu g^uvent^r. Salvis tamen Capitalibȝ d̃nis feodi illius ȝviciis
ʒc̄. In cui⁹ ʒc̄. T. R apud Westm̃. xxv. die Octobr̄.—Patent
Roll 11 Edw. II. pars 1, m. 21.

271. William, who patronised Charmouth, was confirmed
22 Sept. 1219. His successor John appears to have under-
taken the repairs of the buildings of his house, then become
dilapidated judging from his reply to Bishop Grandisson,
who asked for a money grant to enable him to comply with
the large demand of the Court of Rome. John replied that
his buildings and his church were ruinous, and with great
humility begged that the Abbey might not be called upon to
contribute to the subsidy. Still he seems to have acquired
land for the house, as the following from the Patent Roll
shows:—

R̃ om̃ibȝ ad quos ʒc̄ sttm. Sciatis q̃d cum de gr̄a n̄ra   p Abbate de
sp̄ali p· littȝas n̄ras patentes concesserimus ʒ licenciam dederi-   fforde.
mus p nobis ʒ heredibȝ n̄ris q^untum in nobis est dilc̄is nob̃ in
Xp̄o Abbati ʒ conventui de fforde q̃d ip̄i decem libratas t̃raȝ
tenementoȝ ʒ reddituum de feodo suo pprio adquirere possint
hend̄ ʒ tenend̄ sibi ʒ successoribȝ suis imppetuū. Statuto de
ȝris ʒ ten̄ ad manū mortuam non ponend̄ edito non obstante,
put in littȝis p̃dc̃is plenius continet^r nos volentes concessionem
n̄ram p̃dc̄am debito effectui mancipari concessimus ʒ licenciam
dedimus p nobis ʒ heredibȝ n̄ris q^untum in nobis est Wilħo
de Pillaunde ʒ Nicho Portebrief q̃d ip̄i quinquaginta acras
ȝre ʒ viginti acras more cum ptin̄ in Wategh̄ que de p̃dc̃is
Abbate ʒ conventu tenent^r ʒ que valent p annuū in om̃ibȝ
exitibȝ iuxta veram valorem eoȝdem quindecim solid̄ ʒ decem
denar̄ sicut p inquisic̄oem p dilc̄m cticum nr̄m Magr̄m Johem

2 B

Walewayn nup Escaetorem nr̃m vltra Trentam de mandato ñro inde f̃cam ꝗ in Cancellar̃ ñrā retornatam est comptum dare possint ꝗ assignare eisdem Abbati ꝗ conventui habend̃ ꝗ tenend̃ sibi ꝗ successorib; suis imppetuū in ꝑtem satisfaccõis decem libratas̃ tras̃ tenñ ꝗ redditnū p̃dc̃os. Et eisdem Abbati ꝗ conventui q̃d ip̃i tram ꝗ morā p̃dc̃a cum ptiñ a p̃fatis Wiƚƚo ꝗ Nicho recipe possint ꝗ tenere sibi ꝗ successorib; suis p̃dc̃is imppetuū sicut p̃dc̃m est tenore p̃sencium simiƚiꝯ licenciam dedim⁹ sp̃alem statuto p̃dc̃o non obstante. Nolentes q̃d p̃dc̃i Wiƚƚo ꝗ Nicħus vel her̃ sui aut p̃fati Abbas ꝗ conventus seu successores sui r̃one statuti p̃dc̃i p nos vel her̃ ñros inde occonent' in aliquo seu gᵃvent'. Salvis tamen capitalib; d̃nis feodi illius s̃viciis inde debitis ꝗ consuetis. In cui⁹ ꝗc̃. T. R̃ꝑ apud Ebos̃. xxx. die Dec̃.—Patent Roll, 13 Edw. II., m. 24.

272. John de Chidley succeeded John, 24 June, 1330, and seems, although his reputation did not stand high, to have had several legal matters upon his hands in connection with the property of the Abbey.

Devoñ. Johnes Abbas de fforde p at̃t suū op. se iiij die v̂sus Ranulphū Blaunmoster ꝗ Aliĉ vxem eius Ric̃m de Combe ꝗ Walt̃m de Edyngtoñ de p̃lito q"re cep̃nt aulia ip̃ius Abb̃is ꝗ ea iniuste detinuer̃ cont" vadiū ꝗ p̃leḡ ꝗc̃ Et ip̃i nō veñ Et ħuer̃ inde diē hic ad hunc diē ex p̃ħcc̃õe ꝗc̃ Jud̃m attacħ q̃d sit hic in Octab̃ sc̃i Mic̃his ꝗc̃.—De Banco Roll, Easter 17 Edw. III. memb. 26d.

Devoñ. Abbas de fforde p Joħem de Crukerñ at̃t suū op. se iiij die v̂sus Henr̃ de sc̃o Claro vicariū ecctie de Brodewyndesore de p̃lito q̃d reddat ei r̃onabilem compotū suū de tempe quo fuit receptor denar̃ ip̃ius Abb̃is ꝗc̃ Et ip̃e nō veñ Et sicut plur̃ prec̃ fuit vic̃ q̃d cap̃ eū ꝗc̃ Et vic̃ modo mand̃ q̃d nō est inuent⁹ ꝗc̃ I'o sicut plur̃ prec̃ est vic̃ q̃d cap̃ eū si ꝗc̃ Et saluo ꝗc̃ Ita q̃d ħeat corpus eius hic a die sc̃e Trinitat̃ in xv dies p Justic̃ ꝗc̃ Et vic̃ sit ꝗc̃.—Ibid. memb. 88.

Devoñ. Abbas de fferde p Ric̃m Beynyn at̃t suū op se iiij die v̂sus Joħem de Cloptoñ de p̃lito q̃d redd̃ ei r̃onabilem compotū suū de tempe quo fuit receptor denar̃ ip̃ius Abb̃is ꝗc̃ Et ip̃e nō veñ Et p̃c̃ fuit vic̃ q̃d cap̃ eū si ꝗc̃ Et vic̃ modo mād̃ q̃d nō est inuent⁹ ꝗc̃ I'o sic p'us prec̃ est vic̃ q̃d cap̃ eū si ꝗc̃ Et saluo ꝗc̃ Ita q̃d ħeat corpus eius hic a die sc̃e Tⁿitatis in xv dies p Justic̃ ꝗc̃ Et vic̃ sit ꝗc̃.—Ibid. memb. 145.

Idem̃ Abbas p p̃dc̃m at̃t suū op. se iiij. die v̂sus Robt̃m

llmystre ꝗ Adam Rogge de p̄lito qͤre vi ꝗ armis decem boues ꝗ qͧtuor vaccas īpius Abbis p̄cii decem marcaȝ apud Tale inventos cepūt ꝗ abduxerunt ꝗ alia enormia ei intuleꝛ ad gͣue dampnū īpius Abbis ꝗ contͣ pacē ꝉc̄ Et īpi nō veñ Et p̄c̄ fuit vic̄ q̄d cap̄ eos si ꝉc̄ Et vic̄ modo mand q̄d nō sūt inuenti ꝉc̄ I'o sic̄ p'us prec̄ est vic̄ q̄d cap̄ eos si ꝉc̄ Et saluo ꝉc̄ Ita q̄d heat corpa eoȝ hic ad p̄fatū p̄minū p Justic̄ ꝉc̄ Et vic̄ sit ꝉc̄.—Ibid. memb. 145.

273. Adam was confirmed Michaelmas-day, 1354. Abbot John did not undertake the repairs of the church, whatever he might have done to the other buildings, for we find that about this time the edifice required rebuilding. The following extracts from the White Book of Tenures are interesting:—

Octobre Novembr̄ Ian Dengt xxix Cornewaille.
Edward ꝉc̄. A nos chs vadletȝ Robt de Eleford ñre Señ de Touch' labbe de fforde.
Corn̄ ꝗ Devenes ꝗ Johan de Skirbeekꝑ gardein de nos feodȝ illeoq̄s ꝗ a vn de eux saluȝ. N're ch en dieu Abbe de fforde noͥ ad moustree p sa peticion a ñre conseil grevousement compleignant q̄ vous ñre dit feodr̄ lui destreigneȝ de iour en autre pʳ relief a noͥ paier ꝗ seute faire a ñre Court de Bradonessh pʳ c̄toines tres ꝗ teñȝ es villes de lyntoñ Countesbury ꝗ looford en Countee de Devenes queles il tient a ce qil dit en pure ꝗ ppetuelle aumoigne, et en affermance de son estat en cele ptie si ad il moustree devant ñre conseil vn fait p quel Gueras* de Pilesdoñ gͧunta ꝗ p sa chartre conferma a leglise nre dame de fforde ꝗ as Moignes illeoq̄s dieu s̄vantȝ la tre de lefford ꝗ la tre de Cuntebury ove ses appͣtenances ensemblement ove lewe pentre Cuntebury ꝗ lyntoñ quele owe il retynt devs lui pʳ t̄me de sa vie la revision au dit Abbe. A tenir en pure ꝗ ppetuelle Aumoigne quel doun Henri Tracy filz Wiħ Tracy conferma p sa chartre† et auxi vne chartre p quele Henr̄ filz au Countee dona a dieu ꝗ ñre dame de fford ꝗ as Moignes illeoq̄s dieu s̄vantȝ la tre de Cuntebury ꝗ lyntoñ ove touȝ ses appʳtenances. A tenir de lui ꝗ de ses heirs en pure ꝗ ppetuelle aumoigne quits de toutes mañes seculers s̄vices ꝗ demandes en mañe come Henr̄ de Tracy gͧunta meisme la tre as ditȝ Moignes empriant q̄ noͥ lui veuilliens sͣ ce faire droit p quei p avis de ñre conseil vous maundons q̄ vous c̄tifieȝ ñre conseil a londͥs quel estat noͥ avons en la s̄ͣie des dites tres. Et faceȝ diligealment enquerre p quel s̄vice le dit Gueras qi p'mes enfeoffa le dit Abbe tynt les dites tres de Henr̄ de Tracy ou dautre coment ꝗ en quele

* Written (fo. 64) "Gerveys."   † Oliver, p. 347.

mañe, et si le dit Abbe tiegne au̧ļs ļres ᵗt teñʒ es dites villes
q̃ ne sont comp'ses en les ditʒ faitʒ adonq̃ʒ quelles ļres ces
sont ᵗt de qi ces sont tenuʒ ᵗt p queux ṡvices Et ent ƌtifieʒ ñre
conseil entre cy ᵗt la xv de seint Hillair p̧sch avenir. Et
chargeons vous ñre dit feoder q̃ vo⁹ s^u scieʒ de la destresce
quele vous faites v̧s le dit Abbe p^r les choses devantdites entre
cy ᵗt la dite xv. Et ce ne lesseʒ. Doñ ᵗc̃ a Westm̃ le xxix
iour Doctobr̄ lan xxix.
    p ᵗt lev[e]sqʒ de Wync̃ ᵗt p bille endossee
    p Skipwith.
    The White Book of Tenures in Cornwall, 25—39 Edw. III.,
fol. 58.

    ₊ At fo. 64 a letter of the Prince, dated at London,
11 July, 30 E. III., that Robert de Eleford has fully certified
to the Council as to the matters above ordered, and directing
inquiry to be made " si no⁹ cous lestat le dit mouṡ Henri de
Tracy en dit Manoir ou del vn ᵗt del nutre."

Cornewaille.   Juyl   lan xxxj. As audito^rs
Touch' les des accomptes de noʒ Ministres saluʒ. Coment no⁹ feismes
Abbe et   ore tard s^u veer ᵗt examiner p les sages de ñre conseil les
Covent
de fforde. enquestes p'ses a ñre maundement devant Robt de Elford ñre
Soñ de Cornewaiĩl ᵗt Deveneṡ ᵗt Johan de Shirbchʒ Gardein
de noʒ feodʒ illeoq̃s ᵗt devant ñre dit conseil ret^u neer touch
labbee ᵗt covent de fforde avis estoit a ñre dit conseil q̃ p^u
rien q̃ feust Adonqs trove no⁹ ne deyvons seute nautre ṡvice
de eux demander p reson de ļres comp'ses en mesmes les
enquestes si mandasmes p noʒ au̧ļs tres a noʒ ditʒ Señ ᵗt
Gardein de feodʒ qils ne destreignassent les ditʒ Abbe ᵗt Coven
p cause des dites ļres contre reson a ce q̃ semble vous mandons
p avis de ñre dit conseil q̃ s^u la compte du dit Johan lui faceʒ
descharger de la soñie susdite. Et ceste tre vo⁹ ent s̃ra garr̄.
Doñ ᵗc̃ a lond⁹ s en lostiel levesq̃ Dely le xj iour de Juyl lan
ᵗc̃ xxxj ᵗc̃.—Ibid. fol. 76.

    274. John Chylheglys seems to have succeeded Adam. He
was Abbot in the year 1373. His successor, Walter Burstok,
was confirmed 16 April, 1378. The proceedings referred to
in the following extracts occurred in his time.

Som's.   ¶ Abbas de fforde p Joħem Crukerñ aīī suū op. se iiij^{to}
die v̧sus Adam Hodeforde de p̧lito q̃d reddat ei quadraginta
ᵗt duos solid quos ei debet iniuste detinet ᵗc̃ Et ip̃e non venit
Et p̃c̃ fuit vic̃ q̃d sum̃ eū Et vic̃ modo mand q̃d nichil ħet

J'o p̄c̄ est vic̄ q̄d capiat eū si 7c̄ Ita qđ ħeat corpus eius hic
a die sc̄e Trinitatis in xv dies p Justic̄.—De Banco Roll, Easter
9 Rich. II. m. 104d.

¶ Abbas de fforde p Joħem Crukerñ attorñ suū op. se iiij⁽ᵗᵒ⁾   Devoñ.
die v̄sus Robtum Cornu Chiualer de ptito q̄d reddat ei quadraginta solid quos ei debet 7 iniuste detinet 7c̄ Et ip̄e non
venit Et sicut pluī fuit disīr p catalla ad valenc̄ duo₃ solid
Et m̄ p Joħem Hunt 7 Henī Hiłł J'o ip̄i in mīa Et sicut
pluī disīr q̄d sit hic a die sc̄e Trinitatis in xv dies p Justic̄.—
Ibid. m. 151.

¶ Abbas de fforde p Joħem Crukerñ att̄ suū op. se iiij⁽ᵗᵒ⁾ die   Devoñ.
v̄sus Thomā Kernere 7 Elenā vx̄em eius 7 Wiłtm fił cor₃d
Thome 7 Elene de ptito quare cū de cōi consilio regni Regis
Angł puisū sit qđ non liceat alicui vastū vendicōem seu destruccōem faće de ₚ̄ris domib₃ boscis seu gardinis sibi dimissis
ad ₚ̄minū vite vel anno₃ iidem Thomas Elena 7 Witło de ₚ̄ris
domib₃ boscis 7 gardinis in Thorncombe que Joħes de ffar-
yngdoñ nup Abbas de fforde p̄decssor p̄dc̄i nunc Abb̄is eis
dimisit ac vitā ip̄o₃ Thome Elene 7 Wiłi fecerunt vastū vendicōem 7 destruccōem ad exher ecctie ip̄ius nunc Abb̄is be
Marie de fforde 7 cont⁽ᵃ⁻⁾ formā puisionis p̄dc̄e 7c̄ Et ip̄i non
veñ Et p̄c̄ fuit vic̄ q̄d disīr q̄d eos Et vic̄ modo mand q̄d
bīe adeo tarde 7c̄ J'o sicut prius disīr q̄d sint hic a die sc̄e
Trinitatis in xv dies p Justic̄ ad que dīe vic̄ non miś bīe J'o
sicut pluī disīr q̄d sint hic a die sc̄i Michis in xv dies.—Ibid.
m. 228.

¶ Abbas de fforde p Joħem Crukerñ att̄ suū op. se iiij⁽ᵗᵒ⁾   Devoñ.
die v̄sus Thomā Stremynge vicar ecctie de Thorncombe de   (m. 391.)
ptito quare cū idem Abb̄as dn̄s Mań̄ii de Thornecombe existat
7 here debeat ip̄eq₃ 7 omēs p̄decessores sui dn̄i Mań̄ii p̄dc̄i a
tempore quo non exstat memoria ibidē here consueuer quand
cuī de hōib₃ 7 tenentib₃ suis Mań̄ii p̄dc̄i in quodā loco infrā
idem Mań̄iū p cuī p̄dc̄a de trib₃ septimanis in tres septiās
antiquit vsitat p̄dc̄us Thomas Nicħm Bolour balliuū ip̄ius
Abb̄is ad Cuī p̄dc̄m apud Thornecombe in loco p̄dc̄o tenend₃
p p̄fatū Abb̄em deputat quomin⁹ idem Nicħus Cuī illam ibidem
tenere potuit vi 7 armis impediuit p quod idem Abbas pficuū
quod de Cuī p̄dc̄a si ibidem tenta fuisset pcepisse debuisset
amisit 7 alia enormia 7c̄ ad dampnū ip̄ius Abb̄is quadraginta
libra₃ 7 cont⁽ᵃ⁻⁾ pacē Rēğ 7 Et ip̄e non veñ Et sicut prius
p̄ceptū fuit vic̄ q̄d capet eū 7 Et vic̄ modo mand q̄d non est
inuentus J'o sicut pluī p̄c̄ est vic̄ q̄d capiat eū si 7c̄ Ita q̄d

ħeat corpus cius hic a die sc̄e Trinitatis in vx dies d Justic̄.—
Ibid. m. 391.

275. Nicholas was the next Abbot. His name occurs as early as 1388, Oliver says, but without giving his authority; but in one of the following entries from the De Banco Roll we have an Abbot Walter, in Hilary Term, 2 Hen. IV.

Devoñ. ¶ Abbas de fforde p Joħem Sparowe aīt suū op̄ se iiij^{to} die v̄sus Laurenciū Archere de p̄ito quare vi ꝉ armis arbores ꝉ subboscum ip̄ius Abb̄is apud Satteburgħ nup crescentes succidit ꝉ in sepali piscaria sua ib̄m piscatus fuit ꝉ piscem inde ac arbores ꝉ subboscum pd̄cos ad valenciam viginti libra₂ cepit ꝉ asportauit ꝉ alia enormia ꝉc. ad g"ue dampnū ꝉc. et cont^a pacē Regẹ ꝉc. Et ip̄e non veñ Et prec̄ fuit vic̄ qd distr̄ eū Et vic̄ modo mand qd nichil ħet ꝉc p quod potest distr̄i J'o prec̄ est vic̄ qd capiat eū si ꝉc Et salus ꝉc Ita qd ħeat corpus cius hic a die Pasche in tres septimanas ꝉc.—De Banco Roll, 19 Ric. II. m. 166.

Devoñ. ¶ Abbas de fforde p Joħem Sparowe aīt suū op̄ se iiij^{to} die v̄sus Georgiū Crukerñ ꝉ Galfrm Smytħ de p̄ito quare vi ꝉ armis clausā ip̄ius Abbis apud Bromħille ꝉ Wythewylle fregerunt ꝉ arbores ꝉ subboscum suos ad valenciam centū solidor₂ ib̄m nup crescentes succider̄ ꝉ asportauer̄ ꝉ blada ꝉ ħbam sua ad valenciam decem marcaȝ ib̄m nup crescentia cū quibusdam aliis depasti fuerunt conculcauer̄ ꝉ consump̄s ꝉ alia enormia ꝉc ad g"ue dampnū ꝉc et cont^a pacē Regẹ ꝉc Et ip̄i non veñ Et p̄c fuit vic̄ qd attacħet eos Et vic̄ modo mand qd nichil ħent ꝉc. J'o prec̄ est vic̄ qd capiat eos si ꝉc. Et saluo ꝉc. Ita qd ħeat corpora eoȝ hic a die Pasche in tres septimanas ꝉc.—Ibid. m. 167.

Devoñ. ¶ Abbas de fforde p Joħem Sparowe aīt suū op̄ se iiij^{to} die v̄sus Georgiū Knyf ꝉ Thomā Crukerñ cticum de p̄ito quare vi ꝉ armis in sepali piscaria ip̄ius Abb̄is apud Shyterok piscati fuerunt ꝉ piscem inde ad valenciam decem marcaȝ ceper̄ ꝉ asportauer̄ ꝉ alia enormia ꝉc ad gu"e dampnū ꝉc et cont^a pacē Regẹ ꝉc. Et ip̄i non veñ. Et p̄c fuit vic̄ qd attacħet eos. Et vic̄ modo mand q̄d nichil ħent ꝉc. J'o prec̄ est vic̄ qd capiat eos si ꝉc. Et saluo ꝉc. Ita q̄d ħeat corpora eorȝ hic a die Pasche in tres septimanas ꝉc.—Ibid. m. 167.

Devoñ. ¶ Abbas de fforde ꝉ fraꝑ Henr̄ Kernere cōmonacus eiusdem Abb̄is p Joħem Sparowe attorñ suū op̄ sc iiij^{to} die

Ṽsus Johem Crawolegh de ptito q̃d reddat eis quadraginta ⁊ sex solidos ⁊ octo denar̄ quos ei debet ⁊ iniuste detinet ⁊c̄. Et ipe non ven̄ Et sicut plur̄ fuit distr̄ p catalla ad valenciā duodecim denar̄ Et ilt p Jnonē Donne ⁊ Lucā Monne l'o ipi in mīa Et sicut plur̄ prec̄ est vic̄ q̃d distr̄ eū p om̄es tras ⁊c̄ Et. q̃d de exit̄ ⁊c̄ Et q̃d heat corpus eius hic a die Pasche in tres septimanas p Justic̄ ⁊c̄.—Ibid. m. 167 d. m. 167 d.

¶ Abbas de fforde p Johem Spwe att̄ suū op̄ se iiij^to die Ṽsus Johem atte Wille de ptito quare vi ⁊ armis bona ⁊ catalla ipius Abbis ad valenciā quadraginta libraȝ apud fforde inuent̄ cepit ⁊ asportauit ⁊ Walr̃um Whyte natiuū ⁊ śuientem suū in śuic̄o suo ibid existent̄ cepit ⁊ abduxit p quod idem Abbas śuiciū natiui ⁊ śuientis sui p̄dci p magnū tempus amisit ⁊ alia enormia ⁊c̄ ⁊ cont'" pacem Regis ⁊c̄. Et ipe non venit Et p̄c̄ fuit vic̄ q̃d attach eū Et vic̄ modo mand q̃d nichil het l'o p̄c̄ est vic̄ q̃d capiat eū si ⁊c̄. Ita q̃d heat corpus eius hic a die Pasche in tres septīas p Justic̄.—Ibid. m. 186. Devon. m. 186.

¶ Walr̃us Abbas de fforde Robtus Borde Bocher Wilts atte Horsmylle Johes Baker ⁊ Stephus Eueray attach fuerunt ad respondend Edwardo Osborne vicario ecctie de Thornecombe de ptito quare vi ⁊ armis clausum ipius Edwardi apud Thornecombe fregerunt ⁊ quatuor vaccas ⁊ sexaginta porcos suos ibidem inuentos cum quibusdam canibȝ fugauerunt canes illos ad mordend vaccas ⁊ porcos p̄dc̄os in tantum incitando q̃d p fugac̄oem illam ⁊ morsus canū p̄dc̄oȝ due vacce ⁊ quadraginta porci pcii decem marcaȝ de vaccis ⁊ porcis p̄dc̄is int'ierunt ⁊ vacce ⁊ porci residui multiplicit' det'iorati fuerunt ac vaccas ⁊ porcos residuos ibidem ceperunt ⁊ imparcauerunt ⁊ eos ibidem sic imparcatos quousq̃ idem Edwardus finem p quadraginta solidos p delibac̄oe vaccarȝ ⁊ porcorȝ residuorȝ p̄dc̄oȝ henda cum p̄fatis Abb̄e Robto Wilto Johe ⁊ Stepho fecisset. detinuerunt Et alia enormia ei intulerunt ad g'"ue dampnū ipius Edwardi Et cont'" pacem dn̄i R̄e nup Regis Angt sc̄di post conquestum ⁊c̄ Et vnde idem Edwardus p Johem Goold attorn̄ suū querit' q̃d p̄dci Abbas Robtus Wilts Johes ⁊ Stephus die lune px̄ post festū sc̄i Michis Anno regni dn̄i R̄e nup Regis Angt t'ciodecimo vi ⁊ armis scitt gladiis arcubȝ ⁊ sagittis clausum ipius Edwardi apud Thornecombe fregerunt ⁊ quatuor vaccas ⁊ sexaginta porcos suos ibidem inuentos cum quibusdam canibȝ fugauerunt canes illos ad mordend vaccas ⁊ porcos p̄dc̄os in tantum incitando q̃d p fugac̄oem illam ⁊ morsus canū p̄dc̄oȝ due vacce ⁊ quadraginta porci pcii ⁊c̄ de vaccis ⁊ porcis p̄dc̄is int'ierunt Devon.

⁊ vacce ⁊ porci residui multiplicit̃ det̃iorati fuerunt ac vaccas ⁊ porcos residuos ibidem ceperunt ⁊ imparcauerunt ⁊ eos ibidem sic imparcatos quousq̃ idem Edwardus finem ꝉc̃ p̃ delibat̃oe vaccaꝫ ⁊ porcoꝫ residuoꝫ p̃dcorꝫ ħenda cum p̃fatis Abb̃e Robt̃o Wilt̃o Joħe ⁊ Stepħo fecissot⸗ detinuerunt Et alia enormia ꝉc̃ ad g᷈ue dampnū ꝉc̃ Et con᷈ pacem ꝉc̃ Vnde dic̃ q̃d det̃ioratus est ⁊ dampnū ħet ad valenciam quadraginta libraꝛ Et inde pduc̃ sectam ꝉc̃.

Et p̃dc̃i Abbas Robtus Witt̃s Joħes ⁊ Stepħus p Thomam Martyn attorñ suū ven̄ Et defend̃ vim ⁊ iniur̃ quando ꝉc Et dic̃ q̃d ip̃i in nullo sunt culpabiles de t᷈nsgr̃ p̃dc̃a put p̃dc̃s Edwardus supius v̄sus eos querit' Et de hoc p̃ōn se sup p̃riam Et p̃dc̃us Edwardus similit̃ I'o p̃c̃ est vic̃ qd̃ venire fac̃ hic a die Pasche in xv dies xij ꝉc p quos ꝉc Et qui nec ꝉc ad recogñ ꝉc Quia tam ꝉc.—Ibid. 2 Hen. IV., Hilary, m. 138d.

As I have said, it will be noticed that here we have Walter mentioned as Abbot. The explanation may be that the proceedings were commenced in Walter Burstok's time, and his name continued on the pleadings after his death.

Devoñ. ¶ Abbas de fforde p attorñ suū op̃ se iiij^{to} die v̄sus Thomam Splent de p̃tito q̃d reddat ei rōnabilem compotum suū de tempe quo fuit balliuus suus in Westforde ⁊ receptor denarioꝫ ip̃ius Abb̃is Et ip̃i non ven̄ Et prec̃ fuit vic̃ q̃d suñ eum ꝉc̃ Et vic̃ modo mand̃ q̃d nichil ħet ꝉc I'o prec̃ est vic̃ q̃d capiat cum si ꝉc Et saluo ꝉc Ita q̃d ħeat corpus eius hic a die Pasche in vnū Mensem ꝉc.—Ibid. m. 459.

De Banco Roll; Trin. 2 Henry IV.

Devoñ. ¶ Abbas de fforde ɛ̃ attorñ suū op se iiij^{to} die v̄sus Thomam Splent de p̃tito q̃d ei reddat ei rōnabilem compotū suū de tempore quo fuit ballivus suis in Westforde ⁊ receptor denarioꝫ ip̃ius Abb̃is Et ip̃e non ven̄ Et sicut prius prec̃ fuit vic̃ q̃d capet cum ꝉc̃ Et vic̃ modo non misit br̃e ꝉc̃ I'o sicut plur̃ capitat᷈ q̃d sit hic in Octab̃ sc̃i Micħis ꝉc̃.—Ibid. Trin. 2 Hen. IV., m. 2958.

Devoñ. ¶ Abbas de fforde p attorñ suū op se iiij^{to} die v̄sus Joħem Smyth de Tale ⁊ Joħem Seger de Taletoñ de p̃tito quare vi ⁊ armis clausa ip̃ius Abb̃is apud Tale fregerunt ⁊ libam warrennā suā ib̃m intraverunt ⁊ in ea sine licencia ⁊ voluntate sua fugaverunt ⁊ in sepali piscaria sua ib̃m piscati fuerunt ⁊ piscem inde ad valenc̃ centū solidoꝫ ac lepores cunic̃los phasianos ⁊ pdices de warrenna p̃dc̃a ceperunt ⁊ asportaverunt et alia enormia ꝉc̃ et cont᷈ pacem ꝉc̃ Et ip̃i non ven̄ Et prec̃ fuit

viĉ q̄d attach cos ℔ĉ Et viĉ mand q̄d nichil hent ℔ĉ I'o capiant"
q̄d sint hic in Octabis sĉi Michis ℔ĉ.—Ibid., Trinity, 8 Hen.
IV., m. 409.

276. Of the succeeding abbots until the last we know very little. John Bokeland was confirmed 10 June, 1419. Richard succeeded him. Robert occurs in 1448.

¶ Abbas de fforde p attorñ suū op se iiij^to die v̂sus Gilb̂tum   Devoñ.
Pyper alias dĉm Gilb̂tum Boteswayñ de Elleworth in Coñ
Dorš husbondman de ṕtito t"nsgr̄ Et iṕe non veñ Et preĉ fuit
viĉ q̄d attachet̃ oū ℔ĉ Et viĉ retorñ q̄d iṕi nichil het ℔ĉ p quod
℔ĉ I'o preĉ est viĉ q̄d capiat eū si ℔ĉ Et salvo ℔o Ita q̄d heat
corpus eius coram dno Rege a die sĉi Hillar̄ in xv dies vbicūq̃
℔ĉ Et vnde in xv sĉi Martini ℔ĉ.—Coram Rege Roll, Mich.
1 Hen. VI., m. 35.

277. The next entry in the De Banco Roll relating to Ford gives the name of Walter, and thus enables me to add a new abbot to the list. This is on the Roll for Michaelmas term, 38 Hen. VI.

¶ Walr̂us Abbas de fforda p attorñ suū op se iiij^to die v̂sus   Devoñ.
Walr̂um Colebroke de parochia de Columptoñ in Coñ ṕdĉo
Gentilman de ṕlito quare cum idem Abbas in feodo suo apud
Colbroke p cons̃ ℞ šuiciis sibi debitis p Walr̂um Holway
šuient̃ suū quedam alia capi fecisset ℞ idem Walr̂us Holway
alia illa sĉdm legem ℞ cons̃ regni Regis Angt̃ imparcare
voluisset ṕdcus Walr̂us Colbroke alia ṕdĉa vi ℞ armis res-
cussit Et alia enormia ℔ĉ ad g"uo dampnū ℔ĉ Et cont"
pacem Regis ℔ĉ. Et iṕe non veñ. Et preĉ fuit viĉ sicut
prius q̄d distr̄ eum ℔ĉ. Et viĉ modo mand q̄d distr̄ est p
catalla ad valenĉ duodecim denar̄. Et manuĉ p Edm̄ Mate
℞ Riĉm Ware. I'o iṕi in mīa. Et sicut pluŕ distr̄ q̄d sit hic
in Octabis sĉi Hillar̄ Ad quē diem viĉ non mis̃ bŕe I'o sicut
pluŕ distr̄ q̄d sit hic a die Pasche in vx dies ℔ĉ.—De Banco
Roll Mich. 38 Hen. VI. m. 52d.

278. My last extract, too, refers to a claim made in the time of Walter, the newly found Abbot.

Walr̂us Abbas de fforde p attorñ suū op se iiij^to die v̂sus   Devoñ.
Robtum Cammett de ffytelford in Coñ Dorš Gentilman alias
dĉm Robtum Cammett de Cammett in Coñ Dorš Geñosum
de ṕtito q̄d reddat ei decem libras quas ei debet ℞ iniuste

2 c

dotinct ꝉc̃. Et ip̃e non veñ. Et prec̃ fuit vic̃ sicut prius q̃d capet cum ꝉc̃. Et vic̃ modo mand̃ q̃d non est inuent̃ ꝉc̃. I'o sicut pluꝭ capiatꭈ q̃d sit hic in Octabis sc̃i Hillaꝭ ꝉc̃.— Ibid. 253.

279. Then comes Elias, in 1462, and William White, who was apparently Abbot for upwards of thirty years, from at least as early as 1490 to 1521.

280. The last Abbot, Thomas Chardo, otherwise Tybbes, has left something more than a name. He was one of the most distinguished men of whom the Abbey could boast. He was not only an eminent scholar and divine, but the buildings at Ford show him to have been an artist of no mean capabilities. Dr. Oliver has given a memoir, and Dr. J. H. Pring has dealt with the history of his life in fuller detail.* He succeeded in 1521. An account of his various preferments, some probably of great value, and given him to support to some extent his dignity as Suffragan Bishop to his Diocesan, Oldham, will be found in the memoirs to which I have referred. He was evidently fond of building, and remodelled the domestic buildings at Ford on a scale of great magnificence. The beautiful tower, the north walk of the cloister, all that now exists, and the new refectory, with his initials, mitre, and abbot's cap, were as much admired by his contemporaries as by succeeding generations. He surrendered his house 8th March, 1539, at which time there was the full number of thirteen monks. He did not survive the fall long, dying full of years and honours early in 1544.

281. Thus Ford shared the fate of its sister houses. They were all surrendered in 1538-9, but in all probability no buildings were so perfect, and none were abandoned with greater grief than this important foundation. Its revenues amounted to £374 10s. 6½d., according to Dugdale, and its possessions, besides those in the immediate neighbourhood of the Abbey, extended into the adjoining counties of Somerset and Dorset, and as far as Lynton and Countisbury on the north coast.

282. The history of the Abbey after the dissolution is well known, as it became the home of many distinguished families. It and the adjoining land was first leased to Richard Pollard for a term of twenty-one years, at an annual rental of £49 6s. 6d., but the following year, 23rd June, 1540, the lessee obtained from the king a conveyance in fee. Sir John Pollard succeeded his father, and sold Ford Abbey to his cousin, Sir Amias Poulett, of whom William Rosewell, Queen Elizabeth's

* *A Memoir of Thomas Chard, D.D.*, by James Hurly Pring, M.D., 1864.

Solicitor-General, bought it; and his son, Sir Henry Rosewell, sold it to Edmund Prideaux, who, employing Inigo Jones, proceeded to convert the domestic buildings of the convent into a mansion, at what must have been a great expenditure. In the Prideaux, Gwyn, and Frauncois families the Abbey continued down to 1847, when on the death of John Frauncois Gwyn it was sold to G. F. W. Miles, Esq., by whom however it was not long retained, the present owner, Herbert Evans, Esq., becoming its possessor by purchase.

283. No Cistercian building in England, perhaps none in the world, remains in so perfect a state as that of Ford. The site is on the south of the Axe river, the formation of the ground compelling the monks to take that bank of the river instead of, as they preferred, the north. The stream flowing into the river rises in the ground south of the Abbey, and the fish ponds which were constructed in its course still remain, although somewhat altered in shape. The principal entrance is now from the east, and the visitor approaching the Abbey walks over the foundations of the antient church, and treads under foot the dust of stately ecclesiastics and noble founders.

284. Not a vestige remains of the monastic church. The entrance road crosses the north aisle, and the south side of the cloister. This was not consecrated until 1239, but it must not be supposed that there was no building for divine service until that time. The whole of the buildings were in all probability laid out from the beginning, and the work completed as the bounty of the faithful allowed. It was the finished church no doubt that was consecrated nearly a century after the monks left Brightley. Within its walls the remains of Richard the Viscount, Richard the Abbot, Adelicia (1142), Hawisia de Courtenay (1209), Reginald or William de Courtenay (1192-94), Robert de Courtenay (1242), and John de Courtenay (1273), found resting places.

285. Turning to the right we shall enter a building fitted up as a chapel, and usually considered to be the church of the Abbey. This is a chamber of the greatest interest, it being in fact no other than the chapter house of the monks. It is of twelfth-century work, transitional Norman, with pointed vault of two bays. In the extensive alterations of the Abbey made by Edmund Prideaux, this was converted into the domestic chapel of the mansion, and here Cromwell's Attorney-General was buried in 1659. On the walls are various memorial tablets.

286. Over the chapter-house would be originally the library. This is now completely altered into a spacious modern room.

Through the library the monks passed from their dormitory to the church, the staircase leading down to it being probably in the north transept.

287. Still passing northward we enter a vaulted chamber originally nearly 170 feet long, and divided by a central row of eleven columns, all of which with the vaulting are perfect. This building is of rather later date than the chapter-house, and the work is of an elegant and delicate description. Over it is the dormitory of the monks, almost perfect, although now divided up to furnish sleeping apartments for the servants of the mansion.

288. Retracing our steps we come to the south front of the house, and find ourselves in the north walk of the cloister. This is eighty-two feet in length. All but this side is destroyed, and the beautiful Perpendicular work is that of Charde the last Abbot, whose memory is so intimately interwoven with Ford. He did not scruple here to mingle his initials, T. C., and his episcopal and abbatial insignia, with the arms of the Abbey and the King, on the many shields which decorate the spaces between the buttresses and between and over the tracery. Within the existing portion of the cloister and on the north may be traced the ancient refectory (of the later we shall speak presently), although it is blocked up with modern partitions. The kitchen of the monastery remains the kitchen of the mansion.

289. We now come to the *domus conversorum*, but a small portion only of it remains. In its original state it extended northward from the church, probably as far as the diverted stream, which formed the common sewer of the house, and was therefore at least two hundred feet long, the breadth being twenty-six feet. The whole of this however was not occupied by the convent, as traces of divisions can be made out. Over were the dormitories of the lay brethren.

290. We now enter the hall, which is really the eastern end of the new refectory of Abbot Charde. In its original state this fine room was one hundred and fifteen feet long. The western part was divided and altered by Inigo Jones to form the state apartments, and, shorn as it is now of its fair proportions, it still remains a very fine apartment.

291. The barn still remains, and between it and the western end of Charde's refectory may be found remains, probably of the gatehouse; for it was on this side, not on the east, that the entrance formerly was.

292. The alterations made by Inigo Jones, while to a great extent destroying many of the ancient features and disfiguring

the fine work of Charde, and mutilating its proportions, tended to make the abbey a convenient and commodious residence. The dining and drawing rooms are good apartments with elaborate ceilings, and the staircase and saloon are finely designed. But still, in spite of the interference with his architecture and the incongruities of Inigo Jones's additions, Charde's work remains pre-eminently beautiful, and renders Ford Abbey perhaps the most interesting building architecturally, as it is archæologically, in the west country.

293. The property of the Abbey was not of great extent, although at the dissolution its annual value was second only to that of Buckfast. It was, as I have said, situated in the immediate neighbourhood of the Abbey, in the north of the county, at Lynton and Countisbury, and in Somerset and Dorset. Besides Adelicia, the later Courtenays endowed Ford with some of their wealth and the Pomeroys also were its benefactors.

294. The arms of the Abbey were a stag's head caboshed, and the shields containing them may be found in various parts of the buildings of Charde.

295. The seals of the Abbey so far known are but two. One described by Oliver is oval, "divided into three compartments. In the upper part, between two pointed windows, a bell appears suspended in a steeple. In the canopy beneath, is the Blessed Virgin and Divine Infant. On the dexter side is the Courtenay shield, Or, three torteaux, with a label of three points. On the sinister is the shield of Beaumont, Barry of six vairy and gules. Below is an Abbot erect, holding his crozier in his right hand and a book in his left, and three persons on their knees." The legend is,

S. Commune Monasterii Beate Marie de Forda.

Another seal, and one not hitherto described, is said to represent the Abbot between two shields, on the dexter that of the Courtenays, and on the sinister a lion rampant. A legend surrounds the device. This seal is appended to a grant from William Toterigge and Mabilla his wife to Edward Blakforde, John Forde Capellanus, and others, of tenements in Sperhay. This deed was for sale by a firm of London booksellers in 1875, but I have not been able to trace its present owner.

296. With this brief account of Ford I bring to a close this series of papers on the Cistercian Houses of Devon, and trust that I have been enabled to add a little to their somewhat meagre history.

APPENDIX.

LIST OF THE ABBOTS OF FORD.

Name.	Date.	Authorities.
Richard	1136	Harleian MSS.
Robert de Penynton .	1137-1168?	Do.
Baldwin	-1181?	Various.
Robert	. .	Harleian MSS.
John	1191-1120	Leland and Various.
John	Until 1236	Feet of Fines and Documents.
Roger	In 1236	Documents.
John de Warwick .	Died in 1246	Harleian MSS.
Adam	. .	Do. Oliver.
William . . .	Died 1262	Oliver, Dugdale, and various.
William of Crukerne	1262	Various.
Nicholas . . .	From 1283	Episcopal Register.
William de Fria .	Resigned 1297	Various.
Henry	In 1312	Oliver.
William	From 1319	Episcopal Registers.
John	. .	Do.
John de Chidley .	From 1330	Do.
Adam	From 1354	Do.
John Chylheglys .	In 1373	Do.
Walter Burstok .	From 1378	Do.
Nicholas . . .	In 1388	
Walter? . . .	. .	See par. 275.
John Bokeland .	From 1419	Episcopal Registers.
Richard	. .	Oliver.
Robert	In 1448	Oliver.
Walter	In 1460	De Banco Roll.
Elias	In 1462	Oliver.
William White .	In 1490	Various.
Thomas Charde .	1521-1539	Various.

NEWENHAM ABBEY.

Mr. Davidson has very kindly furnished me with a transcript from the Cartulary of Glastonbury, in the Bodleian Library, relating to Newenham Abbey, which I am very glad to be able to add here.

The following seems to have been the substance of the dispute.

The manor and hundred of Axminster, which belonged at the Conquest to the King, were, by a donation in the year 1246, granted by Reginald de Mohun to the Abbey of Newenham. The grant of the hundred carried with it the right to have suit (*secta*) and service (*servitium*) from the owners of the several tithings in the hundred, at the hundred court, when the sheriff made his visitation or tourn. One of the tithings in Axminster hundred was Uplyme, of which manor the Abbot of Glastonbury was lord; and it is to be presumed that from and after 1246 the seneschal of the Abbot of Glastonbury, on each occasion of a sheriff's tourn being held at Axminster, presented himself and did suit (*secta*) to the Abbot of Newenham for the tithing of Uplyme. This "doing suit of court" had been and might be commuted to a payment of ten shillings a year for the sheriff's tourn, and a yearly rent of 6s. 8d. for horderisgold, "hordarii geldum," or treasurer's tax, which seems to have been a peculiar impost payable to a religious house when lords of a manor. It happened, however, that upon the death of an Abbot of Glastonbury, the fruits of the Abbey possessions became vested in the crown during the vacancy, and the seneschal neglected either to do suit of court, or to pay either the fee due at the hundred court to the lord of the manor, or the treasurer's tax, due to the Abbot of Newenham. Thereupon it was alleged, a number of persons, twelve of whom are named, went over from Newenham and its neighbourhood to Uplyme, entered an enclosed field belonging to the Abbot of Glastonbury, and there burnt some growing rushes and other standing crops. At the same time one Robert Tudde, bailiff of Axminster, seised and carried off 37 beasts belonging to the Abbot, by way of distress for non-payment of the fees due at the last sheriff's tourn. This led to a process of law being instituted. A writ was issued to the sheriff to inquire into the truth of the alleged enormities, and to attach the wrong-doers. The return made by the jurors on the 25th of January, 1275, established the truth of the charges, and on the 5th of February following a writ was issued by the Crown, dated at Reading, which was in the nature of a decree or judgment. It took the form of commanding the Sheriff of Devon to take bail for the appearance of the following persons—John, Abbot of Newenham, Brother Henry de la Boneie, Luke le Messer, William Russel, William Todde, Richard de Cleyhulle, Nicholas Pin, and Nicholas Dare, to shew cause why they, together with Richard le Berker, Richard the son of Amiable of Shapwick, John of Egelcumbe, John the son of Richard Care, and William Salomon, and others, committed the acts above mentioned; also to shew cause why they did not appear on the morrow of the Purification of the Virgin (2nd February) as summoned by their sureties. The names of the sureties, are then given.

For the Abbot	Robert Squirel. Reginald Fayth.
For the Friar Henry of Bouere	Adam Scurel. Thomas Fait.
For Luke le Messer	Reginald Gladewine. William Velfais.
For William	Reginald Copiner. William Blonoch.
For Robert Tudde	Hugh Douile. Thomas Bal.
For Nicholas de Cleihulle	Richard le Pottere. Nicholas Pin.
For Nicholas Pin	Richard Humas. Walter Grey.
For Nicholas Dare	Thomas Grugg. Thomas Tannur.

The writ goes on to direct the sheriff to take bail for Richard le Berker, and the other delinquents named, to appear and shew cause together with the eight defendants for whom bail had been taken before.

The narrative of the law-suit is here interrupted in order to introduce an agreement, made in October, 1275, between the Abbots of Glastonbury and Newenham, with regard to the boundaries of some contiguous lands, whereby in consideration of thirty marks paid by the Abbot of Newenham to the Abbot of Glastonbury, the dispute was settled, and all legal proceedings stayed.

We then find an entry of a deed of release and quit-claim on the part of the Abbot of Newenham to the Abbot of Glastonbury of the hundred suit and sheriff's tourn due to the former in respect of Uplyme, in consideration of forty

marks paid by the latter to the former. This last mentioned deed is to be found in the register of Newenham, and has been already observed upon.*
This is a transcript of the original—
MSS. Bodl: Wood i. 212 b.

¶ Processus placiti inter dm̄n regem et abbatem de Newenham pro t̃ras in manerio de vplim abbis Glastonie.
Breve originale.

Rex vicecomiti Devonie salutem quia accepim^9 quod quidam malefactores ꝉ pacis nr̃e perturbatores nuper uenerunt ad quendam seperalem pasturam in vplim que pertinet ad abathiam Glastonie in manu nr̃a existentē racione vacionis cuiusdam ꝉ de qua vltimus abbas eiusdem abbathie obiit scisinū et jaunꝑ ꝉ alia in eadem pastura crescentia combusserunt ꝉ alia enormia ibidem perpetrauerunt ad graue dampnū ipius abbathie in nostri contempt^9 manifestum ꝉ contra pacem nr̃am tibi p̃cipimus quod per sacramentum proborum ꝉ legaliū hoim̃ de balliua tua per quod rei ueritas melius sciri poterit diligenter inquiras qui predictā transgr^9 fecerunt ꝉ omnes illos quos per inquisicionem illam inde culpabiles inueneris attachies ita quod hc̃as corpora eorum corā nobis in crastino Purificacois beate Marie vbicumq̨ tunc fuerimus in anglia ad respondend̃ nobis de transgressioc̃ p̃dicta et habeas ibi hoc breue. Teste me ip̃o apud Marleberghe ꝉc̃.

Ib. 212 b.
Inquisicio capta apd^9 exoniam per p̃dict̃ brē.   Friday, 25 Jan. 1275.
Inquisicio capta apud Exoniam die veneris in festo conuersionis sancti Pauli anno regni Regis Edwardi tercio qui malefactores ꝉ pacis Domini Regis perturbatores nuper uenerunt in quandam seperalem pasturam in vplim que pertinet ad abbathiam Glastonie et janta et alia in eadem pastura crescentia combuscerunt ꝉ alia enormia ibidem perpetrauerunt in p̃judiciū Domini Regis ad dampnum ip̃ius abbīe manifestum ꝉ contra pacem domini regis per sacram̄tum Johannis de Hitone, Johannis fil Galfrid̃, Rog̃ de Clauile, Hugonis de Raleigh, Willi de la uerge, Willi Vinorthcheie Willi de Cranesweye, Henrici de Hayuile, Philippi de Combe, Willi de esse, Roberti Russel, Roberto Puꝛ, Waltero Wering, Henrico de Wicrofte, Henrico de Halc, Ricardo de Boclande, Roberto Beuener. Nicholai de la Forde, Jordano de la Roche, Jordani de Harecumbe et Walteri de Fraunceis Qui dicunt super sacramentum suum quod Henricus de la bouecte

* Davidson, *Hist. of Newenham Abbey*, pp. 24, 25.

de Niwenham frater Ricardus de la Beker⁹, Lucas le messer de Nywenham, Willm̃ Russel de la bate, Robertus Todde Ric⁹ filius amiable de schapewik, Johannes de Egelcumbe, Johannes filius Ricardi Care de Egelcumbe, Henr⁹ filius Dauid de Egelcumbe, Johannes de la Sale, Ricardus Wrange. Ric⁹ faber ⁊ Willm̃s Salomon ⁊ alii multi quorum nomina ignorant vi ⁊ armis venerunt ad terram abbïe Glastonie in vplim que est in manu domini regis racione uacationis abbathie predicte ⁊ janta iṗius abbïe Glastonie in eodem manerio crescentia contra pacem dn̄i regis [combusserunt]. Et dicunt quod Robertus Tudde balliuus de Axminstre alia enormia ibidem fecit videlicet cepit triginta ⁊ septem au⁹ia iṗius abbie Glastoñ pro quadam secta quam exigit abbas de Niwenham ab abbatem Glastonie ad turnū quod senescallus iṗius abbīs tenuit in vltimo hundredo suo quod tenuerunt post festum sancti Michaelis vbi p̃dictus abbas Glastonie nullam sectā debet nec homines sui nec etiam homines de feodo iṗius abbatis Glastonie eo quod quieti sunt per cartā abbatis et conuentus de Newenham. In cuius rei testimoniū huic inquisitioni sigilla sua alternatiui apposuerunt. Dat̃ dictis die ⁊ anno.

¶ Breue judicii.

Rex vicecomiti deuonie salutem. Pone per uadium ⁊ meliores plegg̃ Johannē abbatem de niwenham fratrem henricū de la bonei, lucam le messer, Willm̃ Russel, Willm̃ Todde, Richm̃ de cleyhulle, Nicholaum Pin ⁊ nichm̃ dare quod sint coram nobis a die pasche in quinta septim̃ ad rn̄ded' nobis de placito quare iṗi simul cum fr̄e Ricardo le berker, Riċċo filio amiable de schapewik, Johñe de egelcumbe, Johanne filio Riċċi Care et Willm̃o Salomon et alii nuper uenerunt ad quamdam seperalem pastur⁹ in vplim que pertinet ad abbathiam Glastonie in manu nr̄a existente occasione vacationis eiusdem ⁊ de qua ultimus eiusdem abbathie obiit seisiau et janet ⁊ alia in eadem pastura crescentia combusserunt ⁊ alia enormia ibidem perpetrauerunt ad graue dampnū iṗius abbie et nostri contemptum manifestum et contra pacem nostram ut dicitur. Et ad ostendendum quare non fuerunt coram nobis in crastino purificationis beate marie sicut attachiati fuerunt ⁊ sūmoniti per bonos sum̃. Robertum Squirel ⁊ Reginad' fayth primos uel p'dicti Johannis abbis de Newenham ⁊ adam Scurel ⁊ Thoma fait primos pl'p̃dicti fratris henrici de la bouer⁹ Et regni⁹ Gladewine et Willm̃ velfais ṗmos pl'predicti luce le messer. Et reginaldus copiner et Willm̃ blonoch primos plegg̃ predicti Will'i ⁊ hug̃ douile ⁊ thom̃ bal. primos pl'predicti Roberti

Tudde ⁊ Ricm̃ le pottere ⁊ nichm̃ pin primos pl'pdicti nich'i de cloihulle ⁊ ricrm̃ humas ⁊ Walterum Grey p̃mos pl'pdicti nich'i pin. Thom̃ Grugg⁹ ⁊ Thom̃ tannur primos pl' p'dicti nĩchi dare quod sint coram nobis ad prefatum terminiū ante iudiciū suū de hoc quod non ꝼuerunt predictos Johannem abbatem de Niwenham ⁊ alios coram nobis in crastino purificc.tionis beate marie sicut eos pleg̃ precipim⁹ tibi quod no ommittas propter libertatem abbatis quin ponas per vad' ⁊ saluos pleg̃ p̃dictos fratrem Ricardum le berker, Ricrm̃ filium amabile de schapwik, Johannem de Egelcombe ⁊ alios quod sint coram nobis ad p̃fatum terminū ad respondendum nobis simul cum p̃dictis Johanne abbate de Niwenham ⁊ aliis de predicto placito. Et vnde tu tp̃e nobis mandasti in crastino pur⁹ bc̃ mar⁹ quod preceperas balliuis predicte libertat⁹ quod attachiar̃ p̃dictos frc̃m Ricc̃m le berker ⁊ alios quod ec̃nt coram nobis ad eundem terminū ad respondendum nobis simul cum p̃dictis Johanne abbate de Nievenham ⁊ aliis de predicto placito qui nichil inde fecerunt ⁊ habeas ibi nomina secundo⁊ pleg̃ ⁊ sum̃ pleg̃ ⁊ hoc br̃e. Test⁹ Ƃ de hengham apud Ꝛadinge v° die febr̃ī anno regni nr̃i tercio.

Memorandum quod cum eēt contencio inter uiros religiosos dominum Johannem abbatem ⁊ cōuentum Glastonie ex una parte ⁊ Johannem abbatem ⁊ conuentum de Niwenham ex parte altera super terrarum suarum sese contingenaciū terminis atq, metis tandem pdictus abbas de Niwenham volens nec sufferens diucius durare sed omnino uolens dirimere litis materiam ãnte moto pro se ⁊ conuentu suo uadiauit p̃dictis abbati et conuentui Glastonie triginta marcas pro bono pacis ⁊ ob captandam ab eisdem graciam ⁊ fauorem. Ita quod p'dictus abbas ⁊ conuentus de Newenham predictis abbati ⁊ conuentui Glastonie dabunt et soluent Decem marcas argenti de summa p'dictarum triginta marcarum citra nat' domini proxim̃ futu⁊ et residue xx marcarū de summa eadem ex predictorum abbis ⁊ conuentus Glastonie tali condicione ⁊ modo sunt posite in respectu ut si bene se gesserunt abbas ⁊ conuent⁹ de Newenhã erga abbatem ⁊ conuentum Glastonie nominatim in negocio perambulationis utriusque partis assensu inter terras suas faciendis quam neutra pars ullo malo ingenio impediet nec peruertet. Statim peracto negocio penitus remittentur nec alterutri parte competet actio per p̃sentes. Dat̃ londoñ menş oct̃ anno dñi mᵖ.cc. septuagessīo q̃nto.

¶ Carta abbĩ de Newenhã de quietaclamancia secte hundr⁹ ⁊ torno vicecom̃ de vplim.

5 Feb. 1275.

Oct. 1275.

Omnibus has literas visuris uel audituris Henricus dī gratia abbas de Niwenham ⁊ ciusdę loci conuentus salutem eternam in dño. Nouert uniuersitas uestra nos pro nob' et successoribus nõis imperpetuū remisisse et quietumclamasse domino michi abbati glast⁹ et eiusdem loci conuentui ⁊ ecclie Glastonie totum ius ⁊ clameum quod ħuimus uel ħere potuimus versus ipm abbatem glastonie ⁊ successores suos ⁊ omnes homines suos ⁊ oȝ homines dę feodis suis de manerio suo de vplim de sect̃ hundred' ⁊ torno vic⁹ que nos exegimus ab eis ad hundred' nostrum de axeminstre quod habemus de dono reginaldi de moun ⁊ confirmacione domini henrici regis filii regis Johannis ⁊ similiter de sexdeceim solid' ⁊ octo denar⁹ quos exegimus ab eisdem per annū vnde decem solidos sunt de turno vicecom̃ et vj sol' et viij d' sunt de quodam redditu qui uocatur horderesgeld' vnde inplacitauimus predictum michaelem abbatem per breue domini regis in comit̃ exon̅. Ita quod nec nos nec successores nostri unquam in posterum clamare uel exigere poterimus de predictis abbate nec conuentu Glastoñ nec eorum successoribus nec etiam ab hominibus suis nec ab hominibus de feod' suis de p̃dicto manerio de vplim aliquam sectam aut p̃dictos sexdecim solidos ⁊ iiij denar⁹ per annū uel aliquod aliud quod ad nos uel successores nostros aliquo occasione tempore predicti hundredi nr̃i de Axeminstre accidere poterit. Hec solumodo saluo nobis ⁊ successoribus nr̃is quod si balliuos nroȝ abbatis ⁊ conuentus de vplim in executione mandati dñi regis quod per br̃e suum vicecom̃ deuonie demandat⁹ fuerit ⁊ postea nobis per returnū per ipm vicecom̃ de mandat⁹·fuerit ⁊ nos postea idem mandatum per returnū p̃dictis ballivis ipius abbatis de vplim demandauerimus negligentes ēo constiterit ita quod mandatum domini regis in hac parte non fuerint (sic) execuṭi, bene licebit tunc ballivo de axeminstre qui pro tempore fuit tanquam balliuo vicecom̃ ⁊ non tanquam balliuo nr̃o predictum manerium de vplim intrare ⁊ mandatum illud ea uice executioni demandare, ita quod nec p̃dictus abbati ⁊ conuentui Glastonie nec ecciē Glastonie nec hominibus suis de vplim per mandati illius executioni aliquod unquam in posterum preiudiciū generetur omnes autem proscriptas libertates predictis abbati ⁊ conventui Glastonie ac eccl̃ie Glastonie contra omnes homines ⁊ feminas imperpetuū warantizabimus ⁊ pro hac remissione ⁊ quietaclamancia ac warentia iddem abbas ⁊ conuentus Glastonie dederunt nob̃ quadraginta marcas. In cuius rei testimoniū huic scripto sigillum nr̃m apposui hiis testibȝ dominis Reginaldo de moun, Henrico de traci, Johē balon, Waltero de bathoñ tunc vicecom̃ deuoñ, Willmo de leighe militibȝ, Willm̃o le bray, Ricr̃o de Craswelle ⁊ aliis.

www.ingramcontent.com/pod-product-compliance
Lightning Source LLC
Chambersburg PA
CBHW020812230426
43666CB00007B/972